Genocide, Torture, and Terrorism

Genocide, Torture, and Terrorism

Ranking International Crimes and Justifying Humanitarian Intervention

Thomas W. Simon

palgrave
macmillan

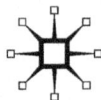

GENOCIDE, TORTURE, AND TERRORISM
Copyright © Thomas W. Simon 2016

First published 2016 by
PALGRAVE MACMILLAN

The author has asserted their right to be identified as the author of this work in accordance with the Copyright, Designs and Patents Act 1988.

Palgrave Macmillan in the UK is an imprint of Macmillan Publishers Limited, registered in England, company number 785998, of Houndmills, Basingstoke, Hampshire, RG21 6XS.

Palgrave Macmillan in the US is a division of Nature America, Inc., One New York Plaza, Suite 4500, New York, NY 10004-1562.

Palgrave Macmillan is the global academic imprint of the above companies and has companies and representatives throughout the world.

Hardback ISBN: 978–1–137–41510–3
E-PUB ISBN: 978–1–137–41512–7
E-PDF ISBN: 978–1–137–41511–0
DOI: 10.1057/9781137415110

Distribution in the UK, Europe and the rest of the world is by Palgrave Macmillan®, a division of Macmillan Publishers Limited, registered in England, company number 785998, of Houndmills, Basingstoke, Hampshire RG21 6XS.

Library of Congress Cataloging-in-Publication Data

Simon, Thomas W., 1945–
    Genocide, torture, and terrorism : ranking international crimes and justifying humanitarian intervention / Thomas W. Simon.
        pages cm
    Includes bibliographical references and index.
    ISBN 978–1–137–41510–3 (hardcover)
        1. Jus cogens (International law) 2. Torture (International law)
    3. Terrorism (International law) 4. Genocide. 5. Genocide–Rwanda.
    6. International crimes. 7. Humanitarian intervention. I. Title.

KZ1261.S56 2015
345'.025—dc23   2015016498

A catalogue record for the book is available from the British Library.

Dedication
to
Nora Visscher-Simon
and
Dashuai Yang,
my cherished youngest ones
without comparisons
from west and east

Contents

Figures

Acknowledgments

esignation, discrimination, and brutalization—marked out by
Raul Hilberg to divide the phases leading up to the Holocaust.
My works have examined each phase in depth. This book
marks the end of a unofficial series that began with *Democracy and
Social Injustice* (Rowman & Littlefield, 1995), which examined the
injustice of discrimination primarily in the context of American constitutional law. *The Laws of Genocide* (Praeger/Greenwood, 2007) took
on the brutalization of genocide in the context of international criminal
law. *Minority Protection and Ethnic Identity* (Rowman & Littlefield/
Lexington Books, 2012) explored the first designation or identity phase
within comparative law. In the present work, I turn to a comparison
of different types of brutalization, particularly genocide, torture, and
terrorism.

The book has been a long time in the making. No book is an island.
Many hands have contributed, but none deserves blame for the final product or any part therein. The following persons have provided construc-
tive suggestions on form and substance: David Duffee, Chad Flanders,
Kevin Gray, David Lea, Larry May, Bruno Simma, Eva Visscher-Simon
(daughter!), Adam Webb, and Rebecka Zinser. Special merit badges go
to Jeffrey Reiman and William Slomanson. who never give up the rather
hopeless task of getting me to write and think better.

The Hopkins-Nanjing Center (HNC) has become an ideal place to
write, pursue scholarship, and, of course, teach. I wish to express publicly my gratitude to HNC colleagues and administrators, especially
Carolyn Townsley, for believing in me and to co-director Cornelius
Kubler for creating an academic atmosphere. Special thanks goes to the
library staff, particularly Yu Xiaoxia from HNC and Sheila Thalhimer
from the School of Advanced International Studies (SAIS).

The ones who deserve thanks for putting up with and stimulating
my critical compassions are the students, too numerous to mention,

from Illinois State University, American University of Sharjah, and, of course, HNC. Most importantly, Wang Yue (Jenny) has once again performed yeoman copy editing services. Friends Dottie Cohen and Joel Friedman provided sanctuary for undisturbed contemplation (except for a dog and a rooster) in beautiful town down Roscoe, Georgia, for the summers of 2013–15.

An earlier version of Chapter 1 on comparing injustices was presented at the International Scholars' Conference on Remembering the Future at Oxford (2000). The original source of Chapter 2 on comparing genocides comes from *Contemporary Portrayals of Auschwitz: Philosophical Challenges*, ed. Alan Rosenberg, James R. Watson, and Detlef Linke (Amherst, NY: Humanity Books, 2000), pp. 83–94. Copyright © 2000 Alan Rosenberg, James R. Watson, and Detlef Linke. (All rights reserved. Used by permission of the publisher.) I had the honor of presenting an earlier version of Chapter 3 on the Rwandan genocide before a Rwandan diaspora community at the University of Notre Dame. Regarding Chapter 4 on torture, I acknowledge the generous permission of the *Denver Journal of International Law and Policy* for permission to reprint "The Iconography of Torture: Beyond the Tortuous Torture Debate," 43(1) *Denver Journal of International Law and Policy* (Fall 2014): pp. 45–90. I presented earlier versions at: the XXVI World Congress of Philosophy of Law in Belo Horizonte, Brazil (2013), the 4th Global Conference on Pain in Prague (2013), and the Neuro Law Conference in Sydney (2012). I made a number of presentations over the years covering segments of the material in Chapter 5 on terrorism: University of Northern Colorado (2003), National University of Malaya (2006), and American University of Sharjah (2007). Finally, an earlier version of Chapter 6 on universal prohibitions was given at the XXIV World Conference on Philosophy of Law in Beijing (2009).

Last but far from least, a heartfelt note of love and gratitude goes to my wife Mengkun Yang (Sarah). She has faithfully managed to give care and sustenance despite some trying moments. She has literally kept me not only alive but also lively enough to compare for another day.

Introduction

"My pain is worse than your pain."
"Our suffering is greater than your suffering."

W e seldom say these things, but we often make these kinds of judgments. Humans have a built-in device that judges just about everything. We constantly evaluate and compare. Of course, we pretend otherwise. We do not want to be seen as imposing our values on others—or at least stand accused of doing this. We like to think of ourselves as professing and practicing value neutrality.

This book steers the analysis in the opposite direction by making a case for judgments and comparisons. However, the object of the judgments and comparisons is not about individuals but about international crimes. The arguments in this book center on the following tersely put claims: International crimes have greater significance than transnational crimes. Some international crimes rank above other international crimes. Genocide qualifies as the worst international crime, a universal prohibition (*jus cogens*), followed by torture. Terrorism does not even qualify as an international crime. Genocide ranks above another international crime, namely crimes against humanity. Some acts (killing for genocide and inflicting pain for torture) within each international crime are more central than other acts.

Before proceeding, it is important to understand some basic concepts of international law. This work focuses on international crimes in contrast to transnational crimes. Transnational crimes such as drug smuggling cross over borders. International crimes rank as worse than transnational crimes because they involve extremely grave or heinous harms against not only state interests but also the interests or morality of the international community as a whole. The international crime of genocide undermines the very foundation of a civilized international

community. *Jus cogens* are universal prohibitions, peremptory norms
that take precedence over all others in international law. "The essence
of the *jus cogens* doctrine is the recognition of the need to establish
common values and standards which will have precedence over state
sovereignty and which will accordingly restructure international
society."[1] *Jus cogens* should provide the ethical underpinnings for some
international crimes. *Jus cogens* should trigger certain kinds of obligations. These obligations *erge omnes* are owed to the entire international
community. Universal jurisdiction gives effect to the obligations *erge
omnes* to prosecute universal prohibitions without regard to classical
grounds for jurisdiction. The exercise of universal jurisdiction entails
the prosecution by any state for individuals for the violations of *jus
cogens* norms. The state should undertake this prosecution not for
its own interest but in the interest of the international community.
The prolific use of the word "should" here serves as a warning of the
deeply normative character of this book. While making every effort to
describe international law, this project goes beyond the descriptive to
the prescriptive.

No other work has taken the track adopted here of ranking international crimes. Instead of providing a ranking among international
crimes, jurists and philosophers lump the crimes together. Then, they
try to figure some way, for example, to justify universal jurisdiction.
One jurist argues that crimes against humanity affect the interests of all
people since anyone could be a potential victim.[2] Yet, genocide should
not lose its status as an international crime on a showing that some
individuals would never be its potential victims. Another commentator
locates international crimes among those harms perpetrated by a state,
largely, against its own citizens.[3] But this would have the consequence
of including famine as an international crime. Finally, more recently,
one philosopher has argued that an enforcement gap provides the justification for a harm being an international crime.[4] This, however, puts
piracy on an equal moral footing with genocide.

It is a far more sensible and fruitful strategy to recognize the legal and
moral distinctions among international crimes. "One of the main functions of criminal law is to express the degree of wrongdoing, not simply
the fact of wrongdoing."[5] This incorporation of degrees of wrongdoing has not happened, at least explicitly, in international criminal law.
Jurists seem unable to agree upon the gravity of international crimes
and the harshness of their punishments.[6] This work attempts to forge
an agreement by beginning from the top of the injustice scale, from the
worst international crime, namely, genocide.

Ranking crimes in this way may seem like an idle academic exercise. Yet, even the Nuremberg tribunal implicitly (and wrongly I argue) ranked the crimes by, among other things, giving crimes against peace (aggression), and not crimes against humanity, central place.[7] Moreover, ranking international crimes has important payoffs. National (municipal) criminal justice systems rank crimes with an eye on having the most serious crimes receive the most severe punishment. The international criminal system does that but only to a limited extent. Ranking crimes has a far more important benefit than establishing different degrees of punishment. It establishes a framework for determining when to intervene in the affairs of another country. If genocide qualifies as the worst crime, as the most unimaginable atrocity, then that should provide a justification for other international organizations and states to intervene to stop it. If terrorism does not even qualify among the ranks of international crimes, then it should not provide any pretext for intervention.

International crimes cross a threshold of harms and injustices that demand the attention of the international community. The type of harms and the extent of these harms mark the category of international crimes. The phrase "widespread or systematic," used to define crimes against humanity, serves as a way to distinguish international crimes in general. International crimes do more than transcend national boundaries. They represent a set of internationally unacceptable harms that spread their contagion globally.[8] However, within the general category of international crimes, some rank as worse than others. The concept of *jus cogens* carves out a subset of particularly heinous crimes among the international crimes. These *jus cogens* crimes should be genocide, torture, and slavery.

Jus cogens international crimes are unconditional prohibitions, the violations of which are, in principle, unjustifiable and/or historically unjustified. "Justifiability" and "justified" provide criteria for sorting out the elements of each crime. Genocide proves not only unjustified in any instance but also, in principle, unjustifiable. No seemingly rational analysis could ever find a justification for genocide even in any plausible hypothetical scenario.

Torture presents some conceptual conundrums. It proves more complicated for the infamous ticking bomb scenario that may provide a hypothetical justification. In that hypothetical scenario, the victim knows the when, where, what, and how of a ticking bomb hidden somewhere. More problematically, the torturer knows that the victim knows. So, the scenario requires the acceptance of some highly implausible assumptions about, for example, the degree of knowledge that the torturer has about the reliability of the victim's knowledge. These implausible assumptions make torture practically unjustifiable.

There is still another argument to demonstrate the unjustifiability of torture. That argument draws on a similarity between genocide and torture. Perpetrators perform these respective criminal acts because of the status of the victim. *Genocidaires*, to use the hideously polite French term, target individuals because of their group status, that is, their actual or perceived racial, ethnic, national, or religious identity. Likewise, torturers inflict pain upon their victims because of the actual or perceived knowledge status of the victims. Genocide and torture are both status crimes and as such there is a prima facie argument for the unjustifiability of both.

Moreover, torture only becomes arguably justified retrospectively. Even then, it becomes suspect, given that alternatives generally remain untried. Torture has no independent prospective justification.

Slavery may be in principle unjustifiable. Genocide and torture are status crime; perpetrators target individuals not for anything they did, but because of to what group they (the perpetrators) perceive them to belong. Slavery, historically and in its most vicious forms, flourished primarily as a status crime. Perpetrators enslaved others based on the victim's race. However, slavery could be and also has been a nonstatus crime. Throughout history, perpetrators enslaved others not because of who they were but because of what they did as, for example, enemy combatants. Nevertheless, the modern form of "status slavery" is not justifiable nor has it ever found a morally acceptable justification in the past.

Some international crimes such as the many acts listed as crimes against humanity do not qualify as *jus cogens* crimes. *Jus cogens* crimes all have a formulation where a case can be made for their being unjustifiable in principle. Ethnic cleansing, as an example of a crime against humanity, is defined as the forced removal of an ethnic group. It does not necessarily involve killing. It may even, in principle, be justifiable if it is forcibly removing a group from harms way. I do not know of any solid historical case of this, but a jaded view of the Serb ethnic cleansing of Albanians from Kosovo offers an illustration. Indeed, Milosevic argued before the International Criminal Tribunal for the Former Yugoslavia (ICTY) that, by forcing Albanians to leave, he wanted to save the Albanians from NATO's bombing of Kosovo.

Terrorism does not qualify as a *jus cogens* crime (or, for that matter, as an international crime) even assuming that it has an acceptable legal definition. If acts of terrorism are put into a political and war context, then constructing an argument for their unjustifiability becomes difficult, indeed. For, those cases depend, in part, on a prior assessment of the political legitimacy of terrorist causes.

The commission of *jus cogens* crimes, primarily genocide, provides strong grounds for humanitarian intervention. In contrast, the commission of most crimes against humanity provides warrant for a duty to protect. However, certain crimes against humanity are so close to genocide so as to be in the same category. In sharp contrast to these, terrorism finds no place in the hierarchical scheme of injustices, because, in part, it has no acceptable definition.

Another method used throughout the book differentiates among the purported international crimes. An international crime must have a clear definition that breaks the crime into its elements. This method for ranking crimes consists of comparing the seriousness of the elements of each crime. Each crime has a definition in terms of its *actus reus* and *mens rea*, criminal act and criminal "mind." Some criminal acts, such as genocide, done with a particular type of criminal "mind" rank as the worst, most despicable crimes.

Genocide and torture, each has core acts (i.e., essential ingredients or necessary conditions) that lie at the very foundation of these crimes. For genocide, it is mass killings, and for torture, the infliction of pain. Analyses of the *mens rea* elements of each of these crimes reveal a critical limitation of the analogy to national criminal law systems for international law. The *mens rea* element for each makes better sense not as an individual criminal mind, as it does for national systems, but as an organizational policy, primarily, as state policy.

In contrast to genocide and torture, a comprehensive survey uncovers no generally acceptable definition of terrorism. As an international crime, terrorism remains in perpetual flux, in a state of continuous indeterminacy. That, of course, makes it impossible to place it on the same level of seriousness as genocide or, even, torture. However, this state of affairs serves state leaders quite well. For this creates enough space for manoeuvring and manipulating definitions when purported acts of terror occur. In short, it provides just the analytic space needed for states to promote fear among their populace.

Using definitions in terms of elements of the various crimes will have its critics, but few commentators would object entirely to this approach. The same does not hold for using iconography as a ground for comparison. No one, to date, has used iconic images to differentiate among the purported crimes. Although it proves difficult to measure the role of iconic images in these debates, no one would deny that they have an effect.

Icons are model images of events. Icons play a critical role, positive and negative, when it comes to evaluating the seriousness of international crimes. Torture has a clear legal definition and an icon (the medieval rack) that helps keep the horror of torture at the forefront of global injustices. Use of this icon enables courts to reject refined distinctions. These distinctions include what some have called "torture light." These distinctions undermine the universal repulsion against all forms of torture. Iconic images, then, actually help to crystalize torture as a *jus cogens* crime, as a universal prohibition.

Genocide, likewise, has a core definition in terms of elements of the crime. However, its icons tend to obscure rather than illuminate. For, the icons of genocide are almost exclusively the icons of the Holocaust (gas ovens, cattle cars, and barbed wire). These icons played a role in the international recognition of the degree of atrocities being committed in the Balkans in the 1990s since those icons either matched or overlapped with the icons of the Holocaust. However, the icons did not match as well for the Rwandan genocide. The Holocaust icons have unjustly elevated the Holocaust to a unique status and, even more unjustly, have helped to devalue the Rwandan genocide.

The collective psychological impact of model images or icons is notoriously difficult to demonstrate. However, it provides at least some explanation for the backlash reaction recently directed at the Rwandan genocide. Admittedly, some previously obscured facts have been more fully acknowledged. Some new facts also have come to light, particularly with regard to the atrocities carried out by Tutsis against Hutus. However, the same kinds of arguments and concerns have never made it to the level of legitimate discussion when it comes to the Holocaust. Few commentators even talk about the retaliatory killings of German sympathizers that occurred at the end of World War II in Yugoslavia. Yet, Tutsi retaliations or revenge killings get immediately labelled as genocide.

While torture and genocide have solid definitions, terrorism does not. Further, while the torture icon illuminates and the genocide icons distort their respective crimes, the terrorism icon trumps any attempt to define it. Terrorism gains, in part, its strength from its iconic images. There is something perverse and disturbing about a purported international crime that remains largely legally undefined and gets its strength primarily from iconic images (and associated ideological rhetoric). These phenomena create a perfect open space for instilling global fear.

The War on Terror has created unforgiveable distortions (and seriously flawed rankings) by exaggerating terrorism and minimizing torture.

The ranking of crimes puts the debates over the old concept of humanitarian intervention and the new idea of a duty to protect in a new light. The duty to protect does not represent a progressive step taken by the international community. It marks a step into darkness. Earlier, particularly in the late 1990s, after the Bosnian war and the Rwandan genocide, jurists increasingly recognized that an impending or ongoing genocide provided ample justification for outside intervention into a state's internal affairs. That no longer holds true because, in part, a duty to protect has replaced humanitarian intervention. The duty to protect has not replaced humanitarian intervention with something better. Instead, it has stifled hope for establishing clear standards for humanitarian intervention. Ranking injustices, by first establishing genocide as the consensual grounds for duty to act, rehabilitates humanitarian intervention by placing it on sound footing.

Part I of this work engages in the controversial task of comparing injustices, arguing for the centrality of genocide. Chapter 1 uses domestic criminal law, which treats intentional murder as deserving greater punishment than negligent homicide, as an analogy for international criminal law, which should treat genocide, in the sense of mass killings, as the worst crime. Chapter 2, then, makes comparisons among genocides, arguing that the Holocaust, rather than qualifying as unique, ranks as the worst recorded genocide. Chapter 3 completes the comparisons by applying the analysis to the Rwandan genocide. It ends by questioning why that horrific genocide, still today, does not receive the recognition it deserves.

Part II takes the comparative project on the road, so to speak, by focusing on two serious distortions from the War on Terror. The War on Terror has managed to downgrade or minimize torture and to upgrade and maximize terrorism. Chapter 4 uses not only legal and moral analysis but also the iconic image of the medieval rack to put torture back in its rightful place as a universal wrong, irrespective of the irrelevant distinctions used to differentiate torture from, for example, cruel, inhuman, and degrading punishment. Chapter 5, then, examines terrorism, arguing that since terrorism remains undefined, it should have no legal recognition. Despite its legal nonexistence, terrorism's political and global persistence unfortunately makes most sense as a mechanism of fear widely employed by nations throughout the world.

Part III draws a solid connection between theory and practice. Chapter 6, the most abstract of any of the chapters, makes the case for universal wrongs (*jus cogens*). It demonstrates that genocide qualifies as a universal prohibition. Chapter 7, then, concludes by showing how a consensus about the *jus cogens* status of genocide, as narrowly defined, serves as the foundation for rehabilitating humanitarian intervention as a new doctrine of a duty to act. That duty should replace the impotent doctrine of a duty to protect.

The world seems increasingly torn asunder by horrifying conflicts and inexcusable injustices. The international community already has forged a consensus over genocide as a universal wrong. The disarray on the ground should not be matched by conceptual confusion in the law. The international community needs to use the consensus about genocide as a first step in constructing a clear and justified criterion for humanitarian intervention. This should serve as a firm foundation for developing a saner response to those injustices that resemble genocide (crimes against humanity) and to those purported injustices (terrorism) that look either nothing like an international crime or look exactly like a war crime (ISIS).

PART I

Comparing Injustices: The Centrality of Genocide

CHAPTER 1

Comparing Wrongs

Humans make judgments and comparisons. They especially compare to determine which human characteristic or act is best and which is worst. These comparative judgments, if not unavoidable, often guide action and policy. Emergency Medical Technicians (EMTs) sort out accident victims according to triage principles, attending to the most critically injured first. They treat unconscious victims before those victims with less severe injuries.

Sorting out victims of a traffic accident pales, conceptually, in comparison to sorting out and ranking global injustices. How can we rank the following injustices: genocide, slavery, mass killings, torture, ethnic cleansing, rape, war crimes, famine, human trafficking, disappearances, human rights violations, refugees, asylum, female genital mutilation, child abuse, terrorism, and political repression? Yet, that is exactly the task facing the construction of an international criminal code. This chapter tries to make some headway toward accomplishing that daunting task. Then, Chapter 2 shows how comparisons and rankings can even be made among purported cases of genocide. Finally, Part I ends with an analysis in Chapter 3 of why the Rwandan genocide has not been given its proper recognition as the worst genocide since the Holocaust.

Comparative Domestic Criminal Law

Every domestic criminal justice system ranks crimes. Let us see whether and how these rankings can serves as models for ranking international crimes. Domestic criminal codes reflect the individual comparative evaluative judgments at a broader societal level. State criminal codes contain, largely unquestioned, evaluative or normative comparisons of harms. Legislators met out more severe punishments for first-degree, premeditated murder than for non-premeditated forms of murder such as negligent homicide. Felonies receive more severe punishments than misdemeanors. The criminal codes provide greater criminal liability for first-degree serial murders than for a single murder.

One way to differentiate these crimes is in terms of the harmful nature and extent of the act and degree of intent. The number of victims and the intent of the perpetrator make a legal and moral difference in state criminal codes as applied to individual actions. State criminal law practice opens the gateway to similar issues in international criminal law.

In national legal systems, disagreements persist over what punishment best fits each crime. Disputes also arise over whether one crime (treason) should have a more severe penalty than another crime (rape). Yet, despite many contentious issues in criminology, the following comparative judgments would most likely find quick assent:

1. A manslaughter that results in the deaths of many is worse than one that results in the death of a few or in the death of a single individual.
2. Premeditated murder is worse than non-premeditated murder.
3. An individual who has killed more than one person has committed a worse wrong than an individual who has killed one person.
4. Multiple killings aimed at a particular group are worse than random multiple killings.

The word "worse" in these claims translates into criminological terms into "should receive a more severe punishment."

Law and morality overlap in criminal law. Criminal law functions in public daylight. A criminal justice system transforms seemingly private matters among individuals into public ones. A punishment of children within the privacy of the home becomes public when it turns into criminal abuse. Criminal law's public nature goes beyond collective concerns and encompasses moral judgments. Criminal law reflects society's morals. A list of criminal acts represents a codification of what society regards as morally reprehensible. A criminal stands guilty not only of having broken the state's laws but also of having violated society's morality. Someone murders another person. Obviously, the perpetrator directed the wrong at that individual. However, the murderer also committed a crime against the state and society. Murder constitutes a public wrong. Although a certain individual or specific individuals feel the direct impact of a criminal act, crime has a collective moral element. Criminal acts indirectly harm other individuals who are not themselves the immediate victims of the crimes. Criminals chip away at collective security. Criminal acts become matters of collective concern.

Consider, then, a translation of three of the previous criminal law judgments into moral judgments, where the word "worse" means "more wrongful, in a moral sense."

1. It is worse to commit lethal acts than it is to commit nonlethal acts.
2. It is worse to kill many (i.e., massively) than to kill a few or to kill a single individual.
3. It is worse to kill intentionally than unintentionally.
4. It is worse to kill massively and intentionally than to kill massively and unintentionally.

The normative judgments (1) through (4) depend on the claim that the number of victims and the intent of the perpetrator affect the severity of the offense. The statements constitute reasonable and justifiable moral judgments. Almost every state criminal code contains a version of these judgments. The burden of proof lies on those who would deny the relevancy of victim numbers and intent for individual criminal liability. Let us now see the extent to which these comparative judgments in domestic criminal law translate into rankings for international criminal law.

Comparative International Criminal Law

Every criminal system breaks down each crime into its elements. In this section, we examine the *actus reus* and the *mens rea* for the international crime of genocide. We shall find limitations to drawing parallels with the crime of murder in domestic systems as well as some important additions.

However, first,, it is important to establish at least the plausibility and viability of normative comparisons. Parallels between state and international legal systems should help make a normative comparative project more academically respectable. If state criminal codes contain defensible comparative normative judgments about different kinds of serious crimes, then, analogously, an international criminal code includes defensible normative comparative judgments about different kinds of grave injustices. The task ahead is twofold: (1) construct provisions for an international criminal code, and (2) defend a particular ordering of grave injustices according to their degree of severity.

A crime has at least two elements, *actus reus* (a wrongful act) and *mens rea* (a wrongful mind or purpose). Domestic criminal law designates certain types of crimes as worse than other types of crimes. The law bases its rankings on a number of different grounds. First, criminal codes rank crimes according to the different degrees of wrongfulness ascribed to each of the crime's elements (act and purpose). The different penalty provisions in a criminal code provide ample evidence of normative comparative judgments. Some wrongful acts are more wrongful than other wrongful acts; some wrongful purposes are more wrongful than other wrongful purposes. International criminal law must add a few important elements to the domestic criminal law list. The status of the victims and the justifications permitted in international criminal law prove very important.

Actus Reus (Act): Killing

What exactly are the core wrongs, that is, the necessary components, of genocide? The two major international treaties on genocide agree on the five types of acts that constitute genocide. Article II of the Genocide Convention (1948) specifies five types of acts (a–e) that constitute genocide:

(a) Killing members of the group;
(b) Causing serious bodily or mental harm to members of the group;
(c) Deliberately inflicting on the group conditions of life calculated to bring about its physical destruction in whole or in part;
(d) Imposing measures intended to prevent births within the group;
(e) Forcibly transferring children of the group to another group.[1]

Article 6 of The International Criminal Court repeats the acts listed in the earlier Genocide Convention:

(a) Genocide by killing.
(b) Genocide by causing serious bodily or mental harm.
(c) Genocide by deliberately inflicting conditions of life calculated to bring about physical destruction.
(d) Genocide by imposing measures intended to prevent births.
(e) Genocide by forcibly transferring children.[2]

Since there are five acts listed, a key question is whether each act independently would qualify as an act of genocide, as some commentators contend.[3] Or, alternatively, as argued here, whether one of these acts is more important than the other acts. For example, are "killing members of the group" and "imposing measures intended to prevent births within a group" both equally genocide acts? In short, are killing and sterilization legally and morally on par? The way to answer these questions is first to note that the acts (a) through (e) appear in a particular order, an order that is legally and morally relevant. "Genocide by killing" appears first on these lists and on all national codifications because it alone constitutes the core ingredient of genocide. In other words, if the criminal act did not include killing, then it would not qualify as genocide.

Notice that, among the five listed acts, (a) is the only lethal, physical act. All of the others are nonlethal acts. That difference constitutes a priority ranking, which reflects a judgment that, in general, lethal acts are worse than nonlethal ones. Otherwise, the lethal act of killing would be legally and morally comparable to any one of the other four nonlethal acts. This would lead to the bizarre conclusion that the Nazis' sterilization campaign against the "mentally defective" should rank on the same level of severity and gravity as the Holocaust killings. Again, I must emphasize (as I have to do throughout—demonstrating a real danger of comparisons) that this ranking does not diminish the condemnation of sterilization. Rather, it elevates the condemnation of killing.

If the claim that the crime of genocide, minimally and centrally, includes acts of killing, that argument accomplishes a great deal. Rather than extending the notion of genocide to include cultural genocide and other nonlethal acts, as many have proposed, this narrow definitional interpretation retains killing as the core act of genocide.[4] The other nonlethal acts listed in Article II of the Genocide Convention and in the ICC's Articles occur on the list along with the lethal act of killing because they often occur in concert with these killings, not because they stand or should stand as independent genocide acts.[5]

In short, this interpretation supports claim (1) ("It is worse to commit lethal acts than it is to commit nonlethal acts."). Claim (2) ("It is worse to kill many (that is, massively) than to kill a few or to kill a single individual") should need little defense. Few would argue against handing out more severe sentences for a serial killer than for someone who murdered only one person. In short, this provides one reason for ranking (4) above (3):

3. It is worse to kill intentionally than unintentionally.
4. It is worse to kill massively and intentionally than to kill massively and unintentionally.

Further, what may have seemed like a difference between the crime of genocide and torture turns out not to be a difference. The *actus reus* of genocide seems to come in a variety of types of acts, ranging from killings to sterilizations. Within the Torture Convention or other laws on torture, the most plausible interpretation, as argued in Chapter 4, would not find a comparable range of acts, only a single type, namely, the infliction of pain.[6] However, this turns out not to be a difference at all. Genocide, like torture, has a single prototypical *actus reus*, namely, killings, even if the laws do (mistakenly!) recognize variations on that *actus reus*.[7]

Mens Rea (Institutional Intent)

Second, the *mens rea* or intent element makes a difference in judging the severity of a crime. Compare the following two cases. The first case involves a carefully planned mass murder. The second is a case of a random mass killing.

On December 6, 1989, Mark Lépine murdered 14 female college engineering students at the University of Montreal's École Polytechnique.[8] While yelling, "I hate feminists," he killed nine females in a classroom after asking the males to leave. His suicide note contained a list of 19 "opportunistic" women, including public figures in Canada. Would it make any moral difference to the severity of the offense if Lépine had randomly killed 14 otherwise anonymous individuals?

On April 23, 1987, William Cruse randomly murdered six people in a Palm Bay, Florida, shopping mall. The jury rejected his insanity plea and found him guilty of first-degree murder. For purposes of this analysis, the most salient feature of the case is the fact that "there was no evidence that Cruse contemplated his attack for any longer than a few moments."[9] Whatever intent Cruse had, it was far more short-lived and flimsier than Lépine's intent. From the evidence, Lépine carefully planned to kill individuals because of their group affiliation. In part, because of the premeditated aspect of Lépine's acts and the relative randomness of Cruse's, many criminologists would argue that the former deserves greater punishment than the latter.

The different legal and moral judgments in these two cases help to support claim (3) ("It is worse to kill intentionally than unintentionally.") (or, as argued below, that "It is worse to kill with great well-formed intention than lesser."). Claim 4 ("It is worse to kill massively and intentionally than to kill massively and unintentionally.") follows from (2) and (3), since it simply combines those claims. All four claims find further support when applied to the crime of genocide.

The *mens rea* of genocide involves more than thinking about and planning the crime. The intent required for genocide includes plans that depend on organizational structures for their development and execution. The phrase "institutional intent" should constitute the *mens rea* element of genocide. Institutional intent consists typically of state policies and state-sponsored organizations that carry out the killings. Institutional intents manifest themselves in different degrees. The concept of well-formedness provides a rough comparative measure of institutional intents. Some criminal acts are better planned, that is, better formed, than other acts. The deliberate and purposeful employment of the massive machinery of the state, for example, makes, *ceteris paribus*, genocide a more heinous crime than other forms of mass atrocities, which do not take place at the direction of a state. Analogously, the Nazi intent was more well formed than that of perpetrators in other genocide cases, such as Rwanda.

The intent element for genocide applies to individuals in their capacity within authoritative structures.[10] The placement of intent within an authoritative structure moves the international crime of genocide away from the common understanding of crimes in national systems. States commonly construct relevant authoritative structures embedded within organizations.[11] The idea of authoritative structure helps to deindividualize the crime of genocide. In national criminal law, individuals have responsibility for murder in their capacities as individuals with a particular mental state.[12] In international law, individuals should have responsibility for genocide in their capacities as leaders and members of organizations.[13] Legal suits against organizations serve as a good analogue in state criminal systems. A suit against a corporation might include a named individual both in the person's individual capacity and in her or his role within the organization.

For the crime of genocide, the "perpetrator" must have the requisite *mens rea*, but this mental state differs from the mental state required for individual criminal responsibility in state criminal law systems. The *mens rea* for individual responsibility has a relatively direct connection to the criminal act. A national criminal court wants to determine whether the accused thought about the act. The *mens rea* for genocide has a less direct, more mediated connection to the criminal act. An international criminal court should focus on determining not just whether the accused thought about the criminal act but also whether the accused planned or knowledgeably acted according to a preconceived plan developed within an (often state-sponsored) organization.[14]

The *mens rea* for genocide includes a knowledge test.[15] The defendants must have had the requisite intent in the sense that they had or should have had knowledge of the alleged crime.[16] The jurisprudence on intent for the crime of genocide has taken some odd turns on the knowledge issue. In *Akayesu*, the Tribunal for Rwanda made a questionable distinction between knowledge and intent.[17] Supposedly, under the Court's interpretation, individuals could know that their acts contributed to the destruction of a group and yet not have the intent or specific goal of destroying the group.[18] The intent requirement for the crime of genocide goes beyond a determination of an individual's actual or imputed knowledge. Courts should assess the individual's knowledge according to how the individual functioned within an organizational structure.[19] The structure consists of policies formulated according to procedures set forth in an organization. For example, presumptions about an individual's knowledge would vary according to the individual's formal and actual role in the organization.

Scholars should pay closer attention to how to make sense of intent in cases of crimes like genocide. The laws of genocide require intent for a conviction.[20] The intent in question does not reduce to an individual intent or to the intent of a specified number of individuals. A determination of the intents of individual perpetrators, although relevant, does not determine the prosecution of individuals for the crime of genocide. A successful prosecution of an individual for the crime of genocide must prove the individual's complicity in the forming of an institutional intent.[21]

Next, we begin to see even further differences between murder as a domestic crime and genocide as an international crime. Victim status is an essential element to the crime of genocide, whereas it is not (but perhaps it should be!) for murder.

Victim Status

The Lépine and Cruse cases highlight a critical but controversial element of murder in domestic law, notably the nature of the victims. Both perpetrators committed lethal acts against innocent victims. However, Cruse should be less culpable not because his acts differ from Lépine's acts regarding the innocent status of the victims nor because both were status crimes, but because, unlike Lépine, Cruse did not intentionally target a vulnerable group.[22]

Oddly enough, the status of the victims clearly does make a difference for genocide, but it remains problematic in domestic criminal law. Would it make any moral difference if Lépine had manifested the same or a greater animus toward college students or engineers that he had toward women? College students and engineers do not qualify as disadvantaged or vulnerable groups in any state legal system, whereas, on some accounts, in some state legal systems, women do constitute a relatively powerless group discriminated against because of their status as women.

The vulnerable group status of the victims should make a legal and a moral difference. Individuals become more vulnerable to harm because of their perceived affiliation with a disadvantaged or vulnerable group. The word "innocent" often appears in descriptions of certain types of victims. The language reflects a comparative moral judgment about the crime. Many people would judge the murder of innocent children as morally worse than the killing of adults. The same well-entrenched moral intuitions at work in judging the innocence of children should extend to other vulnerable groups, including women. Women constitute a vulnerable group. They have a particular vulnerability to violence (e.g., rape as a crime of violence) directed at them because of their gender (group affiliation). Further, being-a-woman adds to vulnerability beyond what being-a-college student or what many other group descriptors would add. These arguments and considerations help support the following, more contentious, comparative moral judgments: It is more morally reprehensible intentionally to kill ten individuals because of their group affiliation than intentionally to kill ten individuals irrespective of their group affiliation. It is more morally reprehensible to kill ten individuals because of their disadvantaged group affiliation than to intentionally kill ten individuals because of their non-disadvantaged group affiliation.[23] Minimally, this analysis makes a case for the relevancy of group affiliation to the severity of an offense based primarily on the relative vulnerability of that group.

Let us round out the previous list of moral judgments, which prove easier to defend in international than in domestic criminal law:

4. It is worse to kill massively and intentionally than to kill massively and unintentionally.
5. It is worse to kill massively and intentionally when killings are carried out because of the victims' status group affiliation than to kill under conditions in (4).
6. It is worse to kill massively and intentionally when the killings are carried out because the perpetrators intended to eliminate

  partially the victims' status group than it is to kill under conditions in (5).
7. It is worse to kill massively and intentionally when the killings are
  carried out because the perpetrators intended to eliminate completely the victims' status group than it is to kill under conditions
  in (6).

(5) adds the factor of a victim's group affiliation. In this chapter, we shall concentrate on (5), which seems counterintuitive, and, in the next chapter, on (6) and (7). There are two defenses of (5). The first, more controversial defense focuses on the victim, while the second one emphasizes the perpetrator. Regarding the first, the following question arises: why should the victims' group affiliation affect the severity of the offense? Even granting that numbers matter, a murder is a murder. Yet, murder is not simply murder. Who-was-murdered makes a moral difference. A comparison of two murder cases will illustrate how a vic-tims' group affiliation makes a moral difference in determining how strongly to condemn an act.

An argument for (5) depends on whether information about a victim's status significantly changes interpretations of a perpetrator's intent. If a perpetrator consciously targeted members of a specific group, then a case of mass murder begins to look like genocide. Generally, an intent that targets a specific group is more well formed than one that does not. If the accused targeted a group itself, this indicates that a certain degree of conscious thought and planning went into carrying out the actions. True, a perpetrator might target a group on the spur of the moment.[24] However, generally speaking, to single out a group, the perpetrators must have deliberately reflected upon the actions before undertaking them. It takes at least a modicum of thought to identify the group even when the target group's identity is relatively well known (females, for example). In some cases, it would take a great deal of time and effort to construct the contours of a group (lesbian feminists, for example). Lépine had a better-formed intent than Cruse, in part, because Lépine targeted members of a group. Generally, state criminal codes hold individuals (Lépine, for example), with their well-formed, malign intentions, more responsible than they do those (Cruse) who act out of rage and passion.

The issue of victim group status is not only less controversial in inter-national criminal law but it is also a critical element of the crime of genocide. Genocide has an element that makes it distinct from any other crime and that raises it to the status of the worst crime. That element concerns the targeted victims of genocide. Even if other harms might exceed genocide in terms of sheer numbers of victims and the degree of institutional intent, genocide remains distinct. Unlike any other form of mass deaths, genocide has no reasonable justification because of the status of its victims. Even if the Nazis claimed to kill Jews because of their acts such as carrying out mercenary business deals or killing Christ, those acts cannot be ascribed to all, if any, members of the group except by means of highly unjustifiable group association.

Conceptually, genocide's definition, unlike a definition of homicide, includes an element of moral condemnation. Homicide is defined, in part, as the killing of a human being, but the definition does not automatically invoke a moral condemnation. It would not be redundant to state "This act was the killing of a human being" and "This act was morally wrong." An instance of killing a person might have a justification, such as self-defense.

Genocide is defined (in part) as killing group members because of their group membership. The reason for the act is built into the definition of the act. That reason (group status of victims) never provides a justification for the act. Group membership never suffices as a reason for the killing members of the group. Membership in the Mafia does not excuse the police killing Mafia members. Even in cases where the nature of some criminal acts, for example, criminal conspiracy, extends the boundaries of responsibility, inclusion in the constructed group does not provide law enforcement officials with an excuse to killing coconspirators. The "*genos*" aspect of genocide (unlike the "*homo*" component of homicide) contributes to (1) the description of the act (killing group members), (2) the description of the perpetrator's reason for committing the act ("because of the victims' group status"), and (3) the formulation of the moral wrong ("killing individuals because of their group status").

Like homicide, regicide (the killing of a monarch) conceivably might find a defensible justification. True, it would never suffice to justify regicide on grounds that a person deserved to die because he or she served as a monarch. However, the monarch might have done something deplorable, such as murdering thousands of subjects, and only regicide can stop the atrocities. Under these circumstances, the perpetrator might have a reasonable justification for committing regicide. A parallel analysis does not apply to genocide. Genocide does not have exceptional circumstances that morally would permit its undertaking. The victims, that is, the "*homo*" or the "*rex*, could have conceivably done something to deserve death. All members of the "*genos*" never could have conceivably done something to deserve their deaths.

The key to the difference lies with the term *"genos,"* which designates a status, namely, group membership, and not an action. Even if members of a group engaged in criminal action, the group designation extends beyond those individuals to other clearly innocent group members. An individual's status and not an individual's action provide the reason an individual becomes a genocide victim. Individuals killed in genocide have not done any action that would even remotely warrant their death. Therefore, the collective designation *"genos"* automatically carries with it a degree of innocence not shared by other similar terms, for example, by the terms *"homo"* and *"regis."*[25] This conceptual analysis does not constitute full-fledged proof of the nonjustifiability of genocide. Nevertheless, it shifts the burden to those who entertain the possibility of finding a defensible (and nonfanciful) justification for genocide.

To further accentuate conceptual differences between genocide and other types of killing, compare the following sets of statements:

(1a)   X committed homicide.
(1b)   X killed a human being.
(1c)   The killing done by X was unjustified and inexcusable.
(2a)   X committed genocide.
(2b)   X killed some individuals because of their group affiliation.
(2c)   The killings done by X were unjustified and inexcusable.
(2d)   X killed members of a *"genos,"* and X was justified or had an excuse.

(1b) partially defines the term "homicide" in (1a). Although (2b) also partially defines (2a), it does something more as evidenced by the word "because" in (2b). (2b) provides a reason for the killings and thereby sets the grounds for a condemnation of the act, making (2c) largely redundant. Given (2a) and (2b), (2c) adds little other than a clarification of what (2b) already contains, namely, an acknowledgment that the killings were unjustified and inexcusable. In comparison, (1c) does add important new evaluative claims to (1b). (1b) specifies that a killing took place, but (1b) leaves open the issue whether the killing was justified or excused. (1c) conceptually includes an assessment of the act. (2b) specifies that the killings were unjustified and inexcusable. (2c) clarifies (2b) without adding new evaluative information. So, the statement: (1d) ("X killed a human being, and X was justified or had an excuse") consists of two statements that both provide information. However, the statement: (2d) ("X killed members of a *'genos'*, and X was justified or had an excuse.") contains a second statement ("X was justified or had an excuse.") that does not provide new evaluation. In fact, if justifications and excuses do not apply to cases of genocide, then the second statement is false. In the case of the killing a person, X might appeal to a justification based on the victim's actions. For example, the victim may have threatened X in such a manner as to raise a self-defense justification for X. In the case of genocide, X may not appeal to a justification based on the victim's actions. The nature of genocide precludes defenses based on a victim's actions. Individuals do not become genocide victims because of any of their actions. Rather, individuals become genocide victims because of their status as members of a group.

Mother Teresa applied the label Holocaust to abortion. Elie Wiesel, a Holocaust survivor, responded, "I resent the violence of the language—the words that they use like Holocaust—no it [abortion] is not a Holocaust. It is blasphemy to reduce a tragedy of such monumental propositions to this human tragedy, and abortion is a human tragedy."[26] Echoing these sentiments, I reject the equivalence of abortion and genocide. Abortion, unlike genocide, is subject to a rational and ethical debate, with rational proponents on opposite sides of the question. There should be no debate over the justifiability of genocide. Unlike the abortion issue, holding a debate where one side defends genocide would be a debate that must be boycotted and condemned.

Domestic criminal justice systems generally do not consider victim status to be an element of homicide, whereas the charge of genocide does. Finally, domestic criminal justice puts a great deal of emphasis on defenses the accuse can raise. Should international criminal law do the same?

Justifications

Domestic criminal codes also differentiate crimes according to the latitude permitted for defenses, justifications, and excuses. Let us call this element "strictness of criminal liability." The perpetrator of genocide should not (even though, under current practice, they can) be able to appeal to excuses involving circumstances or to defenses about mental states. In homicide cases, a defendant may bring exculpatory claims based, for example, on proving coercion or entrapment. In genocide cases, a defendant should not be able to use an appeal to circumstances as exculpatory. The reasons for the asymmetry regarding homicide and genocide are conceptual and pragmatic. In a state criminal justice system, when a defendant uses aspects of the circumstances for a defense, the case brings only a small portion of the structure of the entire political and legal system into question. If a state official coerces someone into committing a homicide, a defense based on the official's actions does not call into question the entire state structure. If a court grants a defendant an excuse based on circumstances, it may lead to an indictment of part of the political and legal system. If a perpetrator of genocide tries to justify genocide by focusing on the circumstances, the perpetrator may bring the entire government, for example, all of the heinous rules, regulations, and acts employed by the Nazi regime, into the question. In genocide cases, if a court grants a defendant an excuse based on circumstance, it may result in excusing all individuals similarly accused. The circumstances at stake in genocide cases can cover the entire system.

An insanity defense raises a host of issues. For a charge of homicide, a defendant may plead insanity at two junctures, namely, with respect to the ability to stand trial and with regard to the charge itself. The second type of insanity plea relates to the intent element. A successful plea of insanity undermines the state's burden to prove that a suspect had the requisite intent needed for criminal liability. There is a particularly telling aspect of the insanity issue that emerges when applied to genocide cases. An insanity type of plea in genocide cases should address the appropriate type of intent, namely, institutional intent. A successful insanity plea in that context would undercut an attempt to prove institutional intent. In genocide cases, then, an insanity defense would take the form of claiming that irrationalism had engulfed an entire society. As with the case of excuses based on circumstances, if insanity pleas functioned in genocide cases as they do in homicide cases, they then permit excusing an entire population that found itself caught in a wave of irrationalism. Genocide acts would then become excused by reason of an insanity writ large. If an international criminal justice system permitted a form of insanity defense in genocide cases, its action would have a serious implication not found if excuse of circumstances were permitted. If the legal system even entertained something like a "collective insanity plea," then it would have effectively dismissed the very idea of a crime of genocide.

Accused perpetrators of genocide direct their actions at victims. To direct actions at a group requires sane, rational calculation. Genocide killings are not collateral damage. Historically, genocide acts have not arisen from spontaneous mass hysteria. Acts of genocide unfurl in a relatively orderly manner. Genocide, in many ways, is quite sane. If a legal system accepts a plea based on some claim of collective insanity, it, in effect, buries genocide as a crime. Admittedly, while people wonder how any sane person could kill a person under any circumstances, the criminal law allows for insanity pleas in some homicide cases. Then, a parallel to genocide cases seems to make sense. Indeed, people wonder how any sane nation could engage in genocide. Yet, the initial puzzlements in the two situations differ. While people may wonder about sane people committing murder, people have little difficulty accepting circumstances where sane people kill in self-defense. A study of genocide's history challenges attempts to question a perpetrator-state's sanity since, in many cases, they seem all too sane, in the sense of being a product of rational calculation. The case of Nazi Germany particularly unsettles partially because of the detailed calculations that went into implementing the genocide. Meticulous records, for example, calculated the costs of transporting each Jew to the death camps.

The on-going process of constructing an international criminal code should incorporate the comparative judgments similar to those found in state criminal codes. An international criminal code should contain comparative judgments about the wrongfulness of the acts, the wrongfulness of the intents, the nonjustifiability of targeting status victims, and the strictness of the liabilities. The case for designating genocide as the worst international crime depends on these comparative judgments. The argument contains the following comparative claims: First, the *actus reus* of genocide generally outstrips all other crimes by its massive numbers of victims. The sheer numbers of deaths involved in genocides provide important comparative measures. Second, genocide is the only international crime to require intent, that is, the policies of an organization, typically, the state. Third, genocide acts, unlike any other international criminal act, target particularly vulnerable groups. Fourth, given a rough equivalence between the first two elements, the nonjustifiability of genocide distinguishes it from other horrific crimes. A morally defensible legal system entertains defenses, excuses, and justifications for killings. However, genocide falls more into the realm of strict liability than any other crimes of mass killings. Genocide, unlike almost any other action, has no defensible justification or, at least, it should not have any defensible justification. The four claims, defended separately later, support the general thesis that genocide has the dubious distinction of being *the* most morally reprehensible international crime. Indeed, "[n]o crime matches genocide in the moral opprobrium that it generates."[27] Torture, as examined in Chapter 4, comes the closest, but torture does not claim the massive numbers of victims and seldom results in death. We reach our "final word," as the philosopher Richard

Rorty calls it, with genocide.[28] There is no higher appeal, nothing outside the universal prohibition itself.

It is important to understand that genocide consists of a combination of factors: killings of massive numbers of victims, a well-formed institutional intent, and an underlying and nonjustifiable motive of group hatred. These factors determine the ranking of one type of grave harm, legally and morally, worse than another harm. The ranking of genocide as the worst crime or among the worst crimes is based on the following: the astronomically high numbers of victims (numbering over 10 million[29] during the twentieth century), the relatively clear-cut purposes supported by organizational structures, the targeting of vulnerable groups, and the inconceivability of finding justifications for the acts. The comparisons of genocide to slavery and war presented in the following sections further clarify and develop these claims.

Comparative Applications

Simply put, genocide ranks, legally and morally, either as among the worst mass harms or as the worst group harm. The terms "group harm" and "worst" need clarification. Genocide is a type of mass or group harm. Group harms are those harms directed against and inflicted on large numbers of people or on members of a specific group. "Worst" means, in a legal context, "deserving greater punishment." Moreover, punishments have moral underpinnings. Genocide deserves greater punishment than other international crimes because of its greater number of victims, more clearly formed institutional intent, and the nonjustifiability of the motives for the acts. Other "grave harms"—slavery and war-related deaths—challenge this ranking claim. To address these issues, the procedure will be to assess one differentiating element of genocide against a comparable element from each of these other grave harms. For countless reasons, slavery proves to be the most troubling harm to compare to genocide. The analysis uncovers a surprising measure that makes slavery more of a competitor to genocide than originally thought. Slavery (claiming an estimated 20 million deaths[30]), like genocide, has claimed countless numbers of victims of killings. However, given that deprivation of liberty lies at the core of slavery, genocide as mass killings still ranks as worse than slavery. Finally, the commission of genocide should rank as a worse crime than causing deaths under war conditions. The "nonjustifiability" factor helps to establish the controversial claim that genocide "outranks" slavery.

Slavery

Slavery, according to some analysts, successfully vies with genocide as the greatest moral wrong inflicted upon groups. Laurence Thomas is one of the few theorists to compare slavery and genocide. He argues that American slavery and the Holocaust involved two different types of harms. According to Thomas, the Holocaust was coercive in a way that slavery was not, but slavery was alienating in a way that the Holocaust was not. Thomas echoes a commonly held view that genocide kills, whereas slavery restricts liberty. Simply put, the Holocaust exterminated millions of people, while American slavery denied freedom to millions of people. Accordingly, slavery and genocide, each reprehensible, harm people in different ways. Both, however, are coercion in that a fate is imposed on people against their will, but the fates are different.[31] Moreover, this comparative judgment overlooks an activity that slavery and genocide share, namely, killing. The institution of slavery did more than restrict freedom. Slavery also killed. During the slave trade, over 20 million people of African descent lost their lives. Given that victim numbers matter when comparing harms, the suffering and deaths associated with slavery and genocide make them comparable harms.

For the sake of argument, let us leave aside the fact that slavery indeed killed and kills. So, the task becomes to compare genocide's killings with slavery's restriction of freedom. Perhaps, then, killing does not always rank as the worst crime. Sometimes it seems that the living hell of suffering outranks even death. As the saying goes, "It is better to die than to suffer." The old adage reflects situations where suffering ranks higher than dying on a scale of harms. Let us make another controversial assumption that plantation owners in the South rarely physically mistreated their slaves. The noted historian Stanley Elkins conceded that it would not stretch the truth to accept the "sympathetic picture of a just regime tempered with paternal indulgence on the majority of well-run plantations."[32] Even if slavery involved few instances of overt physical suffering, it still would rank, along side genocide, as one of the worst wrongs.

Along with saying "We would rather die than suffer physically" goes the saying "Sometimes, we would prefer physical to psychological suffering." A system that condemns a person to eternal servitude because of the person's group identity inflicts a terrible wrong. Even if slavery did not include killings or physically abuse, it eats at the overall fabric of a society that permits and supports it.

Before the Civil War, George Fitzhugh used a comparative ploy to defend slavery.[33] Fitzhugh argued that the Southern plantation system offered freedom to slave at least compared to the real slavery of the Northern wage-labor system. He claimed that Northern capitalists exploited the working class, while Southern communists assumed responsibility for slaves. Even granting Fitzhugh's claims (including the contention that both systems degrade), a slave system's directed degradation still sets it apart from a capitalist system's exploitation. Notice that it makes sense to talk about slavery as a purposeful policy ("institutional intent"). Southern slavery had the explicit purpose of degradation, and it further aimed its degrading practices at members of one type of group. The case for the egregious nature of the harm in slavery systems surfaces after discharging the assumptions and fully acknowledging slavery's brutality. Besides its degrading function, slavery kills and physically maims making it all the worse. Moreover, while many forms of slavery amounted to forms of involuntary servitude, where, after a certain period of indenture, the victim might attain freedom, Southern slavery existed in perpetuity, that is, even a victim's children became slaves at birth, with no hope of freedom.

The comparison between slavery and genocide is not an idle or perverse academic exercise. An acknowledgment of the similarity between the respective group harms might help to heal the wounds between African Americans and Jews in the United States. Members of each community do not seem to recognize fully the other group's pains. A comparative framework also provides a way to evaluate international responses to harm. The mass killings in Cambodia and in Rwanda demanded international action. Yet, these atrocities received far less international attention than apartheid in South Africa did. Even if apartheid is a form of slavery, the situations in Cambodia and Rwanda warranted at least the same degree of humanitarian attention that apartheid received. This does not imply that the international community should not have vigorously attacked racism in South Africa. To the contrary, the international community should have done more. Rather, the comparison highlights a failure to address the great and recurring horror of genocide. If genocide and slavery outrank famine and war on the scale of group harms, then the international community should establish a new set of priorities.

At some level, the harms inflicted by slavery and by genocide may be equally reprehensible. From this observation, it does not follow that, as Thomas concludes, "there are no clear criteria by which one institution could be deemed more evil than the other."[34] Overall, genocide ranks as worse than slavery for one simple reason, genocide necessarily kills but slavery does not. That means that slavery always holds the hope not only of life but also of a better life. No such claim can be made of genocide.

War

International law uses the term "war crimes" as a general category (genocide, crimes against humanity, crimes against peace, and war crimes) and as a specific type of war crime. Violations of the laws of war in armed conflict fit under the specific category "war crimes," which is the subject of this section. Students often scoff at the phrase "laws of war" when they first hear it. They have come to accept, without question, the adage "All is fair in love and war." It, then, comes as a surprise when they learn that, the specific category "war crimes" has a longer history of being subject to international law than any of the other three under the general label "war crimes." Contemporary codifications of the laws of war go back to the 1860s. They begin with Lieber's Code during the US Civil War and the international agreements adopted through the efforts of Henry Dunant (founder of the International Committee of the Red Cross). Despite on-going attempts to lessen the sufferings inflicted through wars, wars still take their toll. The numbers of war deaths, like genocide deaths, are quite high, with World War II claiming over 40 million, which represents a low estimate. Nevertheless, a numerical comparison of deaths shows that genocide now outranks war. Before World War II, the specific category of war crimes ranked above other forms of mass killings. However, since World War II, genocide has overtaken war crimes, again, as measured by the number of persons killed. Rummel has found that genocide deaths are now, "more than all the war-dead of all this century's international and civil wars, including World Wars I and II, the Korean and Vietnam Wars, the Russian and Mexican revolutions, and the Spanish and Chinese Civil Wars."[35]

Comparisons of war crimes and genocide require differentiating them. According to one definition, war is a "large-scale violent conflict between organized groups that are or that aim to establish governments."[36] Genocide differs in that the victims of genocide are "selected for death on the basis of group membership, rather than any transgressions against the killers."[37] Genocide occurs "without regard to whether an individual has committed any specific and punishable transgression."[38] However, the distinction between war crimes and genocide begins to blur when war deaths are included. Civilians targeted in war do not seem any less innocent than members of status groups targeted in cases of genocide. In World War I, civilians accounted for five percent of deaths; by World War II, civilian deaths increased to two-thirds of all deaths. By the 1970s, civilians accounted for seventy-three percent of war deaths, and in the 1980s, they comprised eight-five percent.[39] Civilians, like genocide victims, presumably did not commit any specific and punishable transgressions.

The international community should condemn, unequivocally, the horrors inflicted on innocent civilians. Nevertheless, *"democide,"* as Rummel calls the intentional government killing of an unarmed person or people, is NOT genocide. Article II of the Genocide Convention reads: "The perpetrator intended to destroy, in whole or in part, that national, ethical, racial or religious group, *as such*" (Italics, mine). The drafters inserted the words "as such" into Article II to retain a group focus. Although racial sentiments surfaced during Allied actions against Japan, those responsible for dropping the atomic bombs had not singled out and negatively defined Japanese civilians.[40] Civilians, whether they are Germans in Dresden and Hamburg or Japanese in Hiroshima and Nagasaki, did not constitute a status group, identified in negative ways before the war.[41] The individuals responsible for civilian war deaths did not identify something called a "civilian group" as the target. The inhabitants of the cities bombed during World War II suffered primarily because of the declared war between the Axis and the Allies. They did not die because, before the outbreak of the war, Allied leaders had a low regard for those types of people. Moreover, even if civilians were an explicitly targeted group, their status as civilians carried with it a complicity not found in status groups targeted for genocide. Under war conditions, civilians do not always make up a group of entirely innocent individuals. In the midst of genocide, members of ethnic and other status groups do constitute groups of innocent individuals. As part of a nation at war, civilians have varying degrees of complicity in the war effort. Many civilians make positive contributions to war. To ascribe complicity does not imply that civilians thereby deserve their fate. In contrast, however, the same assessment of complicity does not hold for members of the *"genos."*

The discussion may seem too cavalier about war-related civilian deaths. If numbers matter, then the number of civilians killed during the Leningrad siege in World War II, for example, should provoke deep-seated humanitarian concerns. "More civilians died in the siege of Leningrad than in the modernist infernos of Hamburg, Dresden, Tokyo, Hiroshima and Nagasaki taken together."[42]

During the siege of Leningrad, more than a million civilians died of starvation and disease. Despite these numbers, the Nuremberg War Crimes Tribunal exonerated Field Marshall von Leeb from the charge of war crimes. The tribunal found that von Leeb's actions, which shut out food and medicine from Leningrad, did not violate international rules of war. According to the tribunal, the Nazi siege could have hastened surrender, which is a justifiable war aim.

Michael Walzer, a prominent defender of the just war theory, attacked the tribunal's decision to excuse von Leeb. Walzer accused the tribunal of supporting, with its judgment, a glaring violation of the principles underlying the customs of war. For Walzer, a commander cannot escape responsibility for the consequences of acts of coercion. Yet, even Walzer allows the commander a way to escape responsibility. According to Walzer's reasoning, if a commander offers civilians a free exit from the siege area, the commander thereby frees himself of responsibility for the subsequent civilian deaths of those who voluntarily consented to stay (provided voluntary consent is possible under those conditions). Without going into the specifics of either the tribunal's or Walzer's arguments, one thing remains evident. The tribunal and Walzer provide arguments that justify civilian deaths, even in great numbers, under wartime conditions of siege. The tribunal employs a utilitarian calculation, and Walzer imposes a precondition for a justified siege. It is at least plausible to find circumstances where either or both arguments would prevail.

Genocide cases differ from siege cases in that under no circumstances would genocide becomes justifiable. In contrast to a siege scenario, if those threatened by genocide received an exit offer, their refusal of the offer would not justify genocide. If some targeted Jews had refused to comply with orders to flee in mass to Madagascar, their refusals to flee would not have justified genocide in any form. Allegedly, in 1972, some Hutus refused to escape an impending genocide undertaken by their Tutsi rulers. Even if the Hutus freely consented to their execution, this would never justify genocide nor exonerate the perpetrators from responsibility. Even if a few "voluntary" executions saved many more lives, the result would not justify genocide.

The nonjustifiability of genocide becomes more evident when acts of genocide are compared to the use of weapons of mass destruction. On August 12, 1945, President Harry Truman told the American people:

> We have used [nuclear bombs] against those who have attacked us without warning at Pearl Harbor, against those who have starved and beaten

and executed American prisoners of war, against those who have abandoned all pretenses of obeying international laws of warfare. We have used it in order to shorten the agony of war.[43]

According to many analysts, Truman's strongest justification for dropping the bombs lies in the utilitarian calculation that nuclear bombings would shorten the war and thereby save more lives than the thousands of lives predictably lost from the bombs.

Again, let us turn to Walzer, who rejected Truman's argument on two grounds. First, the greater evil, which the United States avoided by using the bomb, was largely an evil it helped to create. The atomic bombs caused fewer casualties than the threatened dropping of incendiary bombs on Japan's cities. Physically harming someone may help prevent the perpetrator from taking more, longer-term abusive action against the victim, but the positive result hardly serves as a justification for the original beating. Second, the Americans demanded an unconditional surrender from the Japanese. Arguably, a demand for an unconditional surrender had some justification in the case of Germany. Walzer sees the case of Japan as presenting a different set of circumstances. Japan engaged in more typical forms of military expansion than Nazi Germany did. Truman may have correctly calculated that only the show of a devastating force would yield unconditional surrender, but that concession incorrectly assumes that unconditional surrender constituted the only option. Let us grant the historical assessments underlying Walzer's arguments. For purposes of this discussion, it is only necessary to accept the argument's plausibility under certain historical circumstances. Walzer's argument against the use of a nuclear weapon on civilians depends on historical conditions. The challenge, then, lies in constructing a plausible historical hypothetical that would justify nuclear devastation. The case of World War II Japan may not offer the right set of plausible scenarios for constructing a viable hypothetical to justify civilian war deaths by nuclear bombing.

Walzer hints at what a plausible hypothetical might look like. He admits that there are circumstances that justify going beyond the rules and principles governing war:

> Utilitarian calculation can force us to violate the rules of war only when we are face-to-face not merely with defeat but with a defeat likely to bring disaster to a political community.[44]

Genocide brings disaster to a political community. On Walzer's account, dropping an atomic bomb on Germany would have been justified since, with the Nazis, the Allies faced the possibility of not merely defeat but of the destruction of civilization. Accordingly, the greater harm (genocide) should override a lesser harm (civilian war deaths)—and not simply because of the numbers of deaths at stake. A war-time situation conceivably could develop, however remote the possibilities, which would justify killing civilians with atomic weapons.

A similarly constructed hypothetical for genocide does not produce a plausible justification. If it is ever justified to trade some human lives for others, it is never justified if the individuals slated for annihilation are chosen because of who they are and not because of what they did. Consider the following hypothetical: To avoid massive nuclear destruction, it proves imperative to sacrifice a group of individuals. Random selection might offer the fairest procedure available. As an alternative procedure, consider one sometimes heard in medical ethics discussions. A second selection procedure assumes that people destined to die soon anyway would suffer less pain through their sacrifice than they would from their prolonged terminal illness. The two selection standards have independent justifications. The selection criteria (random selection, lesser suffering) each have independent justifications, that is, independent from their application in the case about preventing massive harms. In contrast, a selection procedure based on genocide would never have an independent justification. The selection criterion (victims' group status), at stake in the crime of genocide, does not have some other justification independent of preventing massive harms.

The acceptance of a distinction between war deaths and genocide does not undermine or deflate the reprehensible character of war deaths. A moral condemnation of civilian war deaths does not diminish if the crime of genocide does not include killing civilians in war. Kuper and other jurists who want to conflate civilian war crimes and genocide find themselves defending the German Luftwaffe, which, unlike the Allies, did not engage in pattern bombing. Admittedly, we should balance the victors' justice meted out in the aftermath of World War II with a condemnation of war crimes committed by the victors. Nevertheless, the urgency of condemnation should not blind us to the grounds of condemnation. War crimes of this kind fit best under the category of crimes against humanity and not genocide. The International Law Commission's commentary on Article 20 of the Draft Statue for an International Criminal Court reflected this understanding when they noted that, "crimes against humanity encompass inhumane acts of a very serious character involving widespread or systematic violations aimed at the civilian population in whole or part."[45] The Rwanda

Statute, ignoring the Law Commission's insights, confused crimes against humanity (aimed at civilian populations) with genocide (aimed at negatively identified groups).

Genocide and the other war crimes sometimes accompany one another, but conceptually they must be kept distinct. Wars have some form of justification, even if particular rationales fail. In sharp contrast, genocide never has a justification. Therefore, genocide deaths stand distinct as unjustifiable in principle in contrast to war-related deaths, which, under rare circumstances, have defensible justifications. The consequences of ignoring or rejecting the ranking, where genocide is given moral priority, come into play primarily in the judicial realm. The following violates the rankings: a statute on civilian war deaths has a more severe punishment provision than a statute on genocide does.

These legal consequences pale in comparison to the political consequences for violating the Non-Equivalency Thesis: Genocide is not equivalent to other comparable crimes. The opposite of ranking acts is to treat acts as morally and legally equivalent. The final section of this chapter develops aruments against three prominent versions of the equivalency thesis. The first version treats all the acts (including killing and, what amounts to, sterilization) listed in the genocide laws as equivalent. The second regards all cases of genocide as on par. And the third version refuses to rank international crimes.

Comparative Misapplications

The attempt to avoid comparisons, especially normative ones, becomes futile and disingenuous given the many normative comparisons that go unquestioned. Even more insidious are attempts to argue that harms are morally equivalent. Critics employ this strategy in history and with regard to current conflicts. The strategy consists of attempting to diminish the condemnation of one atrocity by claiming that it is morally equivalent, that is, equally condemnable, to another atrocity: the Allied aerial bombings as morally equivalent to Nazi atrocities during World War II; Palestinian suicide bombings as morally equivalent to Israeli retaliatory attacks; and, a case discussed in detail in Chapter 3, the Tutsi slaughter of Hutus as morally equivalent to the Hutus mass killings of Tutsis.

These and other misapplications considered in this section fall under violations of the Non-Equivalency Thesis. The cases of violations of the Thesis implicitly (or, less commonly, explicitly) accept that genocide killings are morally equivalent to other types of harms. The first type of violation is found within the text of the *Genocide Convention*, which, on one reading, treats all "genocide acts" as morally equivalent. Earlier, we made a case against this interpretation, but the arguments bear repeating in this section. In a second type of violation, all "genocide killings" are treated as morally equivalent. This version often hides in the background of debates over the Holocaust's uniqueness. Since Chapter 3 fully develops the case against this equivalency, only an argument sketch is provided here. A third type of violation holds that all four types of "war crimes" are morally equivalent.

Equivalency of All Genocide Acts

Jurists seem to accept different acts as legally and morally equivalent. This stems, in part, from the misleading structure of Article II of the *Genocide Convention*, which lists the following acts of genocide:

(a) Killing members of the group;
(b) Causing serious bodily or mental harm to members of the group;
(c) Deliberately inflicting on the group conditions of life calculated to bring about its physical destruction in whole or in part;
(d) Imposing measures intended to prevent births within the group;
(e) Forcibly transferring children of the group to another group.[46]

Despite its inclusion with the other acts under the Article's subheading, the act described in section (a) is not equivalent to the acts described in sections (b–e). The genocide act of killing is not morally equivalent to the genocide-related act of sterilization ("imposing measures intended to prevent births within the group"). In general, state criminal codes hold the most severe form of punishment for individuals convicted of murder. As a particularly horrific type of murder, genocide-as-killings should hold a similar place in an international criminal code. Unfortunately, the Rome Statute that established a permanent international criminal court perpetuated the same unjustified equivalency.

Equivalency of All Genocide Killings

Most of the cases considered so far have involved comparisons of genocide with other crimes. Comparisons of different genocides also prove illuminating. All cases of genocide, in the sense of genocide-killings (as distinct, for example, from war-related killings), are not morally equivalent. Some of these genocides were worse than other genocides.

The Holocaust ranks as worse than all other genocides. At the risk of jumping ahead too quickly, I shall once again use the topic explored at length in the next chapter as a further illustration of how a systematic normative comparison helps resolve a highly contentious issue, namely, the uniqueness of the Holocaust. To compare the Holocaust with other genocides we need to determine whether the *actus reus* and the *mens rea* of the Holocaust differ in degree from other genocides. Since I have argued that all genocides are nonjustifiable, there is no need to compare the Holocaust with other genocides on that scale. Let us, then, first turn to the *actus reus* element. No other genocide has approached the numbers of innocent victims than those from Holocaust. No other genocide has matched the nearly six million Jews slaughtered in the Holocaust. It may seem difficult to compare genocides when the numbers approach the millions. However, while sheer numbers should not determine the degree of criminality, numbers are relevant to a legal and to a moral assessment. If two murders are worse than one, then the killing of six million Jews in the Holocaust qualifies as worse than the killing of 800,00 in Rwanda.

Second, regarding the *mens rea* element, no other genocide has involved an institutional intent to exterminate a group that was as deeply embedded and as fully developed within the state as the organizational policies that unfolded within the Nazi regime. Other genocides involved intents to destroy individuals because of their group affiliation, but those "institutional intents" were less well formed than were the ones operative during the Holocaust. The Nazis unleashed a machinery of destruction, with refined parts built to precise bureaucratic specifications. For example, "even though the Jews were carried in freight cars," "the German railroads billed the Security Police for the transport of the Jews, calculating the one-way fare for each deportee by the track kilometer."[47] The genocide in Rwanda lacked these "refinements." Nevertheless, the International Panel of Eminent Personalities to Investigate the 1994 Genocide in Rwanda, created by the Organization for African Unity, concluded that,

> [B]oth physical and rhetorical violence against the Tutsi as a people began immediately after October 1, 1990 and continued to escalate until the genocide actually started in April, 1994. Without question this campaign was organized and promoted, and at some stage in this period these anti-Tutsi activities turned into a strategy for genocide.

However, the Rwandan government's complicity in organizing the extermination propaganda and training the death squads paled in comparison to the industrialized extermination carried out by the Nazi regime. The *actus reus*, which includes millions of victims, together with the *mens rea*, which includes countless policies purposefully implemented, places the Holocaust, not in a unique position, but at the top of hierarchy as the worst genocide. Further, the two elements interrelate. It is difficult to conceive how the massive numbers deaths during the Holocaust could have occurred other than through careful planning. I shall defend these claims in the next chapter. Here, they serve to complete the comparative picture. They also help set a standard to detect bad comparisons.

Equivalency of All War Crimes' Categories

The military tribunals that followed World War II provide many illustrations of illicit comparisons. The Nuremberg trials (1945–1946) did not widely employ the term "genocide." Although the term appears in the indictment of the German war criminals, it did not occur either in the Charter of the International Military Tribunal or in the opinions of the Tribunal. However, the phrase "crimes against humanity" in Article 6(c) of the Charter does include acts of genocide.[48] Consider what atrocity or crime loomed the largest in decisions at the Nuremberg and Tokyo trials. At the time of those trials, genocide had not even been recognized as an international crime in its own right. However, the Allied Military Tribunals did not ignore genocide. What later international documents explicitly designated as "genocide" fit under "crimes against humanity" in the Nuremberg indictments. Note, however, that by placing Crimes Against Humanity, Crimes Against Peace, and War Crimes on the same unranked level, genocide implicitly and incorrectly attains the status of being regarded no worse than Crimes Against Peace. Further, because of its inclusion under Crimes Against Humanity, the acts later designated as genocide became one among many inhumane acts such as enslavement and deportation.

Unlike state criminal indictments, the Nuremberg Tribunal did not have a way to charge greater or lesser crimes. The crucial test for ranking the severity of a crime comes at the punishment phase and not at the indictment phase of a criminal proceeding. In state criminal codes, premeditated or first-degree murder has harsher penalty provisions than vehicular homicide. An analysis of sentences imposed at Nuremberg and Tokyo reveal that Crimes Against Peace ranked far higher in terms of severity than Crimes Against Humanity. The tribunals regarded Crimes Against Peace, which included the "preparation, initiation or waging a war of aggression" as the most severe and most deplorable crime carried out by Germany and Japan during World War II. Moreover, the Nuremberg Charter unduly restricted crimes against humanity to international war situations.[49] Genocide does not always occur in the midst of an international conflict as the case of 1994 genocide in Rwanda vividly demonstrated. Fortunately, the United Nations has cured this defect in Article I of the Convention on the Prevention and Punishment of the Crime of Genocide (Genocide Convention), which explicitly recognizes the potential for genocide to occur "in time of peace or in time of war."[50] Fortunately, the Rome Treaty on the International Criminal Court retains this understanding. Further, problems with even having a definition of Crimes Against Peace or aggression reflect its relative lower status.

Conclusion

Although skeptics may listen to arguments made for ranking group harms, they still might see the entire exercise as futile. They might think that even if one type of group harm is worse than another harm, these comparative judgments have little practical import. Controversies over whether one grave injustice is worse than another one seem to be idle academic exercises.

However, if, for example, the 1994 Rwanda genocide was worse than any other mass killings over the past decade, then we must seriously question, as we do in Chapter 3, the relative silence given to Rwanda in international law, international relations, and related academic studies. Further, while unable to convince the skeptic, international jurists would more readily see the benefits that ranked order of harms has for a global legal system. A hierarchy of group harms provides a framework for the hierarchical codification of crimes under the jurisdiction of the International Criminal Court. The international community faces a serious political and moral challenge, analogous to triage in emergency medical care. It should direct political energies to the worst injustices. Perhaps, this study will contribute, in some small way, to sorting out the many injustices infecting the world.

CHAPTER 2

Comparing Genocides

On January 22, 1941, members of the Legionnaires of the Archangel Michael or Iron Guard, a major political party in Romania, drove 20 Jewish men, women, and children through the automated stages of a local slaughterhouse. After thrusting each body on a hook, they stamped the decapitated and limbless torsos "fit for human consumption."[1]

Descriptions of any genocide sicken the stomach, but the cumulative descriptions of the Holocaust overwhelm. Something about the Holocaust seems to make it different from other horrors. The sense of the Holocaust's unusual place has an academic counterpart centering on the Holocaust's uniqueness. The debate over the Holocaust's uniqueness took center stage with the publication of *Is the Holocaust Unique? Perspectives in Comparative Genocide*.[2] Furious arguments between the anthology's editor and contributors almost derailed its publication. Steven T. Katz, a Cornell University professor of Jewish thought and history, argued for the Holocaust's uniqueness.[3] David Stannard, a professor of American studies at the University of Hawaii and a leading proponent of classifying the decimation of indigenous people as genocide, called Katz the moral equivalent of a Holocaust denier.[4] It may seem that the problems began when the authors received the green light to compare genocides. However, it is critical not to place the blame on the comparative enterprise. It is more a question of the quality of the comparisons than the act of comparing.[5]

This chapter confronts two obstacles to making comparisons among genocides. The first obstacle revolves around claims of Holocaust's uniqueness. We shall reject defenses of the uniqueness of the Holocaust and then go on to compare it with other genocides. However, in terms of the extent of the killings, the development of state policy, and the vulnerability of the victim group the Holocaust surely rank as the worst genocide so far.

The second, and related, obstacle relates to icons. In Chapter 4, on torture I shall defend the use of icons. Here, somewhat paradoxically, I argue against their use. For one thing, the icons surrounding the Holocaust lend support to the discredited uniqueness hypothesis. More critically, these carefully deployed icons tend to undermine otherwise valuable comparative judgments. Nothing else quite lives up to the Holocaust. Nothing matches the cattle cars, the gas ovens, and the barbed wired extermination camps. Letting icons hold sway in debates over genocide has some devastating consequences. Bosnia, sharing more icons with the Holocaust, looks more like genocide than Rwanda, which shares few of the iconic images.

Finally, comparisons among actual and purported cases of genocide produce some important insights. Kosovo, Darfur, and Stalin's famine fail in bids to qualify as genocides. Attempts to downgrade the genocide status, for example, of the Armenian genocide are found wanting. Comparisons among purported and actual examples of genocide demonstrate the moral priority of the Holocaust. They also put each mass atrocity in its proper historical, legal, and moral place. As a more carefully adumbrated concept, then, genocide becomes a more useful and powerful tool in debates over humanitarian intervention.

Holocaust

The first part of this chapter demonstrates that a comparative analysis, rather than serving as an impediment, offers hope for a rational resolution of some hotly contested issues. A comparative analysis can lead representatives of different victim groups to recognize each other's pain and suffering, accept that some groups have experienced greater injustices than other groups have experienced, and acknowledge that at least one group has experienced worse injustices than any other group. The comparative study undertaken here constructs a hierarchy of harms needed to support the following argument: The Holocaust (i.e., the extermination of Jews during World War II) ranks as the worst genocide in recent history. However, even the Holocaust's highest ranking as the worst genocide does not entail its uniqueness, at least, in any ordinary sense of the term. To give highest status to the Holocaust on the scale of grave injustices does not provide support for its uniqueness. The Holocaust has moral priority over other genocides, which means that the Holocaust has been morally the worst genocide. Unfortunately, the uniqueness debate shies away from moral claims and diverts attention to epistemological issues. The moral comparisons of genocide cases do not deflate the historical, political, and legal importance of the Holocaust. To the contrary, the comparisons bolster the case for directing the strongest moral outrage at the Holocaust.

Scholars who proclaim the Holocaust's incomprehensibility make a powerful case. However, the incomprehensibility thesis, as discussed in the next section, faces insurmountable obstacles. It is precisely the challenge posed by the seeming incomprehensibility of the Holocaust that feeds and ultimately undermines the closely associated claims for the Holocaust's uniqueness. Proponents of the incomprehensibility and uniqueness theses face a dilemma. On the one hand, if they entertain the Holocaust's comprehensibility, then that admission would make its horror "all too human," thereby detracting from the enormity of the horror. On the other hand, if they want to convey the enormity of the horror of the Holocaust, they must make it comprehensible. The next section examines a more precise formulation of this dilemma.

Uniqueness: A Dilemma

According to one philosopher, the debate over the Holocaust's uniqueness generates a dilemma.

> If the Holocaust is the truly unique and unprecedented historical event that it is often held to be, then it must exceed the possibility of human comprehension, for it lies beyond the reach of our customary historical and sociological means of inquiry and understanding. If it is not a historically unique event, if it is simply one more incident in the long history of man's inhumanity to man, there is no special point in trying to understand it, no unique lesson to be learned.[6]

An analysis of this dilemma highlights the problems with this type of formulation. It also exposes misleading aspects of the uniqueness debate.

Both horns of the dilemma contain questionable assumptions.[7] Take the first premise, "If the Holocaust is unique, then it is beyond human comprehension." An event's uniqueness does not divorce it from the realm of human understanding even if we limit the realm of understanding to those items amenable to the investigative tools of the social sciences. The challenge facing the social sciences is to uncover the conditions and circumstances that led to the Holocaust. The origins of the Holocaust are certainly open to empirical investigation. Whether we can generalize from the conditions and circumstances that social scientists find and what form the generalizations take pose entirely different problems. Contrary to the assumptions in this part of the argument, a truly unique and unprecedented historical event does not need to exceed the possibility of human comprehension. A social scientist may not be able to infer any scientific generalities from the occurrence of an unprecedented event nor predict future events from descriptions of the past event. Nevertheless, because universal scientific laws do not govern an event does not mean that the event is beyond human comprehension. The historian, for example, still can make an unprecedented event comprehensible by showing how not only one event specifically led to another in this historical circumstances but also how one type of event led to another type of event.

Let us turn to the second premise. If the conditions and circumstances are not unique in the sense that they have occurred before and after the Holocaust, then, contrary to premise two ("If the Holocaust is not unique, then there is no need to understand it"), the need to understand the Holocaust remains. Knowing the similarities between the Holocaust and other genocides can enrich the historical understanding of them, and the comparisons can provide tools for an early warning system of genocides yet to come. Prevention should motivate some genocide studies. Yet, if "uniqueness" means "unprecedented in the past and non-recurring in the future," then early warning systems become futile. Warning systems assume some similarities between past and future genocides. Logically, warning systems are not incompatible with "unprecedented in the past," since a past unique event could recur in the future, but rationales for warning systems conflict if the past subject of the warning is described as "non recurring in the future." Practically, the more similarities there are among past genocides, including the Holocaust, and the more plausible similarities these have with future genocides, the more reliable the early warning system.

A further analysis of the dilemma reveals advantages and disadvantages of giving priority to some forms of discourse over others. The first horn of the dilemma presumes that the Holocaust's uniqueness debate challenges empirical understanding and says nothing about ethical issues. Yet, supposedly historical lessons as well as greater empirical understanding emerge from these inquiries. History provides the materials for the "lessons to be learned." A lesson might come in the form of a strong warning to exercise caution when considering research programs similar to those that contributed to Nazi ideology and practices. However, lessons like these remain indirect. What, if any, moral lessons emerge from studies of the Holocaust? Perhaps I have focused too much on a single terse statement of a dilemma. However, the single epistemological focus evident in the analyses represents a common approach adopted in Holocaust studies. George Kren and Leon Rappoport, authors of *The Holocaust and the Crisis of Human Behavior*, typify scholars in this field when they proclaim, "[w] hat is at stake here is the necessity to come to grips with the underlying epistemologies of genocide."[8] To the contrary, morality, not epistemology, poses the most important stakes in the uniqueness debate. Researchers present historical material from which to draw moral lessons. However, before they begin, scholars should understand the moral categories they use implicitly. To many researchers, talk of "morality" seems specious, personal, and primitive. Yet, beneath the uniqueness claim lies a moral thesis that nothing compares to the moral reprehensibility of the Holocaust. Perhaps scholars find the moral condemnation of the Holocaust so obvious that it does not bear repeating. More plausibly, the uniqueness debate hides the moral categories within discussions that are seen as epistemological. The use of epistemological categories to frame the uniqueness debates avoids a confrontation with those who fail to or refuse to condemn the Holocaust in the strongest moral terms. In the end, contemporary moral perspectives have more to do with the uniqueness debate than historical empirical views.

The uniqueness debate says more about the participants in the debate than about the perpetrators and victims. The uniqueness debate reflects a groping for understanding. It symbolizes the difficulty in fathoming how and why the Holocaust occurred. The uniqueness debate reflects a reluctance to go beyond attempts to understand to a seemingly more difficult plateau that requires the adoption of an explicitly moral position, such as the following. "Uniqueness" serves, at best, as a misleading term for our highest form of moral condemnation. The Holocaust uniqueness debate wrongly uses surrogates for normative claims and avoids an essential moral analysis. Scholars search history for clues of uniqueness and insulate themselves from the far more daunting moral task. Further, resolution of the uniqueness debates, if any exist, hinges on value judgments, not on empirical findings, although the latter are relevant to the former. The uniqueness debate has implications for how to understand the Holocaust. Yet, the uniqueness debate lacks a telling ingredient, namely, the centrality of a moral framework. This does not thereby insinuate that the debates are devoid of moral sensitivity.

The problem lies not so much in scientific posturing, which portends to exclude the ethical dimension for the analysis. Rather, the difficulty stems more from treating the empirical mode of discourse as more important than the ethical. However, let us first try to clarify the incomprehensibility claim.

Incomprehensibility: A Problem

Survivors often refer to the overwhelming incomprehensibility of the Holocaust. Let us just take one example of this, namely, disrespect for the dead, to show how some aspects of the Holocaust are not morally relevant moral features. A Holocaust survivor, Primo Levi, in his last book, written before he committed suicide, provided one of the more telling accounts:

> The human ashes coming from the crematoria, tons daily, were easily recognized as such, because they often contained teeth or vertebrae. Nevertheless, they were employed for several purposes: as fill for swamp lands, as thermal insulation between the walls of wooden buildings, and as phosphate fertilizer; and especially notable, they were used instead of gravel to cover the paths of the SS village located near the camp, whether out of pure callousness or because, due to their origins, they were regarded as material to be trampled on, I couldn't say.[9]

The Holocaust allegedly pushed civilization's moral categories to the limit or perhaps beyond the limit. The Nazis stretched the previously unthinkable idea of "total destruction" into a now unfortunately imaginable form by ordering the destruction of Jewish bones. Arguably, their actions surpassed those of the serial killer Jeffrey Dahmers. Dahmers ate the hearts of his victims. Yet, perhaps the repulsive acts of this serial killer show, in a perverted sense, more respect for victims than the Nazis' acts of complete annihilation. As the philosopher Emil Fackenheim noted, graves characterize civilization. The Final Solution had no burial for Jews. The Nazis extended "annihilation of the living" to "annihilation of the dead."

For some Holocaust scholars, these actions go beyond the limits of morality. The Nazis took actions beyond any then-known terms of moral condemnation. As proof, these scholars note that expressions of disgust at someone's actions occur within the confines of morality. The Nazis' deeds went beyond disgust. If the Nazis, like Dahmers, had eaten their victims' hearts, that repulsive act would have shown that they had some respect for their victims and that they had some humanity left in them. The Nazis, accordingly, exceeded even those outer limits of morality. The Holocaust stands, then, as incomprehensible.

The problem is the disrespect for the dead is the wrong practice to emphasize about the Holocaust if the goal is to demonstrate the enormity of it as an injustice. First of all, ethicists rationally disagree over burial practices. Ethicists vary over how to assess treatment of the dead. Some moralists would find survivors who ate human corpses to stay alive after a plane crash in the Andes repulsive[10]; other ethicists would find their behavior justifiable. Religions have widely divergent burial practices. Zoroastrians, for example, clean the deceased in bull's urine and leave the corpse on a hilltop ("Tower of Silence") for vulture consumption. Burial practices, then, are a defensible form of moral relativism that, arguably, could encompass the Nazi practices.

Second, treatment of the dead should have almost nothing to do with a moral assessment of the Holocaust. Scholars find one of the first examples of an appeal to a higher moral law in a play by Sophocles. Antigone charged King Creon with violating a natural, higher law when he prohibited the burial of her brother. "Much of jurisprudence simply rings changes on the disagreement between Creon and Antigone."[11] Yet, this is an odd place, ironically over a burial place, to build the historical foundations of natural law. A moral assessment of Creon's behavior toward Antigone's dead brother should not take precedence over a moral assessment of the acts that caused her brother's death. Generally, the morality governing treatment of the living (and the dying) should take precedence over the morality governing treatment of the dead.

Moral condemnation of how some individuals treat the living can be completely independent from a moral condemnation of what those individuals did to the dead. However, the latter moral assessment may support the former. Evidence of how individuals treat their dead victims, for example, may affect an analysis of the perpetrators' intent toward the victims. Grinding Jewish bones and throwing the ashes in the rivers shows Nazi contempt and loathing for its victims. Hatred toward the other, however, takes on many forms. The manifestations of hatred have few bounds. The intents manifested and the deeds undertaken by the Nazis reached the extremes, but given the human capacity to invent evil forms, the intents and deeds lamentably remain within the confines of comprehensibility, both moral and historical.

Another legally and morally irrelevant feature of the Holocaust, especially in comparison to other examples of genocide, is the means of annihilation. The debates over the instruments of genocide can take twisted turns. Dadrian, for example, contrasted the Holocaust's killing operations ("streamlined, mechanized, and systematic through the use of advanced technology") with the more primitive and presumably more barbarous means employed in the Armenian genocide.[12] From this comparison of means, are we to draw "the preposterous claim that Jews had it easier than victims in other genocides did because the death machinery was so efficient"?[13] What exactly are the stakes in comparisons of how atrocities have been committed? First, the stakes should be seen as moral and not as empirical. The disputants appeal to different empirical findings to show what techniques perpetrators actually used; but in the final analysis, the debate over means is a moral one. Some techniques for committing atrocities are deemed morally worse than other means. Lethal injection is supposedly a morally better way to carry out the death penalty than by hanging. On September 11, 2001, terrorists used particularly reprehensible means to carry out their attacks on the United States. However, disputes over the means are largely irrelevant in determining the level of injustice of any particular mass atrocity. The ends prove more important than the means, and that is a value judgment.

Empirical claims are relevant to genocide studies. Scholars on both sides of the uniqueness debate appeal to and interpret historical facts and empirical data. Even the fierce and ideologically charged *Historikerstreit* battle, led by German historians accused of downplaying the Holocaust, had its empirical components. Ernst Nolte, for example, claimed that "with the sole exception of the technical process of gassing" Auschwitz was not unique.[14] Jürgen Habermas attacked Nolte for trivializing the Holocaust. The disputants saw the debate as turning on issues of historical understanding, a form of empirical understanding.[15] The controversy eventually settled on whether Nolte had gotten the history wrong.

However, not all empirical matters are equally relevant. Debates over which were the worst means of committing atrocities are largely irrelevant because the means of killing (e.g., axes or guns) are rarely morally determinative in the condemnation of the acts. Even if the means of annihilation used in the Holocaust was "unprecedented in the past" and is "non-recurring in the future," that would not establish the Holocaust's uniqueness. A moral condemnation of an act begins not with morally evaluating the means taken to achieve the act but with morally condemning the act. The case for an act's wrongfulness does not depend on a moral condemnation of the instruments used to accomplish the moral condemnatory act. A moral (and not an empirical) claim underlies this uniqueness claim. In summary, then, while it is important to specify what would count as evidence in these debates, disputes over means are moral ones. However, moral debates over the means of genocide, for example, prove largely irrelevant since the moral condemnation of the ends (the act) generally completely overshadows the moral case against the means.

As shown in the next section, the morally relevant empirical factors for assessing the Holocaust and other examples of genocide are just those features singled out by the legal definition of genocide, namely, act, intent, and victim status.

Uniqueness: A Phenomenon

Katz has embarked upon an ambitious project, partially completed, which places the Holocaust in historical context. Given the work's serious and scholarly scope, any student of the Holocaust must examine it. Katz provides a definition of the phenomenological uniqueness of the Holocaust.

> The Holocaust is phenomenologically unique by virtue of the fact that never before has a state set out, as a matter of intentional principle and actualized policy, to annihilate physically every man, woman, and child belonging to a specific people.[16]

Despite his philosophical sophistication, Katz commits fundamental errors, involving the concept of "phenomenological uniqueness." Katz fails even to acknowledge difficulties in drawing a sharp distinction, required by his analysis, between facts and values. He unwittingly presents an ethical or prescriptive analysis and not simply a phenomenological or descriptive one. Instead of rehearsing the philosophical critique of a logical positivist distinction between facts and values, it proves more valuable to demonstrate the value-laden character of the empirical categories that Katz employs.

Katz uses the following schema to elucidate "phenomenological uniqueness": "$\emptyset$ is uniquely C. $\emptyset$ may share A, B, D,...X with Δ but not C. And again $\emptyset$ may share A, B, D,...X with all Δ but not C."[17] In a discussion of this schema, Katz proposes two key ingredients for C that differentiate the Holocaust from all other historical events, namely, mass killings (relative to the population base) and intentions. Indeed, taken in tandem and fully fleshed out in the next section on comparisons, these criteria succeed in distinguishing the Holocaust from similar events, but they set it apart phenomenologically (empirically) as well as ethically (in degree and not in kind).

Without the inclusion of ethical judgments, Katz cannot justify his interpretation of what constitutes C. True, other mass killings may have many of the same ingredients as the Holocaust, albeit in different degrees. However, we can characterize C in such a way that no other event shares it, and yet, we would still want to say that C does not really capture the difference. For example, the gassing at Auschwitz, which opponents of the uniqueness position conceded was a unique feature of the Holocaust, may in fact distinguish the Holocaust from all other similar events.[18] This unique feature, however, is not enough of a (moral!) difference to support the uniqueness position. Katz's proposal of the Holocaust's unique features, namely, intent and total extermination, are superior to technique features such as gassing, not because of their historical saliency but because, as ends, they are better moral categories than means. The debate over means is largely irrelevant because the means of murder, individual or group, are rarely morally determinative in the condemnation of the act. A judge may enhance the penalty for a murderer who used a particularly gruesome means to carry out the deed, but the murderer stands guilty of the same crime as the one who employs relatively benign means. Likewise, the relative degrees of moral condemnation of the Bosnian and Rwandan genocides should not depend on the differences in the means employed. Descriptions of the genocide in Rwanda often highlight the relatively crude methods used to kill as if this feature should make a moral difference. Moreover, even if the means of annihilation used in the Holocaust were "unprecedented in the past and non-recurring in the future," that would not establish the uniqueness of the Holocaust since a means analysis fails to capture the morally salient features.

Every uniqueness claim is primarily a moral and not exclusively an empirical claim. Katz's choice of mass killings and intention reflects an ethical judgment about the Holocaust. Katz must choose among the candidates for what constitutes C. Katz could maintain that he made the choice among the candidates on historical grounds, that is to say, the elements of C that he opts for are historically more salient than any other possible ones. Whatever grounds Katz chooses for making the choice, those grounds will involve evaluative judgments. Each historical account of a specific genocide will emphasize certain features over others, and some choices of those features turn on what features the historians value and devalue the most. Scholars emphasize different aspects of a given genocide's history because they value (or more accurately, devalue) those features more. Historians of the Holocaust, despite pretensions to the contrary, cannot avoid making value judgments about the investigated material. Admitting the value-laden aspects of a study does not undermine the account. Katz emphatically (and understandably) denies slipping into an ethical abyss. He correctly notes that distinguishing the Holocaust from other events does not "necessarily entail any hierarchy of immoral acts or events."[19] Denying a necessary entailment gives Katz a logical victory, but he still has not blocked making a case for a hierarchy of immoral acts. The Holocaust differs from other genocides in morally distinct ways. Ironically, Katz provides the ingredients to make just the case that he wants to avoid, namely, that "the Shoah (Holocaust) represents a new and higher level of evil."[20] Crudely put, the ingredients consist of numbers killed (degree of extermination) and perpetrators' intent.

The debate over the uniqueness of the Holocaust may have had the unintended consequence of detracting from recognizing the full severity of other cases of genocide, especially, as discussed in the next chapter, the Rwandan genocide. Further, well-meaning attempts to assure the remembrance of the Holocaust also may have the, again, unintended consequence of creating other obscuring devices—images and icons. Unlike the case of torture, examined at length in Chapter 4, the Holocaust iconography has serious drawbacks.

Holocaust Icons

The Holocaust has some powerful images—gas ovens, cattle cars, barbed wired extermination camps, and mass graves. These icons have become deeply embedded in the collective psyche—much to our detriment. Given the power and promotion of Holocaust images, this may seem like an odd stance to take. It seems to run counter to the concerted and noble efforts to assure that the world forever remembers the Holocaust; especially since soon almost no survivors will be around to remind the world of the horrors. It might seem even more difficult to understand arguments against icons in discussions on genocide when so much was made of their use in the torture debates. Needless to say, we have some explaining to do.

Torture has a clear-cut, core definition, which, as shown in Chapter 4, an icon helps to anchor, solidify, and explicate. The icon of the medieval rack helps to emphasize the core harm at stake in any form of torture, namely, the infliction of pain. Use of the icon helps to assure that more subtle forms of inflicting pain (waterboarding) do not get surreptitiously removed out from under the torture label.

Genocide, like torture, has a clear-cut, core definition. However, the Holocaust icons serve more to distort and obscure. Torture has had a longer history than genocide as a widely recognized evil. The international community has only relatively recently come to treat genocide as a universal wrong.[21] Torture, fortunately (conceptually) and unfortunately (historically), has had a much longer legacy.

Moral models, particularly in the form of images, have played an important role in the progressive development of law and morality. The Holocaust has served as a normative template against which to examine subsequent mass atrocities.[22] It was the Holocaust that led Raphael Lemkin, the Jewish Polish jurist, who first coined the term genocide, to lobby successfully for the passage of the Genocide Convention.[23] The Holocaust, as defined in terms of the Convention, does and should serve as the primary reference point for any historical, sociological, legal, philosophical, or any other scholarly examination of genocide. The Inquisition is definitionally, but not icongraphically, to torture what the Holocaust is to genocide.

The Holocaust has had an enormous impact on the world. Images of the Holocaust have been critical for assuring its lasting impact as a paradigm of injustice. These images have stirred deep-seated reactions of revulsion at the enormity of this injustice in every generation since. One iconic image of the Holocaust is pictures of Jews packed into cattle cars on their way to the death camps.

While pictures of gas ovens and cattle cars have become iconic for the Holocaust, they have not become icons of genocides in general, in part because gas killings and cattle car deportation were particular marks of the Holocaust. However, pictures of emaciated, starving Jews looking forlornly past the barbed wire enclosure, as discussed further, have become icons of the Holocaust as well as of other genocides.

These images are not simply evocative. They have provided a moral template that has helped to bring similar incidents within the folds of genocide, as happened with the war in Bosnia. "The scenes of emaciated and terrified men confined to detention camps in north-western Bosnia and Herzegovina, first discovered by Western reporters in the summer of 1992, indelibly reminded the international public of images last seen in Europe during the Holocaust."[25] The reporting and pictures used by Roy Gutman and made by Patrick Roberts and others helped to mobilize a humanitarian intervention in Bosnia.[26]

Figure 2.1 Young survivors behind a barbed wire fence in Buchenwald Concentration Camp[24]

Making a case for the pivotal role of these iconic images in moral and legal debates does not mean that there are no problems with these iconographies. The use of every icon must be a subject of close scrutiny and vigorous critique. Some raised serious questions about the icons of the Bosnian war, including critics who accused Gutman of having staged his photograph of Bosnians behind barbed wire in order to have it published on the cover of *Time* magazine.[27] Yet there seems to be little evidence of that, especially as the images used by Gutman reflected a grim, gruesome reality that also was captured by other photographers, such as Patrick Roberts.[28]

An even more important icon and finding for both the Holocaust and the Bosnian War were mass graves. Mass graves have proven to be a critical piece of the evidence needed to substantiate the legal charges of not only crimes against humanity, but also genocide. Consider further whether the same or similar icons applied to the later war in

Figure 2.2 Bosniak prisoners behind a barbed wire fence of the Manjaca Concentration Camp near Prijedor, Bosnia[29]

Kosovo. One of the difficulties faced by those who wanted to justify the humanitarian intervention in Kosovo was the lack of gruesome depictions.[30] Admittedly, the massacre of 45 civilians at Racak triggered NATO involvement.[31] However, there has been sparse evidence or images in the form of mass graves.[32] Finally, images also can serve as reminders of where horrific massacres did take place in, for example, Srebrenica during the Bosnian War. Images of abandoned shoes from the Holocaust have become an icon of the mass killings in Bosnia.

Despite the power and many positive uses of these Holocaust images, I want to argue against their use. It is not only important but also essential to compare mass atrocities. It is critical to have a way to determine whether a mass atrocity qualifies as genocide. If it does, then that should start a powerful legal and political machine in motion. A determination of an impending or pending genocide makes outside intervention not only palatable but also morally if not legally obligatory.

Holocaust images block, distort, and obscure the analysis. Holocaust images, for example, helped to make the atrocities undertaken in Bosnia look more like genocide than the mass killings committed in Rwanda. Since the next chapter focuses on Rwanda, let us consider another negative facet of using Holocaust images as moral and legal templates to evaluate other atrocities.

The legal definition of genocide, although as clear cut as the one for torture, has a complexity not found in the torture definition. Victim status is a crucial component of the definition of genocide. It is more difficult to convey that critical aspect of genocide with images.

Comparisons of Genocides: Purported and Actual

The analysis of the Holocaust carried out so far has its own danger of undermining the severity of the Holocaust. This section should set the record straight by defending the following claim: The Holocaust has been and probably will remain the worst case of genocide. The comparisons presented in the previous sections undermine claims of uniqueness for the Holocaust but support claims of highest legal and moral ranking of the Holocaust. *Actus reus* and *mens rea* constitute two aspects of criminality. To maintain the moral priority of the Holocaust over other genocides the proponents needs to show that the *actus reus* and the *mens rea* of the Holocaust differ in degree from other genocides. This burden can be met. First, regarding the *actus reus*, no other genocide has approached the numbers of innocent victims killed in the Holocaust. It may seem difficult to compare any genocide when the numbers approach the millions. However, while sheer numbers should not determine the degree of criminality, numbers are relevant to a moral and legal assessment. No other genocide has matched the nearly six million Jews slaughtered in the Holocaust. Two murders are worse than one. By extension, then, the killing of six million Jews was worse than the killing of 20,000 male homosexuals by the Nazis. Second, regarding the *mens rea*, no other genocide has invoked as pronounced or as well-formed state policy to destroy a group, as did the Holocaust. While this claim may be the subject to debate, its formulation should set the terms for future debate. Anti-Semitism has a long and sordid history, which saw prejudice and discrimination become hatred and extermination. No other viable hypothesis even begins to explain the Holocaust than the claim that Jews were purposefully targeted for extermination. Other genocides involved intents to destroy individuals because of their group affiliation, but those intents were less well formed than the ones operating during the Holocaust. A combination of *actus reus* and *mens rea* places the Holocaust not in a unique position but at the top of a hierarchy as the worst genocide. The *actus reus* and the *mens rea* interrelate. It is difficult to conceive how the massive numbers of Jewish deaths during the Holocaust could have been brought about other than through careful planning. The Holocaust stands as the worst genocide.

Since it would take an elaborate analysis to make comprehensive comparisons among genocides, actual and purported, outlines of the comparisons and sketches of the arguments will have to suffice. The elements of the crime of genocide provide the bases for constructing comparative measures. These elements include the act, the intent, the status of the victims, and the issue of justifications. Acts of genocide, that is, massive killings, have occurred with varying degrees of extensiveness and intensity. Similarly, the institutional intent element of genocide comes in varying degrees. In addition, the comparisons demonstrate the importance of determining the status of the victims in debates over mass atrocities. Finally, we raise the issue of whether perpetrators had any justification for carrying out the killings and whether acts by victims or groups have any bearing on the charge of genocide.

Applications of these measures accomplish a great deal. First, the comparative studies provide counterarguments to Holocaust uniqueness claims. Second, this study makes a strong case for ranking the Holocaust as the worst genocide. Third, the comparisons bolster the status and ranking of the certain examples of genocide such as the Gypsy or Roma Holocaust, the Armenian genocide, and the Rwandan genocide. Further, the analysis also downgrades the status and ranking of, for example, the Bosnia atrocities. The comparative framework provides grounds for deciding which of the mass atrocities, such as Darfur, do not qualify as genocide. Finally, and most importantly, these comparisons illustrate the kind of analysis needed to determine the feasibility of a genocide prosecution and the grounds for intervention. All of the measures, rather than denigrating any mass atrocity, promote understanding by helping to put them into perspective.

Act

Some commentators use the extent and thoroughness of the killings of Jews as a further argument for the Holocaust's uniqueness. Some Holocaust scholars claim that the Nazis, unlike any other perpetrator, sought the total elimination of all Jews. The Jews, unlike other victim groups, never had a possibility of exit. This supposedly supports rendering the Holocaust unique. Yet, it simply highlights differences in degree and not of kind.

Unlike the Jews, the Christian Armenians, for example, may have had some chance of exit by adopting the language, culture, and religion of the Islamic majority during the early stages of the Armenian genocide. However, soon thereafter, the Young Turks found it difficult to distinguish innocent from guilty Armenians, leaving few opportunities for exit from the group. The Armenians in Turkey had relatively more exit opportunities than the Jews in Germany had. Genocides, like the Armenian one and the Holocaust, therefore, differ in degree but not in kind over conditions of exit.

Proponents of the uniqueness hypothesis carry the argument one step further by highlighting the extreme barbarity that the Nazis carried out with ruthless efficiency. The Young Turks and the Hutu *genocidaires* did not have the means of industrial annihilation at their disposal. However, Yehuda Bauer, a leading Holocaust scholar, provided evidence that seems to undermine the uniqueness-of-means claim. According to Bauer, the Young Turks set out, albeit not as blatantly and explicitly as the Nazis, to annihilate the Armenians completely using the full power of the state to carry out the annihilation. The Young Turks made "use of technological advances such as the telegraph that allowed for unprecedented coordination in the genocidal process."[33] Pierre Papazian, an Armenian scholar, parenthetically noted, "[l]acking crematoria, the Turks often turned churches to such use by burning alive the victims locked inside."[34] Thus, although the Young Turks lived in a technologically less advanced age than the Nazis, they made full use of the industrial means of annihilation at their disposal.

While, as argued earlier, debates over the means of annihilation are irrelevant to the uniqueness claim, they do have a salutatory affect on the reputed status of other genocides. The means, however primitive, of carrying out mass killings, should be largely irrelevant to assessing the horror of genocide. On that account, the Armenian and Rwandan genocides were just as horrific as the Holocaust.

A moral condemnation of an act begins not with morally evaluating the means taken to achieve the act but with morally condemning the act. The case for an act's wrongfulness does not depend on a moral condemnation of the instruments used to accomplish the moral condemnatory act. In terms of the act, measured by the extent of the killings, the Holocaust certainly holds the dubious distinction as the worst genocide.

Although "A murder is a murder," the numbers killed does and should make a legal and moral difference. Obviously, fine numerical distinctions become rather silly when comparing mass atrocities. The horror of the terrorist attack on the World Trade Center on September 11, 2001, does not dissipate if the figure of less than 3,000 deaths replaces the originally reported number of 5,000. However, scaled numerical comparisons do matter. The millions killed in the Holocaust, Rwanda, Armenia, and Cambodia put these atrocities on a different comparative plane than the thousands killed in Bosnia or Darfur. If the international community sanctioned intervention for the thousands in Bosnia, why did it not do the same for the millions slaughtered in Rwanda?

The numbers killed in Armenia and Rwanda approach those slaughtered in the Holocaust. The numbers killed in Bosnia pale in comparison, but those atrocities triggered international intervention. Kosovo presents a problematic case. For, even today, it has been difficult to find evidence of mass graves in Kosovo.

Mens Rea (Institutional Intent)

Some Holocaust scholars support the uniqueness hypothesis with the claim that the Nazis sought the total elimination of all Jews. The same difficulty of establishing a difference in kind affects disputes over total annihilation. Holocaust scholars locate uniqueness in the Nazis' intent to exterminate all Jews. This claim has come under a number of challenges. David Stannard, for example, finds the evidence that the Nazis intended to kill all Jews flimsy.[35] A cursory reading of the literature raises serious doubts about Stannard's assessment of the evidence. However, the dispute over partial or total annihilation falls by the wayside once we recognize that the uniqueness debate does not stand or fall on this empirical claim. To see the problem with casting the dispute as an empirical one, consider the question: "Did the Young Turks intend total annihilation of all Armenians?" On the one hand, Steven Katz ascribes "practical and political grounds for anti-Armenian conduct by the Young Turks, who wanted to rid their territory, not the earth of Armenians."[36] On the other hand, Dadrian cites evidence of Young Turks carrying out their genocidal policies of total extermination of the entire Armenian "race" beyond the Turkish borders to the Russian Transcaucasus.[37] Dadrian concludes that for the Young Turk Itthadists "the destruction of the Armenians was and remained a hidden agenda, a top-secret plan."[38]

What would resolve the disputes such as those between Katz and Dadrian? As a first step, we should explore treating the comparative features as "differences in degree" instead of casting them in stone as "differences in kind." The features of the Holocaust, then, would differ in degree, not in kind, from those found in other genocides. As a second step to resolving these disputes, we should construct a defensible ethical theory of genocide. If we agree to rank cases according to degrees of differences, then we need to determine what features to use for comparisons. The comparative features come clearly into view upon the adoption of an ethical framework. An ethical theory provides the moral categories needed to pick out the relevant comparative features. As an illustration, consider "severity of the offense" as a moral (and legal) category to use to pick out the relevant comparative features. However, before constructing a moral and legal framework to bring some closure to the uniqueness debate, a particularly useful but woefully underrated sense of understanding should be highlighted.

Let us return to the comparative judgments set forth in the previous chapter.

4. It is worse to kill massively and intentionally than to kill massively and unintentionally.
5. It is worse to kill massively and intentionally when killings are carried out because of the victims' status group affiliation than to kill under conditions in (4).
6. It is worse to kill massively and intentionally when the killings are carried out because the perpetrators intended to eliminate partially the victims' status group than it is to kill under conditions in (5).
7. It is worse to kill massively and intentionally when the killings are carried out because the perpetrators intended to eliminate completely the victims' status group than it is to kill under conditions in (6).

While (6) jumps to a moral plateau above (5), the same does not hold true for the comparison of (6) with (7). Defenders of the Holocaust's uniqueness must differentiate, empirically and morally, (6) from (7). Yet, (7) is not morally different in kind from (6) for one critical reason. The purposeful policies (institutional intent version of the *mens rea* requisite for criminal liability) and actions (the massive killings required for the *actus reus* element of criminal liability for genocide) designed to annihilate an entire group are not any more morally reprehensible than those actions designed to annihilate part of a group. Admittedly, as Katz says, "the killing of some X may be a greater evil...than killing all Y, where there are more X than Y and the absolute number of X killed exceeds the total number of Y even though the killing of X is not...Holocaustal."[39] Nevertheless, a theoretical possibility should not preclude a strong moral judgment about historical events. Assume that the Nazis clearly adopted a policy to exterminate totally all Jews. Further, assume that other genocides involved partial and not total annihilation of the targeted groups. Finally, assume that the Nazis succeeded in killing far greater numbers of their victims than any other genocide in history. Even by granting these assumptions, which constitute the critical ones in the uniqueness debate, the Holocaust does not differ in kind from other genocides. Judgment (6) does not occupy a different moral level than (7) does. (6) differs from (7) in degree and not in kind. There are different degrees of severity for different offenses. Uniqueness defenders may win the battle to demonstrate the extreme severity of the Holocaust compared to the severity of other genocides, but they fail to win the argument for the Holocaust's uniqueness.

For example, however close the Armenian genocide came to the Holocaust, it probably did not stem from a well-formed institutional intent to eradicate all Armenians everywhere.[40] Even Dadrian's claim that the Young Turks had a hidden agenda to annihilate all Christian Armenians beyond Turkey's borders to the USSR does not match the agenda of the Nazis to annihilate all Jews. Nevertheless, despite these concessions to the unsurpassed severity of the Holocaust, the uniqueness hypothesis does not hold. This is because even if only the Nazis, among all other genocide perpetrators, had intended to annihilate an entire group, that would not place the Holocaust in a different moral category from other genocide cases.

To make (7) morally distinct from (6), someone would need to show that the (attempted) annihilation of an entire group makes a moral difference over and above the number of group members murdered. The loss of a group and the concomitant loss of a culture have many lamentable features, including the loss of the very structure that gives group members their identity and fulfillment. However, the same deplorable losses may accompany a partial genocide. Once perpetrators have crossed the threshold and engage in partial extermination of a group, they have reached the moral plateau that calls for the strongest form of condemnation. Replacing "partial" with "total" could add to the degree of severity by signaling how far the perpetrators would have gone to carry out their reprehensible deeds. Nevertheless, it would not thereby catapult the acts onto a higher moral plateau of condemnation.

Another feature of the Holocaust used by defenders of the uniqueness claim is that the Jews, unlike other victim groups, never had a possibility of exit. This supports rendering the Holocaust unique. Unlike the Jews, the Christian Armenians may have had some chance of exit by adopting the language, culture, and religion of the Islamic majority during the early stages of the genocide. However, soon thereafter, the Young Turks found it difficult to distinguish innocent from guilty Armenians, leaving few opportunities for exit from the group. The Armenians in Turkey had relatively more exit opportunities that did the Jews in Germany. Genocides, like the Armenian one and the Holocaust, differ in degree but not in kind over conditions of exit.

Intents differ in degrees. It is best in genocide cases not to think of individual intent but rather of institutional policy. Some genocide policies are better formed than other ones. The degree of well-formedness of the institutional intent of genocide should make a legal and moral difference. The Holocaust and the Rwandan genocide do show different degrees of institutional intent. The Nazis had a long time to devise institutional policies of extermination and had vast resources at their disposal. They created numerous scientific institutes designed to demonstrate the inferiority of Jews and other races. State agents in Rwanda had far less time and far fewer resources. The Holocaust and Rwanda differ only in degree and not in kind when it comes to the institutional intent element of genocide.

However, the extent and depth of the Nazis regime's genocide policies far outstripped any other before or since. The only historical example that comes close to matching the institutional intent of the Nazis is a little known example of the Herero genocide. This example stands out because it provides one of the few examples of a "smoking gun." In 1904, German General von Trotha issued an explicit order calling for the extermination of the Herero.[41] Historians have not found anything comparable in the cases of Armenia or Rwanda or even in the Holocaust. In those cases, the genocide policies must be inferred from any number of sources. Still, the Nazis managed to outdo all others in terms of those policies.

The issue of intent plays a more prominent role in debates over its presence rather than over its degree of well-formedness. Consider the following, one historical and the other current, cases.

A classical example comes from critics who label the 1932 Soviet famine genocide.[42] Millions of people died because of a disastrous economic policy of collectivization, which included exporting grain and refusing foreign aid under conditions of starvation. The Soviets confiscated and exported millions of tons of grain to earn foreign currency for industrialization, and the government refused even to acknowledge a famine to say nothing of refusing to accept relief. People died because of state policies. Individuals, for the most part, did not die because of their group status as rich peasants (*kulaks*). Yet, despite its overwhelming ferocity, Stalin's acts still did not constitute genocide. Stalin may have intentionally caused indiscriminate starvation, but neither he nor his regime intentionally perpetrated genocide.

The issue of intent came up most pointedly in debates over the atrocities committed in Darfur. The US government and the UN had little difficulty in pinning the genocide label on Darfur.[43] However, the independent Darfur Commission did not find evidence of institutional intent: "Generally speaking, the policy of attacking killing, and forcibly displacing members of some tribes does not evince a specific intent to annihilate, in whole or in part, a group distinguished on racial, ethnic, national, or religious grounds."[44]

Victims Status

Defenders of the Holocaust's uniqueness make the following claim: Throughout history, only the Jews have been the targets of total annihilation. The Nazis exterminated close to 6 million Jews. They targeted other groups (Gypsies, Jehovah's Witnesses, homosexuals, Slavs), albeit in far lesser numbers. The very existence of these other target groups helps to undermine the Holocaust uniqueness hypothesis. That, as we shall see, has not stopped scholars from finding clever ways to differentiate the targeting of Jews from the targeting of other groups.

In the Armenian genocide, around 1915, the Young Turks exterminated 1.5 million Armenians. This provides an interesting comparative case. The Armenian genocide challenges the following claim made by proponents of the Holocaust's uniqueness: Throughout history, only the Jews have been the targets of total annihilation.

In an article published in a premier philosophy journal, Margalit and Motzkin proclaimed that *only* World War II Germans "both systematically humiliated and systematically killed."[45] They hedge their bets with the admission that this combination is "exceedingly rare and *maybe* unique" (Italics, mine). The authors say little about extermination and concentrate on humiliation. They discover the foundations of humiliation deeply entrenched within Nazi philosophy. The authors seem untroubled by whether Nazi ideology warrants the label "Nazi philosophy." Focusing, instead, on the intricacies of the Nazi argument, the authors see the Nazis facing a logical conundrum. If the Nazis inflicted humiliation on the Jews, they would acknowledge their victims' humanity. To avoid a logical trap, the Nazis cleverly decided to punish the Jews for their invention of the idea of universal humanity. Margalit and Motzkin supposedly demonstrate that the Holocaust's uniqueness lies within the interstices of Nazi philosophical analyses, however skewed and distorted the arguments became.

On the Margalit and Motzkin view, Nazi practice supported Nazi metaphysics. The paucity of supporting evidence did not deter the authors from informing readers that other victims of Nazi extermination, such as Soviet prisoners of war (POWs), did not experience humiliation. As this illustrates, the authors are not averse to making comparative judgments. They admit that the Nazis humiliated the Romany (Gypsies), but Margalit and Motzkin see Nazi humiliation of Jews as different-in-kind from Nazi humiliation of Gypsies. The Nazis did not treat the Gypsies "in an elaborate structure of humiliation like the one the Nazis created for the Jews."[46] This qualified generalization typifies the authors' position, and it suffers the same fate as others made by them. The authors conveniently ignore how closely the Nazis came to treating other groups similarly to the ways they treated Jews.

Contrary to what the authors would hope to find, the humiliation experienced by the Gypsies and the Jews differed in degree and not in kind. As indications of the similarities, the authors could have cited a few well-known facts. The Nazis had two agencies engaged in research on whether the Gypsies had Jewish origins. The 1935 Nuremberg laws, which first legally defined Jews, officially identified Gypsies as non-Aryan. Indeed, the Citizenship Law of 1943 omitted any mention of Gypsies since the Nazis did not expect the Gypsies to exist very long.[47] Brutal treatment of Gypsies characterized Nazi treatment of them. When it came to humiliation and extermination, Gypsies often found themselves one fateful step behind Jews: "[I]n January or February 1940, 250 Gypsy children from Brno in the concentration camp at Buchenwald were used as guinea pigs for testing Zyklon B cyanide gas crystals, a lethal insecticide that from 1941 onward was used for the mass murders at Auschwitz-Birkeneau."[48] The Nazis had relatively fluid categories for classifying their potential victims. This claim alone, amply supported by historical evidence, undermines the authors' conclusion that "Jews occupied the precise place at which humiliation and extermination intersected."[49] No precise place of intersection for one group alone existed in Nazi thought or practices.

Within their analysis, the authors made choices about their study's focus. They conjoined humiliation and extermination; they said a great deal about humiliation and little about extermination. The choices reflect a highly questionable stand on morality. Contrary to the implications of their analysis, humiliation does not occupy the same moral plateau as extermination. Whatever the moral condemnation humiliation warrants, it pales in comparison to the moral condemnation demanded by acts of extermination. The authors offer no justification for using humiliation as a comparative measure. Humiliation does not serve as justifiable grounds for comparison or as grounds for the uniqueness hypothesis. Killings, not humiliation, lie at the heart of genocide.[50] The category "extermination," not "humiliation," encompasses the Holocaust's morally important feature.

Nevertheless, historically, Jews do stand out as a particularly vulnerable target group. No other group has lost as many to genocide. The Nazis murdered 2 to 3 million Soviets, but these were POWs. Some 2 million ethnic Poles lost their lives at the hands of the Nazis, but the Nazis rejected a plan of total annihilation for the Poles.

A critical but highly controversial component of genocide debates centers on the group status of the victims. The international definitions of genocide clearly confine the target categories to racial, ethnic, national, and religious groups. Racialization of a group's identity creates a category that is, by definition and, unlike any other category, impervious to change. For the Nazis, Jews were not simply an ethnic or religious category; they were a subhuman race.

The issue of genocide victim groups has proved most troublesome in the case of Cambodia. The Khmer Rouge targeted ethnic (Chinese), national (Vietnamese), and religious (Buddhist, Muslim Cams) groups. Yet, the Khmers also targeted Khmers. How could an ethnic group led by the Khmer Rouge carry out genocide against its own group (Eastern Khmers)? This has led some scholars to construct bizarre labels like auto-genocide. The puzzlement vanishes with a deeper understanding of targeted groups in Cambodia. The Khmer Rouge did target the groups listed earlier, but only secondarily. The Khmer Rouge primarily targeted political enemies. This indeed makes the Khmer Rouge different from the Nazis. They did not primarily target any racial, ethnic, national, or religious group for extermination.

Justifications

The final standard considers any viable justifications for the acts. Genocide constitutes a status crime where perpetrators target victims simply for whom they are perceived to be not for anything that they have done. As a *jus cogens* crime, genocide is in principle unjustifiable and in history unjustified.

Darfur again raises some critical questions. The Darfur case began as a civil war and turned into a rebellion. While the war context certainly does not excuse the atrocities, particularly those inflicted on innocent civilians, it does raise some further problems with pinning the genocide label on Darfur. The Darfur Commission charged members of the Sudan Liberation Army and the Justice and Equality Movement, the rebel forces in Darfur, with war crimes. It turned over charges against 51 individuals to the International Criminal Court (ICC). The ICC only issued warrants for two government officials.[51]

We must be careful here. Darfur does not qualify as genocide primarily because the intent requirement appears not to be met. The justification issue complicates matters, but it alone does not disqualify Darfur as genocide. A war context complicates the analysis, but it should not determine the assessment. The Tutsi-led RPF attacked the Hutu-led Rwanda. That war context may help explain the subsequent genocide, but it in no way disqualifies it as genocide.

Conclusion

The world has paid and will continue to pay homage to the Holocaust and its Jewish victims. Examples come all the way from China. Nanjing University, like many universities throughout China, has a graduate program in Jewish Studies.[52] These and other similar efforts should continue unabated. However, attempts to isolate the Holocaust in terms of its uniqueness prevent giving other atrocities their due recognition. A comparison and ranking provides a way out of this impasse. A more careful assessment shows why and how the Holocaust ranks as the worst genocide on record. Only a ranking of this kind opens the door to including other atrocities.

Giving the Holocaust a high comparative ranking has its own pitfalls. It makes it easier for Holocaust icons to swamp all others. The Holocaust then becomes the template for assessing the status of any future mass atrocity. A comparative framework counters this by going deeper and finding the grounds for ranking any mass atrocity. Some mass atrocities rank as worse than others because of the number killed, the well-formedness of the institutional intent behind the slaughter, the racialization of the targeted groups, and the reasons behind the attack. These criteria demonstrate why the following do not fully qualify as genocide: the Bosnia's War, Stalin's Famine, Cambodia's Killing Fields, and Darfur's Ambiguous Genocide.

Comparing historical cases is no idle exercise. Debates over history continue to this day. Efforts to get recognition of the Armenian massacre as a Holocaust have reached the halls of the US Congress.

Attempts to prove that the atrocities committed in the name of communism far outstrip anything Hitler even imagined in the name of fascism have motivated efforts to purge former Communists of any influence in Slovenia. A campaign, mobilized at breakneck speed, for intervention in Darfur relied on guilt over inaction in Rwanda. A comparative framework can sort out these efforts and expose their underlying inappropriate comparisons.

Most importantly, this analysis provides a framework for assessing whether a future mass atrocity qualifies as genocide. Without an analytic framework, decisions about intervention will continue to be held hostage to political manipulators and media pundits. The Holocaust must not be forgotten but neither should other atrocities, past and future. One past case of genocide besides the Holocaust that should be constantly remembered is the Rwandan genocide. The next chapter attempts to answer why that, unfortunately, has not been the case.

CHAPTER 3

Rwanda

Undervalued Injustice

R wanda represents "the undervalued genocide"—hardly a noble distinction. The phrase brings to the fore something troubling about the Rwandan genocide. Almost everyone pays lip service to this genocide by acknowledging its horror. And anyone who knows the least about it will invariably express regret and bemoan the international community's failure to act. Yet, soon after those with bleeding hearts express these laments, they quickly resort either to some form of Rwanda bashing or, even worse, to complete silence as if Rwanda no longer exists. This chapter attempts to understand it, "it" being not so much the Rwandan genocide as the evaluations of and reactions to it.

Raul Hilberg, the foremost historian of European Jewry, provided a schematic to help understand the processes that led to and that took place within the Holocaust. He devised the phases of designation, discrimination, and brutalization to classify the stages of the Holocaust.[1] Yet, the phases also apply to the Rwandan genocide. The Rwandan genocide roughly fits the phased account of the Holocaust better than any other mass atrocity since the Holocaust. This should bode well for drawing comparisons between the Holocaust and the Rwandan genocide. Yet, Rwanda remains the outlier.

In addition to fitting roughly the same pattern that led to the Holocaust, the Rwandan genocide also fits the legal definition of genocide. Even though it took two decades, the United Nations Security Council designated the atrocities in Rwanda as genocide.[2] Further, the first war crimes tribunal conviction for genocide came from the Ad Hoc

International Criminal Tribunal for the Rwanda (ICTR) in the case of Jean Paul Akayesu.[3] The legal status of the Rwandan genocide case goes unquestioned.

Yet, despite the overwhelming empirical substantiation and its subsequent legal designation as genocide, the Rwandan case remains plagued by controversy. Two notable types of issues fall under the general categories of equivalency and allocation. First, various forms of equivalency or moral relativism have raised their ugly heads to demote and downgrade the Rwandan genocide as just one more instances of Hutus and Tutsis killing one another. Second, the Rwandan genocide has been burdened by unjust allocations on many fronts since the beginning. Overall, the Rwandan genocide sits far below terrorism in the implicit ranking (measured by strength of international responses) of so-called international crimes. This chapter aims to challenge the lowly relegation given to the Rwandan genocide.

Besides giving this injustice its due, why should anyone want to defend the Rwandan atrocities as genocide? The debate over the status of the Rwandan genocide affects a number of other important issues. First, a successful defense of the Rwandan atrocities as genocide undermines the *sui generis* (unique) character of the Holocaust. By drawing specific comparisons between the Holocaust and Rwanda, we shall add more arguments to the previous chapters challenge to the uniqueness claim. For, if the Holocaust ranks a *sui generis*, then its rallying cry "Never again!" holds true only by fiat. Since no other mass killings has or probably ever will match the Holocaust, vigilance then operates more as a periodic gaze to the past rather than as a stark warning about the future.

Further, placing the Rwandan genocide in the same general category as the Holocaust bolsters the case for a sound, fundamental legal definition of genocide. It provides a relatively clear-cut measure to use to evaluate other mass atrocities. Whether other atrocities fit into the genocide classification helps determine whether these other injustices trigger the grounds for—nay the necessity—of an intervention.

This strategy has its dangers. It may simply only increase the number of injustices within the intervention group by one, with only Rwanda being added to the Holocaust under that category. No other mass killings, including recent ones such as Darfur and Sudan, match these two paradigms of genocide. So, getting the international community to act has and will not become any easier with the addition of Rwanda to the litany of genocides.

A more important gain, however, offsets this danger. The international community has yet to accept fully any international crime, however narrowly construed, as triggering intervention. Accomplishing that feat alone would be monumental. No state or policy maker defends genocide, especially as narrowly construed, or in any way attempts to downgrade it. Yet, no one seems to want to accept the consequences of recognizing genocide as the worst injustice. If genocide is a universal prohibition, then obligations are owed to the international community to prevent, stop, and punish it. Only after fully embracing this duty to act, discussed fully in Chapter 7, can we then engage in a discussion of expanding that duty to genocide-like international crimes such as crimes against humanity. But first we need, in a sense, to rehabilitate the Rwandan genocide by examining its similarities and dissimilarities to the Holocaust.

Rwanda as Holocaust

Designation

Anti-Semitism has a long, notorious history. Animosity toward Jews marks the longest running history of hatred. Like most forms of hatred, its longevity makes little sense. Perhaps, it stems from a long-standing belief among Christians that the Jews killed their savior, Jesus of Nazareth. Racism has a more recent vintage. Modern-day slavery marks its inception. Throughout the world, darker skin marks a form of inferiority, a stigma of a lesser being. Oddly, Jews and Tutsis count as different races when compared to Aryans and Hutus, respectively. The inanity of those designations says more about the unscientific nature of the concept of race than anything else.[4]

Things, however, get even more perplexing. Modernity has created a new and perhaps more vicious form of group hatred. A paradox anchors this group hatred. The greater the resemblance among groups, the greater the animosity among them. Outsiders would have had difficulty telling the differences among various groups in the Balkans. Serbs, Croats, and Bosnians shared many features, including language. Yet, in the 1990s, some of the fiercest fighting broke out among these groups during the Balkan Wars. The same held true for the Hutus and Tutsis in Rwanda, except with even more devastating results than those experienced in the Balkans.

Throughout its history, one does not have to search far beneath the allegedly neutral descriptions to find harsh judgments of entire groups in Rwanda. The differentiation between Tutsi and Hutus began to crystalize under its native monarchy in the early nineteenth century.[5] Then, toward the end of that century, the colonial powers in Rwanda passed value judgments on the Hutus and the Tutsi.[6] At first, Germany and then its post–World War I successor, Belgium, had a more favorable outlook on the Tutsis than for the lowly Hutus. So-called science had set the racist foundations. In his 1863 journal, the English explorer John Hanning Speke found little hope for the Hutus, "the true curly-head, flab-nosed, pouch-mouthed negro," whose breed seemed destined for perdition.[7] Subsequent anthropological literature incorporated these nonneutral descriptions.

European explorers helped to solidify the race categories by conjecturing, on slim evidence that the so-called superior Tutsis originated in Ethiopia. Anthropologists, relying on this Hamitic hypothesis, classified the Tutsis as from "the primordial red race" or as "Europeans under a black skin." They conjectured that all forms of civilization in Africa came from the Hamitic race, implying that anything civilized found in Africa must have come from outside Africa. Indeed, the Hamitic hypothesis accords with the Bible. In Genesis, Noah cursed the progeny of his youngest son Ham, who, unlike his brothers, who looked the other way, saw Noah naked. The colonizers discovered a group of superior Africans, the Hamites, or "white-coloreds," which they claimed represented the missing links between the white Caucasoid and the black Negroid races.[8]

While appearing more refined during the early part of the twentieth century, the descriptions never lost their value-burdened origins. Father Pages, in 1933, identified the Tutsis as a lost tribe of Christendom, who had lost their Ethiopian Coptic Christian roots in their migration. In that same year, the Belgium colonial rulers required Tutsis and Hutus to carry identity cards, which they had first introduced in 1926. Rwanda's Belgian rulers, who replaced the Germans after World War I, first favored the Tutsis. Then, in 1962, just before granting Rwanda its independence, they bequeathed power to the Hutus.

The colonialist's sharp differentiation between Hutus and Tutsis has been contested on historical grounds. According to a currently popular interpretation, before colonialization, the region's group classifications were relatively fluid and permeable, permitting individuals to change depending on economic status and occupation.[9] Politics, occupational status, and ancestry defined "Hutu" and "Tutsi." The historical debates are interesting, but the important classifications lie in the dynamics of modern political group formations. Rwanda's recent history uncovers a pattern similar to the one set for Jews in Nazi Germany—designation, discrimination, and brutalization.

Value-ladened descriptions of physical features can be detected even in the current literature. Rene Lamarchand, for example, observed that the Tutsi "physical features suggest obvious ethnic affinities with the Galla tribes of southern Ethiopia."[10] Philip Gourovitch, an ardent defender of the current Tutsi regime in Rwanda, gave the following account: "But nobody can dispute the physical archetypes: for Hutus, stocky and round-faced, dark-skinned, flat-nosed, thick-lipped, and square-jawed; for Tutsis, lanky and long faced, not so dark-skinned, narrow-nosed, thin-lipped, and narrow chinned."[11] Stereotypes infect not only how Hutus and Tutsis view each other but also how outsiders see both groups.

Discrimination

Hutus and Tutsis, inside and outside Rwanda, speak Kinyarwanda (whose speakers number over 10 million), practice the same religion, and have similar cultural habits. Within Rwanda, however, Hutus and Tutsis have constituted radically different political identities. Rwandan independence ushered in varying waves of discrimination against the Tutsi minority under two Hutu-led regimes. The policies in the First Republic (1961–1975) under Gregoire Kayibanda (president until a 1973 coup) functioned as an apartheid system placing quotas on Tutsis in education and government jobs. Unlike South Africa, the international community barely whispered a protest against apartheid in Rwanda (just as it failed to do to Kosovo). Rwanda's First Republic ended with massive slaughters of Tutsis. During the First Republic, Rwanda also lost over one half of its Tutsi population to refugee flight to Uganda and other neighboring countries.

Kayibanda's army chief of staff, General Juvenal Habyarimana, seized power and halted the anti-Tutsi pogroms. As president of the Second Republic Habyarimana ended the First Republic's "national Hutuism" and granted citizenship to resident Tutsi but not to those Tutsis who had fled, mainly to Uganda. In 1986, the Museveni regime in Uganda changed citizenship requirements from ancestry to residence. The Ugandan Diaspora group formed the bulk of the Rwandan Patriotic Front (RPF). However, later, the Museveni government, for internal political reasons, reversed its citizenship policy and made members of the RPF refugees in Uganda. The Tutsi guerrilla fighters found them-selves between the Rwandan devil and the Ugandan deep sea.[12] The RPF invasion of 1990 was, in part, an attempt to escape the closing scis-sors of a postcolonial citizenship crisis in Rwanda and Uganda.[13] The

1993 Arusha Accords, designed to end the civil war brought about by the 1990 RPF invasion, required the repatriation of Tutsi refugees. This brief account demonstrates the critical aspects of the political solidification of Tutsi identity over a roughly 30-year period.

There were ample, immediate warning signs of a genocide brewing in Rwanda, in the form of discrimination. In 1990, President Habyarimana assembled the *Interahamwe*, an armed militia that later carried out systematic massacres of Tutsis. Rwanda's three major radio stations played instrumental roles in solidifying and politicizing the identities and engendering the hatred of Hutus for Tutsis by utilizing the Hamitic theory designating Tutsis as Northern invaders.[14] This discrimination phase set the stage for the next, brutalization phase.

Brutalization

A prosecution for the international crime of genocide requires a showing of intent. The 1994 Rwandan genocide, where Hutu militants massacred 800,000, mostly Tutsis, children, women, and men within 100 days, met the intent requirement. According to the UN Commission on Experts, "there exist overwhelming evidence to prove that the acts of genocide against the Tutsi ethnic group were committed by Hutu elements in a concerted, planned, systematic and methodical way."[15] The report marked the first time since adopting the 1948 *Genocide Convention* that the United Nations had identified an instance of genocide. The evidence further shows that the genocide was organized at the governmental level. It takes an incredible mobilization at the state level to carry out genocide of this proportion. With 333 deaths every hour, one commentator called it "this century's best organized genocide."[16] The ethnic identity cards, first devised and issued by the Belgiums, proved highly useful. Hutu extremists played the tribal card of ethnic identity with ruthless vengeance.

Even attempts by Hutus to counter the brutality as it unfolded could not stem the tide of hatred, insanity, and horror. Many Hutus made valiant efforts to save Tutsis. In one church, Hutus refused to be separated from Tutsis, resulting in the killing of all nearly 300 parishioners. "Kodjo Ankrah of Church World Action recounted to me what happened when soldiers entered a church in Ruhengeri and asked that Hutu step on one side, and Tutsi on another: 'People refused; when they said, Tutsis this side, all moved. When they said Hutus that side, all moved. Eventually, soldiers killed them all, 200 to 300 people in all.'"[17] Hutus became Tutsis; Tutsis became cockroaches. Designation and brutalization became a single act.

The brutalization phase in Rwanda distinguishes it from the brutalization carried out in Bosnia and Kosovo. The extent and severity of the harms perpetrated against Bosnian Muslims and Albanian Kosovars pale in comparison to those inflicted on Tutsis. If genocide legally means the intentional killing, in whole or part, of members of an ethnic group, then, despite difficulties finding reliable numbers, the genocidal toll from the former Yugoslavia probably falls within the order of tens of thousands. The count from Rwanda falls into the order of hundreds of thousands. A great deal of (but certainly not all of) what went under the heading of genocide in Bosnia[18] and Kosovo consisted of uprooting ethnic groups from their homes (so-called ethnic cleansing[19]) and military combat-related deaths (war crimes and crimes against humanity).

In contrast, the Rwanda genocide meets the narrow, legal definition of genocide. About one-third of all Tutsis of Rwanda were intentionally and systematically eliminated. The Rwanda genocide occurred after ethnic cleansing attracted international attention in Bosnia. After Bosnia, Rwanda became second more than in time. More people were killed, injured, and displaced in three and half months in Rwanda than in two years of the Bosnian campaign. Perhaps, the RPF "had effectively been the only force on earth to live up to the requirements of the 1948 *Genocide Convention*"[20] by acting to stop an on-going genocide.

The Rwandan case comes the closest to matching the sequence and the severity of harms within each phase of the sequence experienced by Jews under the Nazi regime. The solidification of Tutsi as a defensive identity occurred earlier in the last part of the twentieth century than did the categories of Bosnian Muslims and Albanian Kosovars. However, the case of the Tutsis in Rwanda also breaks rank with that of the Jews in Nazi Germany. The plight of the Jews became continuously and increasingly serious through the designation, discrimination, and brutalization phases. The plight of the Tutsis did not follow the same, continuously downhill descent into the hells of brutalization. Tutsis fared better under Rwanda's Second Republic than they did under the apartheid of the First Republic. Further, brutalization occurred after outside policy makers imposed a quota system for Tutsis on Rwanda. Well-intentioned policies, especially when they solidify ethnic categories, often have adverse effects. The results of the Arusha Accords now haunt its promoters. In any event, severe group brutalization does not always follow from increasingly severe group discrimination. Brutalization may erupt after discrimination seems to have abated. The

Rwandan case illustrates one clear lesson. Patterns of severe group brutalization, most prominently of genocide, demand swift and immediate humanitarian intervention to stop them. Sovereign immunity should not apply, legally or morally, as a defense to genocide.

Undermining Rwanda

Equivalency of All Mass Killings

Moral equivalence treats two injustices on the same (and typically lower) moral plane. Group A commits atrocities against Group B. The condemnation of A's acts weakens if those atrocities came in response to or in the context of B having committed atrocities against A. The equivalency approach typically lumps together all mass killings, refusing to acknowledge that some mass killings (genocide) rank as worse than other mass killings (crimes against humanity). It deflates one injustice by leveling it with other injustices.

The first attack launched by the equivalency proponents focuses on the 1994 Rwandan atrocities. The first version of this may be forgiven, for it consisted of refusals (since, well recognized as unjustified and regrettable) to use the genocide label for the events in Rwanda as they were unfolding. This version of the equivalency thesis took prominence among the world powers during the 1994 Rwandan genocide.

Policy makers played their version of the equivalency thesis during the crisis, which lasted from April 6 to July 26, 1994, as evidenced by the following incidents. On April 29, 1994, Secretary General Boutros-Ghali described the situation in Rwanda as "Hutus killing Tutsis and Tutsis killing Hutus."[21] In May 1994, the United States pressured the UN to replace "genocide" in a resolution on Rwanda to "systematic, widespread and flagrant violations of humanitarian law," that is, to human rights abuses. On June 10, 1994, the US State Department's spokeswoman, Christine Shelly, assessed the on-going atrocities in Rwanda: "Although there have been acts of genocide in Rwanda, all the murders cannot be put in that category."[22] On June 14, 1994, the US Ambassador to Rwanda, David Rawson, described the situation as one of brother against brother, "Cain and Abel all over again." The policy advocates in each of these examples characterized the situation as a conflict between two equally blameworthy ethnic groups. According to some government officials, the use of the label "genocide" at that time would have meant the acceptance of certain obligatory action according to international law.[23]

While the international community has come to a consensus in recognizing the Rwandan genocide, that has not stopped Rwanda's version of genocide deniers. Some critics, without even having more carefully calculated and recalculated the number of deaths, proclaim that more Hutus than Tutsis were killed in the slaughter. Herman and Peterson even go so far as to accuse the RPF of genocide against the *Interahawame*.[24] The moral equivalence thesis here amounts to a form of denial, a form totally without empirical support or justification.

Two subtler versions of the equivalency thesis—one backward and the other forward looking —find instances of Tutsis committing genocide against Hutus. 1972 Burundi supplies the strongest case for this. No one seriously doubts the fact that in 1972 Tutsis slaughtered perhaps hundreds of thousands of Hutus. Rene Lemarchand has led the charge to get this atrocity recognized—as what remains an open question.[25] Throughout his many writings, he equivocates—not quite willing to reject the genocide label but still set on edging it into the genocide category. In one work, he consciously takes ethnocide as synonymous with genocide; in another, he uses terms such as selective and partial genocide. Despite his protestations to the contrary, the result of Lemarchand's equivocation is that the 1972 Tutsi killings of Hutus in Burundi offsets the 1994 Hutu killings of Tutsis in Rwanda. The 1994 Rwandan genocide becomes just one more example of Tutsis and Hutus committing mass slaughter and genocide against one another. "Cain and Abel all over again."

Yet, a war crimes prosecutor today would have a difficult time pinning the genocide charge on Tutsi leaders in Burundi. A critical element of the crime is missing—organized institutional intent to eliminate ("in whole or in part") the entire group. The Tutsi repression came in response to a Hutu rebellion led by the Burundi Worker's Party, which did issue highly inflammatory statements advocating the annihilation of Tutsis. In response, the Jeunesses Revolutionnaires Rwgasore (JRR), a militant youth wing of the Tutsi ruling party (Uprona), led the killing sprees against Hutus. There is good evidence that these were targeted killings—but they targeted educated Hutu elite, and, most importantly, the JRR acted largely as an independent force.[26]

Even within Rwanda's recent past the label genocide has been misused. In the civil war in Rwanda in the early 1990s, some nongovernmental organizations labeled various killings of hundreds of Tutsis as genocide. They equated civilian war deaths with genocide. "The linking of the deaths of only hundreds to the terms apocalypse and genocide throughout the civil war period diminished their impact as warnings" of an impending genocide in 1994.[27]

Forward-looking versions of the equivalency thesis have continued to gain strength during and since the 1994 genocide. Amnesty International reported that from April to August 1994, the RPF killed "hundreds—possibly thousands—of unarmed civilians and captured armed opponents."[28] This version has extended to the immediate aftermath of the 1994 Rwandan genocide. The current Tutsi-led Rwandan government's "genocide" in northern Congo seemingly has offset the 1994 Hutu militant's genocide in Rwanda. Yet, similar issues are seldom if ever raised about the Holocaust.

Toward the end of World War II and in the immediate aftermath, retaliatory killings of thousands of German sympathizers took place, particularly in Yugoslavia.[29] Of course, these parallels are easily dismissed since the number of German sympathizers killed does not even come close to the number of Jews slaughtered in the Holocaust. The number killed in the so-called second Rwandan genocide does come somewhat closer to the number allegedly killed in the second genocide. But beyond a certain threshold why should these comparative numbers matter? The main comparative point lies in the fact that the retaliatory World War II killings seldom if ever even come up for discussion. More importantly, these so-called retaliatory killings in Rwanda hardly fit the legal definition of genocide.[30] Finally, why do critics immediately jump on the genocide bandwagon without even entertaining the idea that perhaps these killings might be at least understandable if not excusable? Taking retaliatory measures against those who have just committed genocide against your group does not seem particularly outlandish. This line of reasoning becomes even more curious when the 1994 Hutu mass slaughters are labeled as retaliatory, meaning that we should understand them in the context of a country experiencing a full-fledged invasion by the RPF.[31] It is not clear how retaliatory motives excuse the Hutus but not the Tutsi RPF.

Still another group of critics question the planning of the Rwandan genocide. Yet, in contrast, discussions of the planned character of the Holocaust seldom include even an acknowledgment that most of the exterminations took place in the chaos of war's end. This should make one wonder what consequences follow from this regarding the intent element of genocide.

A subtler, less obvious version of the equivalency thesis merely describes the human rights violations committed by Rwanda in isolation—without mention of the genocide context out of which these actions grew. Amnesty International, for example, deplored the human rights violations in postgenocide Rwanda. The Rwandan War Crimes Trials Organic Law 8/96 limited the right to appeal to questions of law and flagrant errors of fact. Yet, over 130,000 suspects awaited trial in Rwanda's overcrowded prisons. Many judges and prosecutors received only six months' training, with little or no prior legal training. The first trial on December 27, 1996, lasted only four hours without assistance from legal counsel. Only a few dozen indigenous defense lawyers practiced in Rwanda. In 1997, Rwandan courts heard over 300 genocide cases and sentenced 103 to life imprisonment and 108 to death. The litany of Rwanda's human rights abuses, however, deflates the horror and urgency of response to the genocide. In a sense, politically, human rights abuses (as evidenced by the Kosovo crisis) sometimes seem to have become accepted internationally as a greater harm than genocide. Amnesty International uses the term "human rights violations" to encompass both the 1994 Rwandan genocide and the US death penalty.

Criticisms of Rwanda's government often fail to include critical factors. While the RPF did carry out reprisal killings against alleged *genocidaires*, it also exhibited remarkable restraint given the circumstances. The Rwandan Patriotic Army tribunal sentenced some of its soldiers to death for reprisal killings before the international tribunal in Arusha tried anyone for genocide. In addition, the genocide decimated Rwanda's judicial system. The United Nations not only failed to act but it also perpetuated the genocide through its relief efforts. Further, the international judicial system did not respond in a timely and effective manner. In addition to a possible serious charge of global racism, global politics have revealed an inadequate, distorted, and morally reprehensible conception of and response to group suffering by the international community. These important factors do not excuse the Rwandan government, but they do make its actions more understandable.

Allocation

The equivalency "game" wrecks havoc in itself but becomes even more troublesome when placed in the context of unfair and unjust allocation of resources devoted to the Rwandan genocide and its aftermath. In terms of overall numbers, for example, of foreign aid dollars, it appears that Rwanda has done quite well since the genocide. Yet, troublesome distributions of resources lurk not far below the surface.

Judicial Resources. A humanitarian intervention did not come "too little, too late" to Rwanda; unlike nearly contemporaneous responses to Bosnia and Kosovo, an intervention never came. More tellingly, instead of stemming the tide of the atrocities, the immediate postgenocide response of the international community greatly exacerbated the conflict. The international community not only facilitated the mass exodus of Hutus from Rwanda into neighboring Zaire (now the Democratic Republic of the Congo), but it also aided and abetted those largely responsible for the genocide, the *Interahawame*, the Hutu extremist militia. These *genocidaires* (as the French so politely call them) used the refugee camps as recruiting grounds to conduct cross-border raids into Rwanda. The RPF retaliated with its own incursions into Zaire.

The history of what later became the Democratic Republic of the Congo is a long, sordid, sad affair that continues its deepening plunge into chaos today.[32] However, it is clear that the *Interahawame*, through its various mutations, has played a destabilizing role in the Congo. Rather than tracing its wretched path of destruction, I shall make instead some general points about the disparate treatment of organizations in the context of international crimes.

Comparisons of organizational responsibility for international crimes in Nazi Germany, Bosnia, and Rwanda provide some fresh insights into these conflicts. The Nuremberg Tribunal included indictments of organizations. The Tribunal found a number of Nazi organizations criminally responsible. While the full thrust of these efforts to hold organizations criminally responsible became stymied, they did result in state actions against aspects of those organizations. The Nazi Party's symbols, for example, remains illegal in Germany to this day.

The Bosnian War also involved vicious criminal organizations, such as Arkan's guerillas, which had carried out a significant portion of the atrocities. Admittedly, the International Criminal Tribunal for the Former Yugoslavia (ICTY) never brought these organizations to justice. However, the international community's "boots-on-the ground" served as a de facto deterrent, assuring that these organizations would never rise again. Further, the ICTY but not the ICTR has made relatively extensive use of a concept known as joint criminal enterprise. For example, a sealed indictment charged Arkan (Zeljko Raznatovic) with Joint Criminal Enterprise before his murder.[33]

The same forces and efforts designed to assure the dismantlement of genocide organizations that operated with varying degrees of success after the Holocaust and after the Bosnian war did not take hold after the Rwandan genocide—and arguably, with far more devastating effects by not only permitting but also facilitating the flourishing of the *Interahawame*. This would be tantamount to doing the same for the SS in the USSR following World War II.

The idea of organization responsibility for genocide and other international crimes should be pursued further. Examining the role of organizations should include expanding the types of suspect organizations to include, for example, churches.[34] A strong case exists for extending the scope of responsibility for genocide to religious organizations, such as the Seventh Day Adventist Church. Pastor Elizaphan Ntakirutimana was president of Adventist Church in the province of Kibuye, where one out of three were Tutsis (compared to a national population of 15 percent Tutsi) before the genocide. Few Kibuye Tutsis survived the genocide.

Ntakirutimana was the first religious leader to appear before the ICTR. Yet, the individualistic premises of the Rwanda Tribunal assured that Ntakirutimana's individual role in the genocide was addressed but not his organization's role. The Catholic and Anglican churches have monopolized the attention given to the role of churches during the genocide. The Seventh Day Adventist Church, unlike its Catholic and Anglican counterparts, has never adequately addressed, voluntarily or otherwise, its role in the 1994 genocide.

An established religious organization has a radically different purpose than a militia. However, justice must address the role of presumably benign organizational structures. More people were slaughtered in churches than any other place during the genocide. Tutsis took refuge in Ntakirutimana's church and hospital compound not simply because of Ntakirutimana's authoritative assurances of safety but also because the place of refuge was a church. Philip Gourevitch's book title, *We wish to inform you that by tomorrow my family and I will be dead*, proves telling for it contains the words of an appeal for safety from a minister lower on the hierarchy to his superior, Ntakirutimana.[35] The church members who were not targeted for extermination occupy a position with moral implications. Given their position, they were no longer simply morally neutral members of an organization. The genocidal nature of the organization's goals and acts, committed at the behest of the organization, transformed membership in the organization into a moral category. Their organization, at least the part of it operating in that province in Rwanda, should have become a suspect criminal organization.

On November 8, 1994, the United Nations Security Council patterned a war crimes' tribunal for Rwanda on the one established, in 1992, for the former Yugoslavia. A tremendous amount of money has been spent on the ICTR, with the dollar amounts being comparable to expenditures on the ICTY. The budgets look relatively comparable; the budget for 2002–2003 gave about $250 million to Yugoslavia and less than $200 million to Rwanda. However, the ICTR and the ICTY began on very different footings. Relative to the tribunal for the former Yugoslavia in The Hague, initially, the tribunal for Rwanda had inadequate resources. The Dutch built state-of-the-art courts for the ICTY in The Hague. However, at the outset, the ICTR in Arusha, Tanzania, did not have a library. Printing materials involved a seven-hour drive to Nairobi, Kenya. Two panels of three judges shared the same courtroom, with no windows or air-conditioning.

The ICTR, in the beginning, was not only plagued with incompetence but it also exhibited organizational viciousness. Sammy Bahati Weza, for example, collected evidence for three years as a defense investigator for the ICTR, on the case of Lt. Samuel Imanishimwe, a Hutu military leader from Cyangugu prefecture. During the trial, witnesses testified that Simeon Nsamihigo, deputy prosecutor of Cyangugu, had ordered and facilitated the killings of Tutsis. Later, informants revealed that Weza, the ICTR defense investigator, was Nsamihigo, the *genocidaire* deputy prosecutor. Another defense investigator Joseph Nzabirinda was arrested in Belgium after a witness identified him as a member of the *Interahawame*. In other words, the ICTR employed *genocidaires*—not a bad job if you can get it—but hardly even imaginable at Nuremberg or the ICTY.

War crimes tribunals, in general, do not have a stellar record for bringing the accused to justice. Moreover, it proves difficult to find meaningful ways to compare the efforts and records of the various tribunals. However, while a few cases do not establish a comparative pattern, they do indicate some worrisome trends.

The US government spared little effort in helping to bring those accused of Holocaust war crimes to justice. There is no better symbol of this than the long legal ordeal of John Demjanjuk, in a case where the United States even outdid Israel. The US government created an office solely dedicated to helping to pursue Holocaust war criminals. In this case, they found Holocaust survivors who, despite investigators' protests to the contrary, identified John Demjanjuk, then a retired steel worker living near Cleveland, Ohio, as Ivan the Terrible, a notoriously brutal guard at Treblinka, a concentration camp in the former Czechoslovakia. These identifications led to the extradition of Demjanjuk to Israel, where a trial court found him guilty of genocide while he served as a guard at Treblinka and sentenced him to death.[36] On appeal, the Israeli

Supreme Court overturned his conviction.[37] Israel returned him to the United States. In subsequent proceedings not only did the United States refuse to reinstate his US citizenship but also extradited him once again, this time to Germany, where he recently died at the age of 88 before he could appeal his conviction.

It is difficult not to be struck by the differences between the Demjanjuk case and the Ntakirutimana case. Ntakirutimana fled Rwanda in 1994 to live in Laredo, Texas, with his son, an anesthesiologist. The ICTR indicted the Seventh Day Adventist minister for the deaths of countless numbers of Tutsis in his Rwandan church. But it took the United States six years to extradite him.

Pastor Elizaphan Ntakirutimana (whose name means "nothing is greater than God"), president of the Seventh-Day Adventist mission at Ngoma, stood accused of the genocide of Tutsis, which began on the Sabbath, April 15, 1994. Before April 1994, Kibuye had the highest Tutsi population of any Rwandan prefecture (252,000). After the genocide, only 7,000 to 8,000 Tutsis remained in Kibuye. The ICTR also indicted his son, Gerard, formerly a doctor in Rwanda.

Ntakirutimana was arrested on September 29, 1996. After awaiting trial for 14 months in the infirmary of the Webb County jail, United States Magistrate Marcel Notzon ordered Ntakirutimana's release. He was rearrested on February 26, 1998. Federal District Judge John Rainey upheld his conviction.[38] The US Supreme Court denied a writ of certiorari.[39] He was transferred to the ICTR on March 31, 2000. He was the first clergyman convicted for the 1994 Rwandan genocide.[40]

These cases simply illustrate a troubling lack of judicial resources expended on Rwanda relative to other atrocities.

Scholarly Resources. The final questionable allocation of resources concerns academic attention given to the Rwandan genocide. Let us take just one anecdotal example. In the summer of 2001, Oxford University provided an academic retreat for over 600 scholars to explore "The Holocaust in the Age of Genocide." The horrors of the Holocaust became stepping stones for not only the usual flash flood of academic papers but also an immersion in music, poetry, film, theatre, and exhibits. For a solid week, the participants experienced what it has taken a generation to convey. On Monday July 17, the ceremony began amidst the splendor of Oxford's Sheldonian Theatre with greetings from political notables who read to an audience that did not need any convincing. The Conference's honorary president, Elie Wiesel, Nobel Peace Prize recipient and Holocaust survivor, issued an impassioned response to *The Holocaust Industry* by Norman Finkelstein, a journalist and academic author, who had charged that an exclusive club had made the Holocaust a lucrative business. The afternoon history session opened with Deborah Lipstadt recounting her successful defense against Holocaust-denier David Irving's libel charge. The publicity stir caused by Finkelstein's attack reminded everyone how short-lived are the victories like Lipstadt's and how continuous are the battles. Right from the beginning, at this scholarly conference on genocide, the Holocaust took center stage, leaving little room for the extensive consideration of other cases of genocide, past and present.

The conference's title "Remembering For the Future" addressed one noble purpose for remembering, namely, so that the world never forgets the Holocaust horror. Conference delegates had the honor of having a private viewing of London's first major permanent exhibition on the Holocaust. Many viewers when confronted with a 40-foot-long model of Auschwitz or the sight of Dr. Josef Mengele's operating table found the experience difficult and moving. The exhibit, taking up 13,000 square feet, maintained a tasteful respect and achieved an emphasis on education. Still, the videotaped testimonies from survivors, many of whom attended the conference, left the deepest impressions. The conference focused on Holocaust survivors passing the torch of remembrance to their descendants. Remembering For the Future conferences occur every six years. The 2006 conference had far fewer survivors in attendance. Their children heard their parent's pleas and have already begun to assure a place for future remembering of the Holocaust. There, however, was little or no remembrance of the Rwandan genocide.

The politics of memory never chart a smooth course even for the Holocaust. The Imperial War Museum provided a discomforting context. Before entering the exhibit, conference delegates sipped wine while roaming among Sherman tanks and a human torpedo (a World War I Italian invention). However troubling delegates found these strange juxtapositions, the complete absence of another goal for exhibits proved even more disturbing. What accounted for a failure to Remember For the Present? Did remembering the past help in any way to increase alertness to any event in the present that might turn into genocide?

Before the conference began, UK's *Independent* predicted that, "papers will debate whether Hitler's 'Final Solution' was something unique or just the worst in a century of attempted genocides in Armenia, Cambodia, Burundi, Rwanda, Kosovo and East Timor."[41] The scholars did address a few other genocides, for example, the ones in Armenia, the USSR, and Nigeria (against the Riverrine). However, talk of other genocides, despite the conference theme "In the Age of Genocides," often stimulates a reaction that comparisons somehow give the Holocaust less than its due. The act of comparing genocides might even bring a muted charge of "denier."

Of the over 300 papers "presented," the program did not include one paper that focused on the 1994 Rwandan genocide. If any contemporary genocide came close to the Holocaust, the state-sponsored slaughter of close to one million people, mostly Tutsis, surely did. The Rwandan genocide holds the dubious distinction as the only genocide officially recognized by the United Nations. The plight of Tutsis survivors has followed a similar trajectory as Jewish survivors did. Six years after a campaign to exterminate them, the Tutsis, like Jewish survivors soon after the Holocaust, have been mostly forgotten. The Tutsis have not had the chance to say "Never Again" because outsiders largely refuse to acknowledge the enormity of the 1994 horror. Why have scholars largely ignored the plight of Rwanda's Tutsis?

At this Remembering for the Future conference, a few participants tried to focus some international light on the Rwandan genocide. They tried to convince the delegates to do something unusual for an academic gathering, that is, to take a political stand. They urged the scholars to adopt a resolution on recent and impending mass deaths in Central Africa. A "Draft Resolution" highlighted current threats to Tutsis in neighboring Congo. Just as actual and threatened persecution of the Jews continued after the Holocaust, the Tutsis continuously faced threats, particularly in the Congo. The Conference's Executive Committee, feeling politically ill equipped, reluctantly refused to present the resolution to a final plenary session.

The last day of the conference moved to London's Westminster Hall. At its final plenary session ("Question Time"), resolution supporters made another effort to take advantage of an unusual gathering of genocide scholars. They tried to remember the future by raising scholars' voices in the present. From the official rostrum, the panelists reflected the conference's dominant sentiments. They presented a version of the equivalency argument: "Many tribes in Africa kill each other. Tutsis and Hutus have killed and continue to kill each other. Therefore, the 1994 Rwandan 'incident' and subsequent developments just fit into the spiral of violence endemic to the region." This and other similar reactions effectively muffle pleas to remember Rwanda's past.

This is not to say that there have no been conferences, books, and articles devoted to the Rwandan genocide. However, the event described earlier symbolizes the secondary status that the Rwandan genocide almost inevitably receives. It seems odd that one can readily find scores of institutes, research centers, and university organizations devoted to the Holocaust in particular and to genocide in general. One can also find organizations focused on a specific genocide (Argentina, Armenia, Cambodia, Kurds, Tamils, and Ukraine). However, no research center focuses exclusively or even primarily on the Rwandan genocide.

The Rwanda genocide still occupies politically, legally, and academically a secondary status relative to other mass atrocities. Perhaps, this is due to the Rwanda genocide not fitting the paradigmatic image of genocide.

Comparative Icons

The Holocaust became well known in the immediate aftermath of World War II. General Dwight D. Eisenhower, Supreme Commander of the Allied Forces, made sure that video footage of the liberation of the death camps played in movie theaters across the United States. For complicated historical and political reasons, those death camp images did not become iconic until decades later.[42] The way the Holocaust images became iconic makes a fascinating story but one outside the scope of this inquiry. For purposes of this analysis, it is important to acknowledge the power and status accorded to the Holocaust icons. The media has played and continues to play an obvious role in promoting and preserving these icons.

Genocide—or, rather, the Holocaust—has a number of iconic images, most notably the gas ovens, the cattle cars, the forlorn faces, and the emaciated bodies looking out through barbed wire enclosures, and, of course, mass graves. Typically, other mass atrocities get in some way measured against these icons. Definitionally, the Rwandan massacre qualifies as genocide; iconically, it does not have the same type of images associated with the Holocaust. The images of the Rwandan genocide include machetes, dead bodies strewn throughout churches, and skulls. These images differ dramatically from those of the Holocaust. Even more telling is the absence in the Rwandan genocide of the very icon of evil—an analogue to Adolf Hitler.

Icons play a role in determining how the international community reacts to an atrocity. Note the efforts to match images of the Bosnian War with Holocaust icons. It is difficult to prove the consequences of the Rwandan icons mismatch. However, it does serve to give a certain degree of plausibility and legitimacy to arguments aimed at diminishing the horrors of the Rwandan genocide. It allows certain kinds of arguments to take hold about Rwanda, arguments that have barely, if ever, surfaced in analyses of the Holocaust. Perhaps, the mismatch between Holocaust and Rwandan icons played a role in the nonreception initially (and since?) given to the Rwandan genocide.

However, something far more sinister took place to displace the otherwise high ranking of the Rwandan genocide among injustices. Simply put, for images to even have a chance to attain iconic status, the media needs, at least, to convey the image. The media failed to disseminate images of the Rwandan genocide. Yet, much more importantly, other images, which immediately became iconic, overwhelmed and supplanted those of the Rwandan genocide. Just as the media, however reluctantly, began to give Rwanda the attention it deserved—images of the Twin Towers under attack became firmly embedded in the collective consciousness.

The political memory of the United States public lasts for only a short time. Television dominates the nation's short-term memory. Many atrocities, especially, those committed outside the United States, vie for the precious few seconds of media attention. The media magnates allow outsiders only short appearances on the American political consciousness screen.

Years after the genocide in Rwanda, the then major news network ABC granted Central Africa a few brief moments in the spotlight. ABC's *Nightline* aired a unique form of investigative journalism. Its host, Ted Koppel confessed to a news media oversight that amounted to an immoral act. While he admitted that the news media generally covered what its audience wanted to see (e.g., the O. J. Simpson trial), he acknowledged the media's responsibility to present what it thought its audience should see. He indicted the media, including ABC, for its inexcusable failure to cover the 1994 Rwandan genocide and its aftermath. To offer some restorative treatment Koppel filmed the reports from Goma in the Democratic Republic of the Congo, where some reports claimed that two to three million people were unaccounted for during the summer of 1999. The first in a five-part series began Saturday, September 8.

During an eight o'clock class on Tuesday morning, I begged my Illinois State University students to give themselves extra credit and watch the second part of the series that evening. However, little did I know at the time that Rwanda and Central Africa would once again be denied their rightful placed in the media spotlight. ABC had scheduled the second segment on Rwanda for Tuesday *September 11, 2001*. Needless to say, images of the Twin Towers under attack flooded the media. In subsequent interviews, Koppel barely mentioned the series on Central Africa, apparently putting it on hold indefinitely. The grave injustices in Africa and elsewhere once again took a back seat.

Nevertheless, the genocides and atrocities in Africa continue to pose a threat to reason, ethics, and law for the twenty-first century in ways reminiscent of what the Holocaust did to the foundations of values in the twentieth century. The hope is that law and morality will be ready to meet the challenge. The first step is to listen to the questions.

Conclusion

Of any atrocity since the Holocaust, Rwanda comes closest to matching it. Jews and Tutsis followed a similar trajectory leading to their respective brutalization phases. In the 1930s, Third Reich courts heard cases to determine whether individuals "qualified" as *Mischlings*, as cross breeds between Aryan and Jewish. At the time, few could have guessed what that designation would later mean. Similarly, a seemingly innocent designation by Belgium colonialists on an identity card as a Tutsi had catastrophic consequences for those caught with it in 1994 Rwanda.

In the 1930s, Jews became the target of a series of discriminatory acts. These laws forbid them to hold government jobs, teach in public schools, or practice medicine. The minority Tutsis also found themselves, to varying degrees, the victims of state-endorsed discriminatory policies under the First and Second Republics. Campaigns of hatred were launched against the Jews in Nazi Germany and against the Tutsis in Rwanda.

Genocide, according to international law, consists of the killings of members of a racial or ethnic group with the intent to destroy, in whole or in part, that group. The insanity of attempted extermination took place with ruthless barbarity in both Nazi Germany and 1994 Rwanda. Yet, despite these similarities, the two genocides stand far apart. Both have had their share of belittlers, distractors, and deniers. Still, these negative campaigns have had a great deal more success when the target has been Rwanda than when it has been the Holocaust. Perhaps, it may take time to correct the record with Rwanda. However, to resort to a legal phrase, time is of the essence. We cannot afford too much time. The stakes are too high.

Giving the Rwandan genocide its proper place among the injustices of the world is not simply an academic exercise. World leaders, in particular, and the international community, in general, seldom agree on anything. Where we find consensus, we should capitalize on it. Let us restate the points of agreement that we have unearthed so far:

1. Genocide is among the worst injustices if not the worst international crime.
2. The Holocaust and the 1994 Rwandan mass killings each qualify as genocide.

The implication of accepting (1) and (2) are granting:

3. Genocide provides sufficient conditions for humanitarian intervention.

With the acceptance of (3), we can turn attention to (4), which we develop fully in Chapter 7:

4. Genocide-like crimes against humanity also provide sufficient conditions for humanitarian intervention.

Perhaps, when discussing highly charged emotional issues, cold logic can help. Comparing horrible injustices may well offend, but it just may help to give Rwanda its due.

PART II

Comparative Applications: War on Terror's Distortions

CHAPTER 4

Torture

Undervalued Injustice

Introduction

Imagine a fully conscious man strapped faced down on a cold steel table. A sharp knife, hovering above, descends to carve descriptions of his hideous deeds into his back. Another device follows the knife to stop the bleeding and cleanse the wound before a third device fills the open wounds with ink. The machine—called the Harrow—"goes on writing, more and more deeply, for twelve hours."[1] With this, the writer Franz Kafka provides a harrowing iconic image of torture in his dark story *The Penal Colony.*

To understand and to condemn torture we need look no further than iconographic images such as that painted by Kafka. Yet, despite the power of images like this, torture has become a victim of countless nuanced analyses filled with distinctions designed to minimize torture's harm. The torture debate is seriously misguided. Fueled by the War on Terror, the torture debate is seriously misguided. It has transformed torture from a universally condemned crime to a regrettable but sometimes necessary state function. This chapter attempts to put torture back to where it should have remained, namely, among other universally prohibited acts such as genocide and crimes against humanity.

The *United Nations Convention Against Torture and Other Cruel, Inhuman, or Degrading Treatment or Punishment* defines torture as:

Any act by which severe pain or suffering, whether physical or mental, is intentionally inflicted on a person for such purposes as obtaining from him or a third person, information or a confession, punishing him for an act he or a third person has committed or is suspected of having committed, or intimidating or coercing him or a third person, or for any reason based on discrimination of any kind, when such pain or suffering is inflicted by or at the instigation of or with the consent or acquiescence of a public official or other person acting in an official capacity. It does not include pain or suffering arising only from, inherent in or incidental to lawful sanctions.[2]

Torture seems to involve any number of elements that cry out for definition and differentiation: severe pain, physical pain, suffering, mental pain, mental suffering, cruel treatment, inhuman treatment, and degrading treatment. Yet, participants in the debate should resist this lure, but the temptation to make distinctions is difficult to resist. Lawyers and philosophers have dominated the torture debate. This should not be surprising since both are heavily invested in the distinction drawing business. Find a distinction; argue a case. Find a distinction; publish an article. Yet, these distinction-infested debates have hindered rather than moved the torture debate forward.[3] Participants in the torture debate have fallen into a definitional-distinction trap. Does torture include physical and mental pain? Is there a difference between torture and cruel, inhuman, or degrading treatment? Does a torture prosecution require a showing of general or specific intent? These questions raise interesting academic issues. However, as we shall see, they only muddy the waters of the torture debate.

The torture debate also manifests a flawed view of international criminal law. International criminal law is not national criminal law writ large. Using national law as a model has disastrous consequences for international criminal law. For example, intent plays a very different role in international criminal law than it does in national criminal law. Overall, international crimes lack nuanced particularity. International criminal law represents the international community's attempt to provide a focus on the grave breaches, the systematic and widespread atrocities, and the clearly reprehensible acts. Making fine-tuned distinctions steers attention away from the big picture—the "unimaginable atrocities" that "shock the conscience."[4]

Keeping the focus on the big picture does not imply throwing away all distinctions. It is how best to make use of those distinctions that are in question. International criminal law does not consist of a conceptual pie that divides neatly into finely grained, detailed, distinct slices. Instead, international criminal law focuses on a set of egregious, central, core wrongs, and injustices. A crime consists of an act (the *actus reus*) and a "mental" component (the *mens rea*). At this stage, let us focus on criminal acts. As shown, in Chapter 1, the core *actus reus* of the international crime of genocide is mass killings. The core *actus reus* of torture, as argued later, is inflicting pain. However, finding a better way of interpreting the claim that the basic act of torture consists of the infliction of pain can help avoid the definitional trap. The strategy is to start with those acts, as represented by, for example, the image of Kafka's Harrow, that almost everyone would agree constitute torture. Then, other acts are evaluated according to how closely they visually and conceptually resemble the core act of torture as represented by the iconographic image.

The infliction of pain lies at the heart of the wrongfulness of torture. The "severe pain" referred to in the Torture Convention is Inquisitorial pain, that is, the brutal pain similar in kind to that inflicted on victims during the Middle Ages and depicted in Medieval engravings of the rack (see Figure 4.1). Refined legal or philosophical distinctions impede rather than move the torture debate forward. As this chapter demonstrates, the following icon of the rack used during the Inquisition will do better than Kafka's imaginary Harrow.

The second part of this chapter introduces this novel iconographical approach to torture. The rack of the Inquisition serves as the icon for determining which acts constitute torture. The first section shows how icons serve as moral and legal templates for evaluating purported harms. The icon of the Inquisition's rack should serve as an icon for assessing what acts qualify as torture. Yet, not every icon is created equal. Some icons, such as the Chinese practice of death by a thousand cuts, should be rejected as inappropriate. The third section demonstrates how to use the iconographical method to determine whether certain acts of neglect qualify as child abuse. This illustrates how the iconographic method applies across a wide variety of group harms.

The third part of this chapter takes on the more traditional legal analysis. It examines the *actus reus* and *mens rea* elements of the crime of torture. The first section defends the claim that, just as killing constitutes the core act of the crime of genocide, so inflicting pain makes up the core act of torture. This section shows how an iconographic approach helps to undermine some troublesome categories of acts that allegedly do not rise to the level of torture, including psychological pain and mental suffering as well as cruel, inhuman, and degrading treatment. The second section defends the claim that the institutional intent of the state is the *mens rea* element of torture. It further rejects attempts

Figure 4.1 Medieval rack[5]

to establish specific intent as the *mens rea* of torture. Finally, the fourth and final part, building on the previous arguments that will have undermined the many refined obscuring distinctions in the torture debate, makes arguments for treating torture as a universal prohibition.

This chapter on torture sets up a comparison with the next chapter on terrorism. The War on Terrorism has had dramatic and opposite effects on each of these harms. Torture has, in a sense, become a victim of the War on Terrorism, which has succeeded in devaluing it. The War has, obviously, bolstered and has, not so obviously, overvalued terrorism. Iconography can help reestablish torture among the top of the hierarchy of international crimes.

Iconography

The law is "part of a distinctive manner of imagining the real."[6] Images play a crucial role in law. Images, models, metaphors, and exemplars also have played and play an important role in science. Not only propositions but also certain kinds of pictures used in science can have truth-value.[7] The billiard-ball model of gas, the double-helix model, the solar system model of the atom—all of these models proved crucial to science.[8]

Icons are symbolic, pictorial, paradigmatic representations.[9] They are, in part, shorthands for descriptive and prescriptive statements. These statements include descriptions of both historically situated events and historical narratives that tie together similar events. Moreover, the statements also are prescriptive that is, moral judgments of condemnation. Yet, these icons are more than just statements. They have a critical emotive content. They represent and trigger a deep-seated moral revulsion. A photograph of a mass grave provides a paradigmatic example of an icon that typically provokes universal condemnation. The shorthand feature of icons is not just a convenience; it marks a virtue of icons. A demand to spell out the statements connected with an icon represents a moral failing. The need to persuade someone of the immorality of mass graves indicates something amiss. This is not to say that there is never a need to defend or expand upon an icon through commentary, but we also need to recognize how deeply embedded some icons are and should be in our moral fabric.

Icons are akin to paradigms (basic standards of judgment). Theorists of justice have difficulties agreeing on paradigms.[10] Theorists of injustice should not have the same difficulties. It would be odd indeed to publish a book on the pros and cons of genocide, a paradigm of injustice if ever there was one. Paradigms, in general, anchor interpretations but are themselves not immune to interpretation and reinterpretation.[11] Paradigms of injustice, however, are more deeply embedded than those of justice.

Icons are pictorial in the way that some examples of photojournalism have become iconic. Nick Ut won a Pulitzer Prize for his photo of a screaming girl (Phan Thi Kim Púc) being burned alive from napalm during the Vietnam War.[12] There has been a long-standing dispute about the efficacy and ethics of photojournalism.[13] In an earlier work, Susan Sontag warned of the public becoming anesthetized by these images.[14] But later she made a much more sympathetic case for them.[15] The use of icons in law avoids these controversies since they do not involve a public display of the images but a judicial and moral use of them.

Academic debates also use images or icons. Images play a role in law.[16] These images and icons, as argued later, do and should play a determinative role in the torture debate. However, anyone perusing any law or philosophy journal would have difficulty finding even a diagram to say nothing of a picture. Yet, if the commentators used pictures more often, the torture debate would have an entirely different character, especially if they carefully deployed certain icons. Icons can serve as the crucial moral models in debates over torture.

Icon of Torture: The Rack and the Inquisition

Throughout history, the Inquisition has supplied critical icons of torture, such as the rack shown in Figure 4.2.[17]

In fact, there were three inquisitions. The first, the Medieval Inquisition (1184), attacked heresies, particularly the dualist beliefs of the Cathars and the Waldensians in southern France.[19] A 1215 papal bull, *Ad Extirpanda*, issued by Pope Innocent IV, outlined the circumstances and methods for the Dominicans to extract confessions through torture.[20] The Spanish Inquisition (1478–1834), initiated by King Ferdinand II of Aragon and Queen Isabella I of Castile, began with a focus primarily on *conversos*, Jews who converted to Catholicism but who had allegedly lapsed back into their former Judaic beliefs and Jewish practices.[21] Finally, the Roman Inquisition, through the Congregation of the Holy Office established by Pope Paul III in 1542, targeted Protestant heretics.[22]

Historical accounts of atrocities typically go through a revisionist period, where critics attack previous accounts as exaggerated.[23] As discussed in Chapter 3, debates over the Rwandan genocide now are

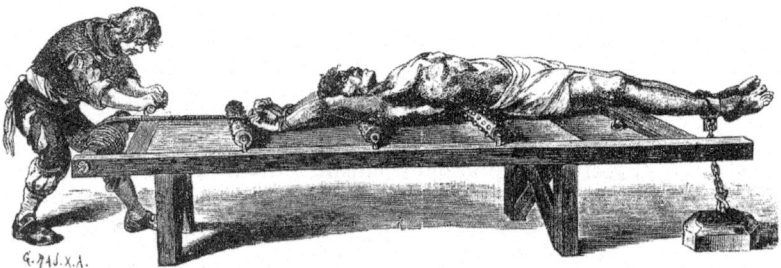

G·PAJ·X·A·

Figure 4.2 Medieval rack illustration[18]

undergoing this period of revision. With regard to the notoriety of Inquisition, perhaps secular authorities engaged in more brutality than the religious ones during the same period. Indeed, European secular courts carried out a brutal regiment of torture, particularly after the Church abolished trial by ordeal in 1215.[24] These and other historical revisions are important, especially since Protestants have had a stake in exaggerating the torments of the Catholic Inquisitions.[25] However, no one has challenged the barbarity of using torture devices during the Inquisition. Therefore, these revisions have not undermined the case for using devices from the Inquisition as icons of torture.

Pictures and descriptions of the torture implements used to extract confessions during the Inquisition create an almost universal reaction of disgust (Figure 4.3).

Three methods stand out. First, the *strappado* (pull, or *garrucha*, pulley, in Spanish), the "Queen of Torments,"[27] by ropes and pulleys raises the accused with hands tied behind the back.[28] The weights would suspend the victim up to five degrees of duration and severity.[29] The *proto* (colt or rack) pulls the victim's limbs in opposite directions until the joints became dislocated.[30] Finally, the *toca* (cloth) or *interrogation o mejorado del aqua* (otherwise known today as waterboarding) "simulates" drowning (Figure 4.4).[31] Before, this also was called the submarine.[32] More recently, former US vice president, Dick Cheney, referred to it as a "dunk in the water."[33]

These icons, particularly the rack, have served and should continue to serve even more in the future as normative templates in judicial decisions. Images from the Inquisition provide the paradigm, exemplars, and models of what is clearly prohibited as torture. When the US Supreme Court, to take a most notable example, has had to interpret the cruel and unusual punishment provision of the Eighth Amendment, it often has invoked images of the Inquisition. In the case of *In re Kemmler*, the Court found that the Eighth Amendment prohibited Congress from allowing punishments such as "burning at the stake, crucifixion, breaking on the wheel, or the like."[35] In *Brown v. Mississippi*, the Court asserted that, "the rack and torture chamber may not be substituted for the witness stand."[36] In *Ashcraft v. Tennessee*, the Court found that, "state and federal courts, textbook writers, legal commentators, and governmental commissions consistently have applied the name of 'inquisition' to prolonged examination of suspects conducted as was the [36 hour] examination [interrogation] of Ashcraft."[37] In *Chamber v. Florida*, the Court found that, "the rack, the thumbscrew, the wheel, solitary confinement, protracted

Figure 4.3 Medieval torture devices[26]

questioning and cross questioning, and other ingenious forms of entrapment of the helpless or unpopular had left their wake of mutilated bodies and shattered minds along the way to the cross, the guillotine, the stake and the hangman's noose."[38]

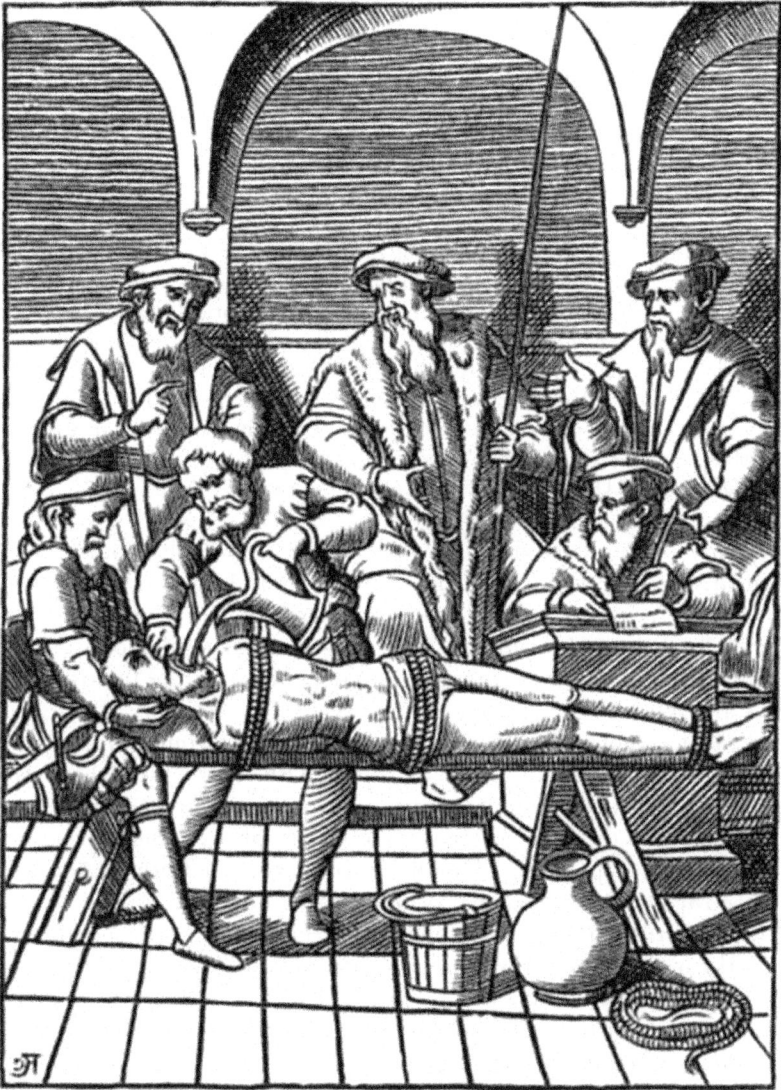

Figure 4.4 Image of a woodcut depicting "Toca" or waterboarding[34]

Invoking images of the Inquisition does not just provide vivid pictures. These images lie at the heart of the decisions to abhor torture. Most importantly, these references serve as normative templates. But they do not draw a bright line around those inflictions of pain severe enough to qualify as torture. Instead, they mark out a category that takes in anything resembling it. *Blackburn v. Alabama*, which is worth quoting at length, best exemplifies this approach:

> Since *Chambers* v. *State of Florida*, 309 U. S. 227, 60 S.Ct. 472, 84 L.Ed. 716, this Court has recognized that coercion can be mental as well as physical, and that the blood of the accused is not the only hallmark of an unconstitutional inquisition. A number of cases have demonstrated, if demonstration were needed, that the efficiency of the rack and the thumbscrew can be matched, given the proper subject, by more sophisticated modes of "persuasion." A prolonged interrogation of an accused who is ignorant of his rights and who has been cut off from the moral support of friends and relatives is not infrequently an effective technique of terror. Thus the range of inquiry in this type of case must be broad, and this Court has insisted that the judgment in each instance be based upon consideration of "[t]he totality of the circumstances." *Fikes* v. *Alabama*, 352 U. S. 191, 197.[39]

Similarly and more recently, in *Pennsylvania v. Muniz*, the Court found that the privilege against self-incrimination "was designed primarily to prevent 'a recurrence of the Inquisition and the Star Chamber, even if not in their stark brutality.'"[40] In the words of legal theorist Seth Kreimer, these modern techniques lie far too close to the Inquisition's rack and screw.[41]

This does not mean that courts should set up a continuum beginning with Inquisitorial torture and ending with torture lite.[42] The now infamous Bybee Memo characterized torture as suffering "equivalent in intensity to the pain accompanying serious physical injury, such as organ failure, impairment of bodily function, or even death."[43] Another Bybee Memo proclaimed that waterboarding does not "inflict actual physical harm" but only "controlled acute episodes."[44] Notice, however, that the methods permitted and promoted by the Bush administration included waterboarding, one of the classic methods of Inquisitorial torture.[45] In other words, the problem is not that the icon method permits "torture creep," where the baseline moves from "never" to "rarely" to "whenever needed."[46] Rather, the difficulty lies with the Bush administration having one and only one icon of severe physical impairment. Instead they should have started with the iconic rack, which includes the full panoply of torture methods, including waterboarding, used by the Inquisitorial. In fact, the Bush administration used most of the primary Inquisition methods:[47] Manadel al-Jamadi received the *strappado*,[48] Khalid Sheik Mohammad[49] and Abu Zubaydah Husayn[50] the *toca*. A condemnation of the Medieval *proto* (rack) entails an outright moral rejection of the Medieval *toca* (cloth used in waterboarding) because of the moral equivalence of the two methods. Similarly, the Bush administration's outlawing of torture causing serious bodily harm entails, what should have been, its rejection of waterboarding.

Inappropriate Icons: Death by a Thousand Cuts

As noted earlier, the icons for torture have a history, a use subject to criticism and change. However, the choice of icons is far from arbitrary. Not all icons are created equal. The choice and use of an icon can be criticized and rejected. Consider the Chinese practice of *lingchi chusi* or death by a thousand cuts, used in the West as an icon of torture in the East.[51] Before a crowd of Beijing onlookers, a few soldiers performed *lingchi* on Wang Weiqin:

> Two soldiers brought forward the basket holding the knives that the procedure required. Others stripped the victim and bound him by his queue to a tripod in such a way that the front of his body was fully exposed to the state executioner and his assistant. The executioner began by slicing off pieces of flesh from the convict's breasts, his biceps, and his upper thighs.[52]

First, note that this report, like so many Western ones, invariably takes practices of *lingchi* out of context.[54] Perhaps the following factors might modify reactions to the case of Wang Weiqin. *Lingchi* is misnamed "death by a thousand cuts."[55] The process did not involve 1,000 cuts on a fully conscious victim.[56] After four slices, the executioner put Wang to death with a swift stab to the heart.[57] Further, this case involved multiple killings by the accused. Wang and his gang killed 12 members of another family (Li Jichang), including a three-year-old, in a revenge feud.[58] Only the subsequent suicide of Li's wife prompted the authorities to pursue Wang.[59] Also, at the time of the execution, Wang probably had been heavily sedated with opium, one of the strongest painkillers.[60] Finally, soon after Wang's execution, on April 24, 1905, the Chinese government abolished *lingchi* and other forms of cruelty.[61] All of these factors show the importance of context when making judgments. They do not, however, undermine the overall condemnation of the practice.

More importantly, throughout the nineteenth and twentieth century, writers used *lingchi* as an icon of Chinese cruelty and barbarity.[62] The

Figure 4.5   The Lingchi of "Pseudo-Fuzhuli"[53]

authors of *Death by a Thousand Cuts* document the many inappropriate uses of this icon in the West.[63] For example, Western portrayals would show the victim tied to a cross.[64] The Chinese never used the Roman/ Christian cross for executions.[65] Archibald Little, a British onlooker, described Wang's "pieces of flesh, as cut away, being thrown to the crowd, who scrambled for the dreadful relics."[66] While these accounts bolstered the European belief in Chinese cruelty and barbarity, even Little's account, in the end based on hearsay, proved inaccurate.[67] These constructions were symptomatic of Westerners reading their own sense of execution into the Chinese context. Executions in the West, contemporaneous with the use of *lingchi*, were imbued with Christianity.[68] Western executions inflicted suffering on the victim and stimulated a cathartic reaction in the onlookers.[69] In contrast, Chinese executions were ritualized enforcements of the law, meant to teach a lesson rather than to lead to redemption.[70]

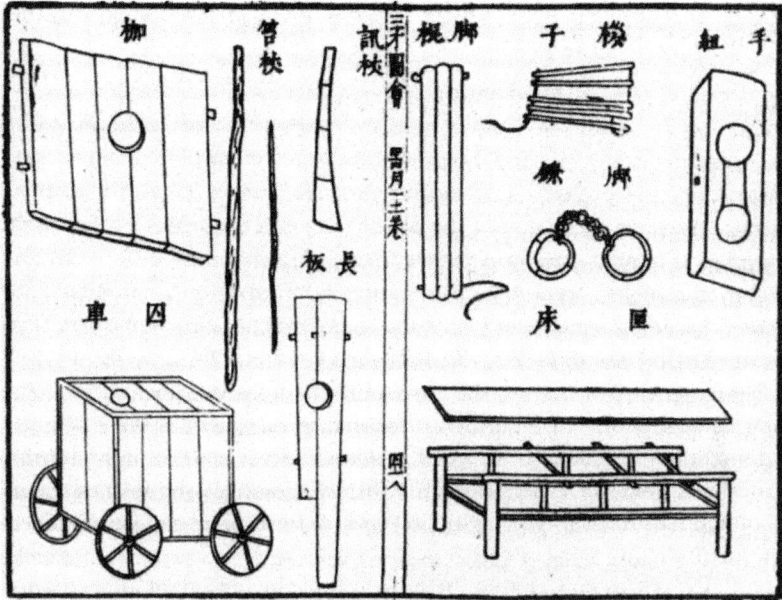

Figure 4.6 Ming Dynasty torture implements: wooden manacles, finger press, ankle press, fetters, "box-bed," interrogation baton, light and heavy flogging sticks, cangue, prisoner's card, restraining board.[75]

For purposes of this analysis, the most important problem is that Westerners used *lingchi* as an icon for cruel torture, when it served no such purpose in China.[71] First, *lingchi* was a form of execution, not of torture, although no one could deny that it involved torment.[72] Second, magistrates in China could and did torture, but the law regulated the implements of torture.[73] The lawful implements consisted of only a few, namely, the baton (*xunzhang*, distinguished from the *zhang* or interrogation stick) as well as the finger (*zanzhi*) and ankle (*jiagun*) presses (Figure 4.6).[74]

These last two were reserved for adult males accused of robbery or homicide, for which the penalty was exile or death,[76] but they could be used no more than twice without special authorization.[77] Compare the Chinese implements of torture with the following list of torture devices used during the Inquisition: "Head crushers, skull-splitters, wrist and leg irons, chain scourges, saws, hanging cages, the *guillotine*, spiked necklaces, self-mortification belts, the oral, rectal, and vaginal pear, the chastity belt, breast rippers. . . . "[78]

Yet, Western commentators avoided these cross-cultural comparative inventories. When they did undertake a single comparison, it was to the detriment of China. George Mason, author of *The Punishments of China* (1801), even mistakenly identified the Chinese ankle press with the Inquisition's rack.[79] When magistrates, in actuality, began to use something resembling the rack, that is, the box bed (*xiachuang*), Emperor Kangxi, in 1679, explicitly forbade its use.[80]

This brief excursion into Orientalism should at least demonstrate how to reject a purported icon of torture. Still, however persuasive readers might find *Death by a Thousand Cuts*, they should not suspend critical judgment. Admittedly, the authors do little in the form of explicit judgment, seeming to describe rather than prescribe. Yet, they assume judgmental inferences from their readers.[81] Even a thorough deconstruction of Western depictions of Chinese practices should not deter a condemnation of *lingchi*, which even as a form of execution matches the torture icon.

Finally, critics may charge the portrayal of the rack as an alleged universal icon of torture with Orientalism, for it treats a western European technique as universal. In China, until recently, cinematic representations of torture were commonplace, whereas sex was taboo.[82] Chinese torture icons, at least those appearing in films, consist mostly of chains and whips.[83] However, most Chinese would have few objections to using the rack as a universal icon, especially since it helps expose problems in the West.[84]

Iconographic Method: Child Abuse

The iconographic method applies to wide range of group harms. An analogy with child abuse will help to clarify how to use these moral icons in legal and moral disputes. Child abuse consists of distinct types of harms: physical abuse, emotional abuse, neglect, and sexual abuse.[85] The case of Mary Ellen Wilson makes an excellent candidate for the icon of child abuse. The child welfare literature places the discovery of child abuse in the United States around the 1870s.[86] The training manual for Court Appointed Special Advocates in child abuse cases begins with the case of Mary Ellen, the "discovery case."[87]

In 1866, Mary Ellen Wilson, slightly over the age of one, was indentured to Mary Connolly, who had divorced her daughter's biological father and remarried.[88] Mary Ellen's caretakers, Mary and Francis

Connolly, whipped her daily and periodically maimed her with scissors.[89] Mrs. Etta Wheeler, a sweet-faced missionary, uncovered the case and, in desperation, approached Henry Bergh to help rescue Mary Ellen.[90] The history of the animal welfare movement, oddly enough, provides additional context for the case. In 1866, Bergh, a member of the landed aristocracy, founded the American Society for the Prevention of Cruelty to Animals (ASPCA), the first organization of its kind anywhere.[91] Although reluctant to divert resources away from animal welfare, Bergh eventually became convinced to intervene on behalf of Mary Ellen, whom he reportedly acknowledged as a "little animal, surely," and he allowed his staff to undertake an investigation.[92] Elbridge T. Gerry, grandson of James Madison's vice-president and counsel for ASPCA, filed a petition on Mary Ellen's behalf.[93]

Judge Abraham Lawrence of the New York Supreme Court sentenced Mary Connolly to one year of hard labor for criminal assault and battery, a lesser crime than the felonious assault charge in the initial indictment.[94] He gave custody of Mary Ellen to The Sheltering Arms, an institution for dependent children.[95] Elbridge T. Gerry went on to help organize the New York Society for the Prevention of Cruelty to Children (NYSPCC), incorporated in 1875.[96] The NYSPCC's board included some of America's wealthiest men (having excluded women until 1921).[97] Bergh also played a pivotal role in the founding of the child welfare movement.[98]

Making physical abuse the paradigm of child abuse does and should not privilege that form of abuse. Rather, it helps to resolve disputes over other forms of child abuse. While sexual abuse receives the most newspaper coverage in the United States,[99] neglect far outstrips the other forms of child abuse.[100] Rates and incidences of physical and sexual abuse have decreased dramatically throughout the United States.[101] Neglect may have declined but not as rapidly or significantly as physical and sexual abuse.[102]

Before examining similarities between assessments of child abuse and torture, it is important to address, however briefly, a critical dissimilarity between the two forms of injustice. Recently, the Center for Constitutional Rights took the Holy See to task for failing to mention, in its Initial Report to the Committee Against Torture,[103] the sexual abuse inflicted by its priests.[104] The Center then contended that sexual abuse is torture, which is in keeping with the position previously adopted by the Committee Against Torture.[105]

Contrary to the Center and the Committee, an implication of this analysis, set forth more fully later, is that generally speaking, sexual abuse, however egregious, is not torture. First of all, the sexual abuse engaged in by priests did not fulfill the purpose requirement under the Torture Convention.[106] Other than their own sexual satisfaction, it is doubtful whether priests had any other institutional purposes when carrying out their morally reprehensible acts. The Shadow Report tried to dodge this objection by noting that, unlike torture, the charge of cruel, inhuman, and degrading treatment does not require proof of a purpose. But the Report cannot have it both ways, for then it has admitted that sexual abuse is not torture. More importantly, and, again, as argued more fully later, pain lies at the core of torture, whereas sexual abuse may not involve any pain whatsoever.[107] This is not to condone any form of sexual abuse. Conflating sexual abuse and torture does not bolster the perceived harm status of either one. Rather, it diminishes the likely perceived impact of both.

It would take a separate book to unravel the complexities of child abuse.[108] However, returning now to the similarities, child abuse presents some of the same difficulties as torture. Most importantly, it is amenable to the same iconography approach advocated in here. Physical abuse, as represented by the icon of Mary Ellen Wilson, serves as the paradigm, the normative template for child abuse.

When neglect can be shown to resemble physical abuse, then, if criminal prosecution is justified for physical abuse, it should be equally justified for similar cases of neglect, as it would be for the following case:

> One of the most severe child abuse cases of the last few years comes out of Plant City, Florida, where in 2005 Plant City Police entered into a child abuse investigation and found a "feral" child. The girl, 7-year-old Danielle, was found naked in a dark closet. Her hair was matted and covered with lice and she was lying on a moldy mattress surrounded by bugs. She had sores, rashes, and bug bites covering her skin.

> She was wearing a diaper that was full of urine and feces and dirty diapers covered the floor of the trailer in which the family lived. Feces covered the walls of the trailer and cockroaches were everywhere. The girl weighed only 48 pounds and was unable to eat solid food. She spent a great deal of time recovering in the hospital.[109]

Similarly, when examining torture, courts (and analysts) should compare the image of Inquisition torture with that of the current practice being called into question. The presumption should be that the practice looks like Inquisition torture. The burden then falls on the alleged perpetrator to show that the practice is nothing like those practices conducted during the Inquisition, that is, that it more closely resembles *de minimis* harm. The Court in *McKune v. Lile* adopted this strategy: "Determining what constitutes unconstitutional compulsion involves a question of judgment: Courts must decide whether the consequences of an inmate's choice to remain silent are closer to the physical torture against which the Constitution clearly protects or the *de minimis* harms against which it does not."[110]

Child neglect statutes are notoriously vague, giving room for the prosecution of *de minimis* harm for neglect.[111] The courts have adjudicated a number of questionable cases of neglect. For example, Dr. Bobbie Sweitzer, then an anesthesiologist at Massachusetts General Hospital, left her one- and four-year-old daughters in her Porsche after cracking the car window and activating the alarm system.[112] She ran into Sam's Club to drop off some film, leaving her girls out of her sight for 20 to 30 seconds.[113] She returned home to find that she had been reported to the Department of Social Services for child abuse.[114] It took eight months and $15,000 in fees to "clear" her name.[115] In another case, parents in Indiana were convicted for loosely taping their children's arms and legs while playing a hostage game with their children.[116] Bridget Kevane, a literature professor at Montana State University, was charged with neglect for leaving her three children and their two friends (ranging in age from 3 to 12) at the mall for a few hours.[117] These cases of alleged neglect look nothing like the physical abuse suffered by the likes of Mary Ellen, and therefore, the courts should have dismissed them as constituting *de minimis* harm.[118]

The same type of analysis, recommended here for child neglect cases, should guide determinations of what constitutes torture. In *Wilson v. Seiter*, an inmate claimed that the following constituted cruel and unusual punishment: "overcrowding, excessive noise, insufficient locker storage space, inadequate heating and cooling, improper ventilation, unclean and inadequate restrooms, unsanitary dining facilities and food preparation, and housing with mentally and physically ill inmates."[119] While the Justices disagreed over the majority's intent requirement in prison conditions cases, they concurred, in effect, finding that these conditions constituted only *de minimis* harms.[120]

With torture, the strategy is similar to that in child abuse cases. First, start with those acts such as the intentional infliction of pain that almost everyone would agree constitutes torture. Then, evaluate other acts such as waterboarding according to how closely they resemble the core act of torture. Following this method, there would be little doubt that practices such as waterboarding qualify as torture.

Elements of Torture

Let us turn to a more traditional legal analysis of torture by breaking it down into its elements. This section argues that the *actus reus* of torture consists of inflicting pain and the *mens rea*, of institutional intent, first introduced in the analysis of genocide in Chapter 1. This legal analysis and the previous iconographic method undermine the distinctions (e.g., physical pain versus mental suffering) that obscure the torture debate and help prevent torture from being recognized as a universal wrong.

Actus Reus (Act): Inflicting Pain

Crimes consist of a criminal or guilty act (*actus reus*) carried out by a criminal or guilty mind (*mens rea*). Statutes in national criminal law systems categorize different crimes and list the elements that prosecutors need prove for each crime.[121] The crime of murder may include the following: killing with intent to kill, killing with intent to cause grievous bodily harm, killing recklessly, and killing in the course of committing a felony (the felony murder rule).[122] Each category of murder involves killing. There are greater and lesser instances of the same act, that is, of killing.

International criminal law has similarities and dissimilarities to national criminal law. Compare the crimes of genocide in international law[123] and murder in national law.[124] Both include acts of killing. However, a national law on murder distinguishes between various kinds of killing,[125] whereas the Rome Statute does not distinguish types of killings under the crime of genocide.[126] Chapter 1 argued that the core act of genocide is massive killings.

However, before proceeding, it is important to note a difference between analyses of genocide and of torture. While killing is the core *actus reus* of genocide, it is not the sole *actus reus*. Genocide is the killings of "national, ethnical, racial, or religious groups."[127] In other words, for killings to qualify as genocide, the prosecutor must not only establish that killings occurred, but also that the victims came from certain types of groups. This is one reason iconography has a limited utility in depicting the *actus reus* in genocide cases. An icon will not provide a complete depiction of the *actus reus* since it generally does not readily identify the victim group. In contrast, a single icon such as the Inquisitorial rack does fully capture the *actus reus* of torture. With respect to the *actus reus*, a prosecutor in a torture case does have to prove anything about the nature of the victim, only the infliction of pain. Nevertheless, despite this dissimilarity, genocide and torture each have core acts. As demonstrated more fully in Chapter 1, the core wrong of genocide is killings. Analogously, the core wrong of torture is inflicting pain.

What is the wrong in torture? To some, the quest to find the wrong in torture would seem easy. The proverbial common person might start by noting, first of all, that torture hurts. The Inquisition rack icon captures the underlying phenomenology of torture, namely, the inflicting of pain. That simple and insightful claim has eluded jurists and philosophers. The infliction of pain lies at the heart of torture.

Opponents of torture find any number of things wrong with torture, over and above the infliction of pain. Surprisingly, few torture opponents seem content with finding that the wrong of torture lies in inflicting pain. They think that something more than pain must be a stake in torture. Parry, for example, sees torture in terms of asymmetrical power relations.[128] Most opponents of torture see it as a violation of the individual's autonomy or agency—in short, torture undermines the very identity that makes the individual human. According to Wisnewski, "[r]ather than being inflicted on the body, torture comes to be directed first and foremost at the agency of the victim."[129] For Shue, torture not only undermines agency, but it also turns such agency against itself.[130] Davis sees torture as some sort of endurance test: "torture is the intentional testing of a sentient, helpless being's ability to bear physical suffering against that being's will and indifferent to its welfare."[131] Sussman takes these philosophical and psychological harms to an existential extreme when he proclaims that "torture turns out to be not just an extreme form of cruelty, but the pre-eminent instance of a kind of forced self-betrayal [colluding against oneself], more akin to rape than other kinds of violence characteristic of warfare or police actions."[132]

Yet, just as physical pain does not accompany every instance of torture, autonomy or agency also are not always lost through torture. In fact, many torture victims not only come through the horror as fully intact human beings, but also many report never succumbing to a point where they entirely abandoned their autonomy or agency.[133] In a recent article, Luban and Shue unwittingly admit this: "Allowing the state to use severe mental pain or suffering is allowing them to employ an inherently awful tool...—the experience of severe mental pain or suffering—that is capable *sometimes* of attaining an awful goal: destroying the psychological identity of its target (italics mine)"[134] So, is torture only wrong when it destroys human identity, which it only does sometimes? To the contrary, the wrong of torture is the intentional (and actual) infliction of pain on a person within a political and legal context.

These characterizations of torture highlight something often inadvertently overlooked in discussions of torture. Most analysts focus on the victim and not on the perpetrator.[135] They zero in on what torture does to the victim. Obviously, any moral assessment must ultimately include what torture does to the victim. However, it should be just as obvious that law and morality should point their accusing fingers at the perpetrator. A perpetrator-centered analysis initially avoids a problem that can easily get the victim-oriented approach off the track. The former delays a debate over whether to subjectively or objectively assess a victim's pain and suffering. Initially, we do not need to care about whether the victim just happens to have an extreme tolerance for pain. What matters is that the perpetrator *intended* to inflict the pain.

Cruel, Inhuman, or Degrading Treatment. Statutes[136] and courts[137] distinguish torture from cruel, inhuman, or degrading treatment. Jeremy Waldron has attempted further to distinguish inhuman from degrading treatment.[138] A victim-oriented sense of the former is "treatment which cannot be endured in a way that enables the person suffering it to continue the basic elements of human functioning."[139] Degrading treatment includes four kinds of outrages to human dignity: bestialization, instrumentalization, infantilization, and demonization.[140] Indeed, these might differ from each other in significant ways. Yet, it is important not to see them as less severe than physical pain.[141] The important thing is to see how they connect to the icon of torture, the infliction of pain, in ways similar to the use of the rack in the Inquisition.

In a study of survivors of the Bosnian War, the researchers noted that, "physical pain per se is not the most important traumatic stressor in survivors of torture."[142] Jessica Wolfendale makes a strong case that so-called torture lite methods can be even crueler than direct physical torture techniques, since the former provides a moral distance between perpetrator and subject, thereby allowing the victim to feel more responsible and the perpetrator less responsible.[143] However, she wrongly accepts the suggestion that the distinction between torture and torture lite depends on an understanding of violence as primarily physical. Torture as paradigmatically physical does not provide more distance—rather, it provides a critical connection.

Thus, arguing for the centrality of physical pain for the act of torture does not entail claiming physical pain as a necessary element of the act of torture. Whatever distinctions made among these experiences, it is critical to note not so much how they differ from physical pain but how closely connected they are to physical pain. Metaphors prove telling in this debate. Waldron partially captures my position of erecting "a sort of *cordon sanitaire* around the much more important prohibition on torture—a 'fence around the wall,' designed not just to keep police, spies, and interrogators from crossing the torture threshold but to keep them from even approaching it."[144]

British forces subjected Irish Republican Army suspects to five methods: protracted standing, hooding, subjection to loud noises, sleep deprivation, and food and drink restrictions.[145] While the European Commission on Human Rights found that these practices amounted to torture,[146] the European Court of Human Rights disagreed but found that they were inhuman and degrading.[147] The Supreme Court of Israel found similar Israeli interrogation techniques—shaking, waiting in Shabach position,[148] tightening of handcuffs, sleep deprivations—unnecessary and unlawful, but refused to label them as torture.[149] As argued earlier, the key move to have these techniques qualified as torture is to show that these diverse techniques are very much like being subjected to the medieval rack. Many forms of cruel, inhuman, and degrading treatment differ in degree and not in kind from paradigmatic forms of torture. A similar case can be made for mental suffering.

Mental Suffering. Those who participate in the torture debate could use a basic course in neuroscience. The discussions suffer, if I can use that word advisedly, from a focus on only a narrow piece of the neurophysiology of pain. Many analysts become stymied after they provide an initial exposition of what they call "physical pain." Law professor Amanda Pustilnik, for example, notes that victims of waterboarding report that it was not physical pain that they felt.[150] What she fails to acknowledge it that what the victims are reporting is that waterboarding is not the same type of pain as they receive when their skin nociceptors respond to intense mechanical stimulation.[151] That does mean that it is not painful.

Similarly, Luban and Shue claim that "[b]ombarding prisoners with earsplitting, culturally repugnant rock music for hours on end would certainly count as mental suffering although some might discount it as constituting physical pain."[152] Contra Pustilnik, these prisoners might not report their experiences of loud noise as the same as their experience of pain from physical stimuli, but they would still label them as painful.[153] Expectations affect both physical, as narrowly construed, and hearing pain.[154]

As examples of experiences that are physical suffering but not pain, Luban and Shue list "freezing cold, unbearable heat, itching, nausea, paralysis," aching all over, and the inability to breathe.[155] If commentators stay focused on monomodal nociceptors, then they miss the richness of the neurophysiology of pain.[156] There are different kinds of nociceptors, including skin and visceral ones.[157] The neurophysiology of painfully cold sensations is complicated. It involves a molecular thermoreceptor called transient receptor potential melastatin 8 ("TRPM8"), which "express markers of nociceptors as well as non-nociceptors and have axonal properties indicative of both A and C fibers."[158] A singular focus on simplified pain pathways blocks recognizing the rich array of pain experiences and the similarities among these.

There is an iconography of pain at work here. Almost every discussion of pain uses the image of pain originating from something like a hammer causing injury to the hand.[159] If that is the sole image or primary icon, then other pathways are either ignored or treated as problematic. Whereas diagrams of sensory pain beginning in the hand after a hammer blow abound, it is difficult to find any diagrams of pain stemming from loud noises or excessive cold.[160] A person's report of pain stemming from a hammer blow to the hand will differ from reports of pain from excessive noise or cold. Those differences, however, do not create different, and thereby problematic, categories. Their neural circuitries are similar enough, especially in the context of the torture debate. Thus, many nuanced distinctions found in the torture debate turn out to be distinctions without important differences.

Mens Rea (Institutional Intent)

The Inquisition rack icon captures the *actus reus* of torture. Yet, its use does not give a full account of torture, which also includes a mental element not captured by the icon. However, there is a distinct time advantage to using icons if only for determining the *actus reus*. Judges and juries would not take a great deal of time to compare the icon of torture to an incident under examination. Similarly, an iconographic approach should short-circuit the plentiful academic debates over the acts of torture. The attention, then, should shift away from the now readily recognized act of torture to the perpetrator. That is where the legal and academic focus should be.

All of the characterizations of torture considered so far highlight something often inadvertently overlooked in discussions of torture. Most analysts focus on the victim and not on the perpetrator.[161]

They myopically set their sights on what torture does to the victim. Obviously, any moral assessment must ultimately include what it does to the victim.[162] However, it should be just as obvious that law and morality should point the accusing fingers at the perpetrator. What seems to matter the most for legal and moral analyses is that the perpetrator intended to inflict the pain. Yet, as shown further, once again, nuanced distinctions about the perpetrator's intent have clouded the torture debate in the same way that distinctions about the act have.

Specific Intent. The United States issued an Understanding to the Torture Convention ("U.S. Understanding"), specifying that "intentionally inflicted" meant, "specifically intended."[163] An analysis of a recent attempt to defend this illustrates the extent to which these efforts and the position of the United States are misguided. In an article ironically titled "Tortured Reasoning," the authors set out to show that a torture conviction requires that the accused inflicted pain or suffering for a purpose prohibited by the Convention.[164]

Indeed, Article 1 of the Torture Convention states,

> …any act by which severe pain or suffering, whether physical or mental, is intentionally inflicted on a person for such purposes as obtaining from him or a third person information or a confession, punishing him for an act he or a third person has committed or is suspected of having committed, or intimidating or coercing him or a third person, or for any reason based on discrimination of any kind, when such pain or suffering is inflicted by or at the instigation of or with the consent or acquiescence of a public official or other person acting in an official capacity. It does not include pain or suffering arising only from, inherent in or incidental to lawful sanctions.[165]

First, the article's authors confuse intent and motive, specific intent and special intent. The crime of genocide requires a special intent or motive.[166] Similarly, the Torture Convention lists a series of plausible institutional purposes or motives.[167] The phrase "for such purposes" indicates examples to follow for illustrative purposes. Interestingly, the purposes listed are activities and functions typically carried out by a state.[168] Therefore, it is a misreading of the plain language to attribute a requirement of specific purposes enumerated in the Convention.

Second, another plausible reading of the intent requirement is to distinguish deliberate from accidental acts. In a deportation case, the US Third Circuit Court of Appeals read the intent requirement contained in the implementing regulations promulgated pursuant to the Torture

Convention, not as a specific intent requirement but as simply exclud-ing "severe pain and suffering that is the unintended consequence of an intentional act."[169] The Court concluded that the intent requirement "distinguishes between the suffering that is the accidental result of an intended act, and suffering that is purposefully inflicted or the foresee-able consequence of deliberate conduct."[170]

Third, the US Understanding is either misleading or effectively empty. Regarding the former, the US Understanding is a backhanded way of getting in a narrower interpretation of torture under the guise of special intent. According to State Department testimony, "the origi-nal [transmittal] package proposed an understanding to the effect that, in order to constitute 'torture,' 'an act must be a deliberate and calculated act of an extremely cruel and inhuman nature, specifically intended to inflict excruciating and agonizing physical or mental pain or suffering.'"[171] It was this severe sense of torture that the United States lobbied for during the drafting of the Torture Convention, a sense rejected by Convention.[172] Alternatively, the Senate Executive Report explained that "[b]ecause specific intent is required, an act that results in unanticipated and unintended severity of pain and suffering is not torture for the purposes of this Convention."[173] This only rules out unanticipated or unintended acts, and the notion of special intent is not needed for that.[174]

Fourth, the notion of specific intent has proven problematic even in US criminal law. It was dropped completely in the 1981 Model Penal Code.[175] Fifth, the idea of special intent lends itself to narrow interpreta-tions. US immigration courts, whose decisions the authors (Hathaway, Nowlan, and Spiegel) cite approvingly, have used this narrow reading in its removal cases.[176] However, this sense of special intent is not the same as the sense of special intent defended by the authors. It is yet another problematic sense, namely, that in removal cases the petitioner needs to prove that he or she has been specifically targeted for torture upon return to his or her country.

The specific intent reading should be rejected. However, that rejection should not result in shifting the focus back to the victim.[177] Replacing the specific intent requirement with some other such as foreseeability will not resolve the problem.[178] The solution is to recognize the ambigu-ous role that intent plays in the Torture Convention, designed to cap-ture the mental state of individual state agents as well as the goals and policies of the state. In the end analysis, the intent required for torture is not individual intent. Rather, just as in the case of genocide, it is institutional intent in the form of state policies.

State Policies. People are more likely to escape prosecution in international law for killing a thousand individuals than they would in national (municipal) law for killing one individual.[179] The justifications for this odd situation lie within the notion of criminal intent. An analysis of intent also will help clarify another paradox in international law. Individuals who directly carry out mass killings are less likely to face prosecution in an international criminal court than are officials far removed from the actual killings.[180] Resolving these paradoxes, however, depends on a radical rethinking of the idea of intent in international criminal law. The need for this reassessment becomes apparent on thinking about another troubling feature of international criminal law. To appreciate the problem, consider the following hypothetical questions. How would prosecutors have charged Adolf Hitler under the current genocide statute that requires proof of intent? Would they have to prove that Hitler had nearly six million intentional states of mind that led to the killing of nearly six million Jews? Something is wrong here. Obviously, there is a need to reevaluate the notion of intent in international law. As we shall see criminal intent in international law, unlike its counterpart in national law, has little to do with individual minds and a great deal to do with organizational policies.

Before proposing a new sense of intent for international criminal law, we need to show why the International Criminal Court should retain any sense of intent. The case for keeping an intent requirement begins with acknowledging the inevitable comparative judgments about the seriousness of crimes in any criminal justice system. No matter how distasteful it might seem, jurists and nonjurists judge some injustices as worse than other wrongs. We might say, for example, that we condemn all killings. However, we do not hesitate to judge the brutal slaying of a child as worse than the compassionate hastening of an adult cancer patient's death. These often unexamined, comparative judgments— particularly when seriously made in legal and moral debates—have important consequences for social policy. For many of the reasons set forth throughout our investigation, we regard intentional crimes as worse than nonintentional ones. If we rely on (often without debate) these comparative assessments, then we are more likely to approve of devoting more resources to the prosecution of those accused of committing intentional killings.

For murder convictions, national criminal laws require not only that defendants committed a criminal act but also that they had a "criminal mind."[181] To convict someone of murder under national criminal law, prosecutors must prove that the accused intentionally committed the act.[182] To convict someone of genocide, should international criminal law require prosecutors to meet the same intent standard or, given the extreme nature of the crime of genocide, should it abolish the intent requirement altogether?[183] Adopting the latter, strict liability approach would be a serious mistake. Stripping the element of intent from the crime of genocide would deflate the extreme moral condemnation that the crime of genocide warrants. However, if we keep the intent requirement for genocide, we can only do so if we accept a radically different sense of intent than the one used in national criminal law systems.

The idea of criminal intent in international law should not mirror the sense of intent that is so central to national criminal law. In the latter, a first-degree murder conviction requires that the accused individual had intent to commit the crime.[184] Cases of genocide involve more than one individual who commits the crime. It might seem appropriate, then, to require proof of intent for each one of these individuals. Yet, this move would seriously distort the nature of genocide. Genocide is not simply killings carried out by many individuals. Genocide is far more insidious than mass killing. It takes far more than the combined intents of a number of individuals to accomplish genocide. Genocide requires considerable organization. Genocide requires institutionalized organization. Acts of genocide involve institutions and organizations, typically governmental institutions and state organizations.[185] To capture the underlying horror of the crime of genocide, international criminal law needs to adopt a more institutionalized sense of intent, which we can label as *institutional intent*. As we shall see this institutional sense of intent makes more sense when interpreted not as a state of mind but as an organizational policy.

When we interpret criminal intent as organizational policy, we resolve many of the oddities created by appropriating the idea of individual intent from national criminal law into international criminal law. Most importantly, if convictions for acts of genocide require prosecutors to prove individual intent, then prosecutors will have a difficult time separating the little fish from the big ones.[186] A small town café owner who suddenly mutated into a militant Bosnian Serb (Tadic) should not have the same degree of criminal responsibility for the acts, however vicious, that he committed as should the leaders of the militant factions that directly encouraged and guided the commission of them (Karadzic).[187] Otherwise, if prosecutors persistently and fully applied the idea of individual intent in these cases, then they would have to call for harsher punishment of the little fish than for the big fish since it is more difficult to establish individual intent for the big ones than for the little ones. In contrast, if prosecutors sought proof of institutional intent, then they would have to make the big fish the primary targets of their indictments.

Admittedly, the choice of institutional over individual intent also has disadvantages. It would lead to situations where prosecutors might let the little fish escape criminal responsibility entirely. In other words, the individuals closest to the criminal acts, that is, the little fish who actually carried out the horrifying deeds of slaughtering massive numbers of people, would most likely not face prosecution under international law. This dilemma warrants serious attention, which must await some further discussion.

The analysis should focus not on an individual torturer but on the state as a torturer. William Schabas has made a compelling case for substituting state policy for the intent, *mens rea* requirement for the crime of genocide.[188] The Torture Convention occupies a middle position between individual and state criminal responsibility in that it make states indirectly responsible by holding its agents individually responsible.[189] Unfortunately, international law does not yet have mechanisms for state criminal responsibility.[190]

The torture debate is about states and about the law. There are many troubling things about the torture debate. Most analysts focus on the victim and not on the perpetrator.[191] Obviously, any legal and moral assessment must ultimately include what it does to the victim. However, it should be just as obvious that law and morality should point their accusing fingers at the perpetrator (the *mens rea*). But who is the perpetrator? What really matters, legally and morally, is not even that an individual perpetrator intended to inflict pain, but that a state perpetrator implemented a policy to carry out acts that constitute universal prohibitions in international law. In short, as an international crime, torture has close affinities to genocide. It is that analogy that should redirect the torture debate.

Universal Wrongs

Where an issue appears in an argument—its argument-place—affects the analysis of that issue. If an article begins with an assessment of the various arguments presented by those who deny the Holocaust, then the presenter has elevated the status of Holocaust denial. If, however, the presenter first provides a detailed, well-documented account of the litany of Holocaust horrors, then a footnote on Holocaust denial toward the end of the piece gives denial little credence. Similarly, giving prominent argument-place to those who try to justify torture has skewed the torture debate.[192] This observation, of course, does not excuse authors from the challenging task of demonstrating that torture constitutes a universal wrong. It merely highlights the difficulty readers should have in giving credence to torture justifications after having been persuaded by the iconography of torture. The structure of this article, which starts with vivid pictures of torture, should make it easier for readers later to accept that the prohibition against torture should be universal. Once the iconographic approach and the legal analysis have successfully dismissed the obscuring distinctions that have dominated the torture debate, the road is open for fully accepting torture as a universal prohibition.

Torture as a Peremptory Norm [193]

What did the drafters of the Torture Convention have in mind?[194] The immediate impetus for moving forward with the Torture Convention came from the efforts of Amnesty International. In its 1973 Report, it clearly recognized the gravity of torture in that there was no act that was "more a contradiction of our humanity than the deliberate infliction of pain by one human being on another, the deliberate attempt over a period of time to kill a man without his dying."[195] Article 2 of the Torture Convention states unequivocally that, "[n]o exceptional circumstances whatsoever...may be invoked as a justification of torture."[196] This absolute prohibition remained throughout the drafting stage of the Torture Convention.[197]

"Why, then, given the rhetorical, moral, and legal status of this prohibition, is torture being debated?"[198] Why, indeed?[199] Even the most jaded pessimist (I hope!) would have difficulty imaging a newly emerging, widespread debate among scholars and the public over whether emergency conditions justify genocide. As noted before, in a disagreement with Mother Teresa, who contended that abortion was genocide, Elie Weisel quipped that at least abortion was debatable.[200]

The Torture Convention prohibits torture absolutely: "No exceptional circumstances whatsoever, whether a state of war or threat of war, internal political instability or any other public emergency, may be invoked as a justification for torture."[201] However, the "no exceptional circumstances" provision does not apply within the Torture Convention to cruel, inhuman, or degrading treatment.[202] Yet, the absolute ban on both practices remains intact if the Torture Convention is read in conjunction with the International Covenant on Political and Civil

Rights because, under Article 4 of the Covenant, neither torture nor cruel, inhuman, or degrading treatment can be justified by a public emergency.[203]

Justifications: Unjustifiable and Unjustified Acts

Genocide and torture do differ, but not in a way that undermines the universal prohibition, the preemptory norm status of genocide and torture. Some acts are unjustifiable, while others are unjustified. An act is *unjustifiable* if there is no coherent possible world where someone could or would defend the act in terms of some rationally defensible moral theory.[204] An act is *unjustified* if there are no actual circumstances under which those acts would be justified within some defensible moral theory.[205] Genocide is unjustifiable. There are no rationally construed hypothetical circumstances that provide an exception to the universal prohibition against genocide. Unlike almost any other crime, genocide is an irrevocable status crime.[206] In an act of genocide, people are killed for what (whom) they are perceived to be, that is, for their alleged membership in a vulnerable group and not for any act that they have committed or are about to commit. This makes genocide unjustifiable.

Torture comes very close to genocide, in that it is difficult to conceive of actual circumstances where it would be justified. However, torture is not unjustifiable. As the Ticking Bomb scenario[207] tries to demonstrate, there may be hypothetical circumstances that might justify torture.

Yet, attempts to argue that torture is justifiable in principle ultimately fail for reasons that they fail for genocide. Both crimes are status crimes. A critical element of each crime is that they are carried out because of the victim's status. With genocide, the victim status is more obvious. Genocide killings are carried out because of the victim's status as a member of a legally cognizable group, namely, their actual or perceived members of a racial, ethnic, national, or religious group. Torture, less apparently, inflicts pain upon victims because of the knowledge status of the victim. Perpetrators inflict pain on victims because of the knowledge perpetrator's think that victims possess. Torture, like genocide, has nothing to do with the victim's past acts; both target the victims because of their status. Status crimes are in principle unjustifiable.

Torture also is unjustified; that is, there are no actual circumstances that would constitute exceptions to the universal ban on torture.[208] Take the following theoretically plausible examples of morally reprehensible acts. First, newborn babies could be strapped to car bumpers to reduce traffic accidents and fatalities. Second, the twin experiments, conducted by Dr. Mengele, the Nazi physician, during World War II yield life-saving results.[209] Third, Wang Weiqin's killings of the Li family members stopped the cycle of revenge killings.[210] These acts might constitute acceptable exceptions in some possible world, but they should not qualify as exceptions in this world. These acts, like some situations with torture, constitute hypothetical circumstances that should be legally excluded if there are any hopes of making this a moral world.

Genocide is unjustifiable in that it does not admit any exceptions, even hypothetical ones. Torture is unjustified in that it does not admit any practical exceptions. The Ticking Bomb scenario mistakenly treats torture as an act that includes hypothetical exceptions.

To justify torture involves finding situations where torture becomes permissible. The Ticking Bomb has become an icon in the torture debate.[211] The issue of justifications appears at the end of this chapter, which is exactly where it should appear overall in the torture debate. Questions of justification have a far lesser impact when they appear after the iconography of torture has done its work. Permitting the Ticking Bomb scenario to sit at the table will result in, what one commentator describes as perpetrators hearing ticking bombs everywhere.[212]

Conclusion

"Law is not brutal in its operation. Law is not savage. Law does not rule through abject fear and terror, or by breaking the will of those whom it confronts. If law is forceful or coercive, it gets its way by nonbrutal methods, which respect rather than mutilate the dignity and agency of those who are its subjects."[213] There are many troubling things about the torture debate. Most analysts focus on the victim and not on the perpetrator. Obviously, any legal/moral assessment must ultimately include what it does to the victim. However, it should be just as obvious that law and morality should point their accusing fingers at the perpetrator (the *mens rea*). But who is the perpetrator? What really matters, legally and morally, is not even that an individual perpetrator intended to inflict pain, but that a state perpetrator implemented a policy to carry out acts that constitute universal prohibitions in international law. In short, as an international crime, torture has close affinities to genocide. It is that analogy that should redirect the torture debate.

Iconography provides a way to reorient the torture debate to its original, saner grounds. The rack has served, serves, and should serve more prominently as the icon of torture. It clearly highlights the central wrong of torture—an institutional or state agent inflicting physical (in a broad sense) pain on a helpless individual. A prosecutor or judge needs only to compare pictures of waterboarding or other ingenious devices to the rack icon to determine their obvious similarity. Torture is not a matter of subtle definitional distinctions. Torture is a blatant, odious scourge that is easy to recognize with open eyes, unobscured by conceptual nuances.

The circle of international crimes has an affinity with the circle of rights. In recent centuries, the circle of rights has expanded dramatically. For many past centuries, a narrowly circumscribed circle of rights excluded certain groups, including slaves and women. That circle has expanded to include these and other groups. Some continue to advocate for expanding the circle even farther to include animals. International law continues to expand the circle of universal, exceptionless prohibitions, beginning with genocide and reaching out to torture. Unfortunately, the current debates over torture represent a backlash against this expansion. Indeed, one very troubling thing about the torture debate is that it is still being debated.

In a sense, this chapter has engaged in a war on the War on Terrorism. It has battled against that War's efforts to undervalue torture. The next chapter takes on the next phase of the battle, to repel the forces of the War on Terror that have overvalues terrorism.

CHAPTER 5

Terrorism

Overvalued Injustice

"The world will never be the same." What place, if any, does terrorism have among the panoply of international crimes? Does it sit comfortably alongside its peers—genocide, torture, and crimes against humanity? Or does it occupy a position of greater stature seated above the others, at the high table? Contrary to current trends, terrorism ranks rather low. It does not and should not even qualify as an international crime.

Few outside of legal circles may have even heard of international crimes such as crimes against humanity. Yet, everyone knows terrorism. They especially know terrorism through the attack on the World Trade Center. The attack on that fateful Tuesday, September 11, 2001, gave terrorism a particularly high level of prominence and preeminence. After that ignominious day, the nations of the world not only joined together to express their sympathies but also to unify to fight the terrible menace. The Israeli prime minister Ariel Sharon, for example, appearing on American television talk shows the next day, lost no time. Israel's message became readily apparent. Americans quickly realized on September 12, 2001, what the Israelis had known throughout their short history. Terrorism requires not only constant vigilance but, more importantly, continuous war as well. The world had become a battleground.

And, indeed, the nations of the world have launched a seemingly never-ending battle against the scourge of terrorism. Given terrorism's elusive nature, nothing qualifies as a final victory over it. Eliminating its most prominent leader (Osama bin Laden) and effectively dismantling its most powerful organization (al Qaeda) does not mark its defeat or even its demise. Fear not. A defeat of ISIS will not bring an end to the war on terrorism. For, the world has been placed on a permanent state of alert. Any one victory only creates a geometrically progressing need for more victories. Terrorism fits the agenda of many politicians and industrialists by putting the world in a permanent, never-ending state of war.

Never has the saying "You know it when you see it"[1] reaped such havoc. For, no one really knows terrorism—at least, in the sense of being able to provide a definition. It may take the form of Palestinian militants engaged in questionable practices of guerilla warfare or perhaps of members of a Palestinian clan kidnapping and murdering three hitchhiking Israeli youths. Still, yet, it might take the form of one environmentalist damaging the property of an animal research facility or of an entire army (ISIS) launching an attack in Syria and Iraq.

However, I will argue that terrorism should not take a seat on the same platform as other international crimes. In fact, it should not even be allowed through the door—especially the door leading to the room of international or even domestic criminal law. The law, especially criminal law, depends on definitions. It makes no sense to treat terrorism as an international or domestic crime if it has no elements, that is, defining parts. Just as the War on Terrorism has unjustifiably succeeded, as argued in the previous chapter, in undervaluing torture, it has even more perniciously overvalued terrorism.

This chapter puts forth the claim that, in many important senses, terrorism does not exist. Yet, the chapter goes on to account for terrorism's persistence, despite, paradoxically, its nonexistence. The first major part of this chapter examines the legal analytic approaches to terrorism. The first section within this part briefly recounts the history of terrorism, revealing an interesting gap that has left state terrorism out of the picture. The second section undertakes the seemingly hopeless task of unraveling the elements of the crime of terrorism. Not only have the international community and the United States failed to reached a consensus on the definition of terrorism but more importantly, as argued in the third section, they have excluded the only viable candidates for the core *actus reus* of terrorism, namely, the killing of innocent civilians.

The second major part of this chapter examines terrorism from various normative and comparative perspectives. The first section demonstrates how analysts have exaggerated the threats of terrorism. It demonstrates that even assuming a consensus on what constitutes a terrorist act, the harms associated with terrorism have been greatly overblown and exaggerated. Moreover, as argued in the second section, terrorism's reach has overextended into so-called eco-terrorism. The third section undertakes the major comparative analysis of the chapter. Comparisons of terrorism to genocide and torture reveal interesting features of all three crimes. Genocide far outstrips terrorism in terms of number of deaths. However, what makes genocide (or any other crime for that matter) particularly heinous is its planned nature, whereas randomness distinguishes most terrorist acts. Torture in comparison to terrorism raises more complicated problems. The analysis reveals a critical difference. Torture is practically unjustifiable, whereas terrorism is not only justifiable in principle but also (perhaps) has been historically justified.

The chapter ends with a final part that uncovers a critical problem in the entire terrorism debate, namely, indeterminacy. This part illustrates the forms of fear that emanate from the indeterminacy of terrorism. This indeterminacy serves state interests well. But before worrying about the future fear, let us understand terrorism's sordid past.

Analyses of Terrorism

History of Terrorism

Terrorism and its close relatives have interesting ties to language. The words "zealot," "thug," and "assassin" began their linguistic development through their association with specific terrorist organizations. The Zealots (from Greek *zelos*, ardor or strong spirit) in the first century (48–73) led a revolt against the Romans. The word "thug" derives from an Indian group by that name, who, in the name of the Hindu goddess Kali, "for over seven centuries killed millions of people" by strangulation.[2] The word "assassins" (which is often thought, mistakenly, to be derived from the Arabic *Hashishhin* or "users of hashish") comes from an Islamic group that operated in Persia from the eleventh to the thirteenth century (1090–1256).[3] They publicly carried out assassinations of political and military figures.[4]

The nineteenth century saw terrorist acts carried out by individuals in the name of groups or movements. Some anarchists promoted propaganda by deed, which included assassinations of those wielding oppressive power: individuals, in the name of anarchism, assassinated a Russian Czar (Alexander II) and a US president (William McKinley).

A history of terrorism, however, cannot remain focused solely on individuals and groups from which we inherited words that describe problematic if not despicable acts. Soon, history has to confront the troubling truth that historical instances of terrorism included some movements that appeared worthy of support. Seldom do revolutionaries and others choose terrorism as a weapon of first choice. The historical problem, the problem of demarcation, infects discussions of terrorism in general. Where does the line demarcate acts that deserve wholesale rejection and those that do not?

During his brutal reign, Hitler experienced at least ten attempts on his life. The Nazis executed prominent Protestant theologian Dietrich Bonhoeffer for his association with the 20 July Plot on Hitler's life in 1944. This occurred two weeks before US infantry liberated the Flossenbürger concentration camp where Bonheoffer's hanging took place. Are political assassinations wrong or just certain ones?

The argument that one person's terrorist or terrorist organization is another person's freedom fighter resonates throughout history. From 1948 to 1990, South Africa adopted a brutal apartheid (which mean "to be apart") regime of racist segregation, where a small white minority ruled over a large nonwhite population. Today, the world celebrates Nelson Mandela and the African National Congress (ANC) for their liberation politics that freed South Africa from the racist throes of apartheid. What is largely forgotten is that the governments of the United Kingdom and the United States branded Mandela a terrorist and the ANC a terrorist organization. These designations had some justification. Admittedly, long-time activist Mandela never directly participated in any activities that targeted civilians, and he remained in prison through the most active phases of the ANC. However, ANC campaigns did result in a considerable number of civilian deaths. Much to the dismay and consternation of the ANC, the Truth and Reconciliation Committee (TRC), headed by then Bishop Desmond Tutu, addressed charges lodged against the ANC. The ANC, for example, had a military wing, *Unkhorto we Sizwe*, better known by its initials MK. MK operatives applied to the TRC for amnesty for acts committed during the apartheid era, including the Church Street bombings in Pretoria that killed 19 and wounded 217. The TRC granted amnesty on grounds that even though MK caused some civilian casualties, it had targeted the military, specifically the South African Air Force (SAAF).[5]

Many analysts try to distinguish the actions of freedom fighters from terrorists by noting that the latter specifically target civilians, whereas the former do not.[6] The MK's acts may have resulted in civilian casualties, but it did not deliberately target civilians. Perhaps, this might hold true for the MK. However, the same cannot be said for organizations such as the Provisional Irish Republican Army, which led an armed campaign against British rule in Northern Ireland. In any event, it proves difficult to make nuanced distinctions among all the multifarious acts committed by an alleged terrorist organization. Groups such as the Catholic Irish Republican Army (IRA) have a long and varied history. To stem public hostility, the IRA often refused to take responsibility for cases of bombings of Protestant civilians. To complicate matters even further, Protestant loyalist paramilitary operations were more likely to engage in indiscriminate killings because of the difficulties in identifying IRA members.[7]

Yet, a history of terrorism that included only individuals and groups would be misleading. After all, the word "terrorism" itself was coined during the French Revolution and its aftermath, aptly dubbed the Reign of Terror (June 1793 to July 1794) by the British statesman Edmund Burke. That terror was a government policy. The Jacobin dictatorship executed from 17,000 to 40,000 French citizens in the name of virtue and democracy.[8] And these were not only single executions by the guillotine. Some 700 alone were massacred in the town square of Lyon.[9] In short, the roots of terrorism, linguistically and historically, lie in state action.

Most analysts conveniently overlook or adamantly deny the existence of state terrorism.[10] In a political and legal world dominated by states, it should come as no surprise to find the phenomenon of state terrorism a neglected field of study. States blocked efforts to include state terrorism within international law, for example, within the *UN Convention for the Suppression of the Financing of Terrorism* (2004).[11] Yet, the killing of innocent civilians by state agents proves all too common. To keep with examples from Northern Ireland, British soldiers unjustifiably massacred civil rights protestors on January 30, 1972, now known as Bloody Sunday. In the 1970s, many countries in Latin America, particularly Chile and Argentina, used terrorist tactics against their own people.

Primoratz claims that state terrorism ("wholesale terrorism," in the words of Chomsky and Herman)[12] is morally worse than nonstate terrorism (retail terrorism).[13] The state, generally, can amass far more resources to carry out killings than any individual or group. Only states possess weapons of mass destruction.[14] However, states also have far more readily available means at their disposal. States use arbitrary detention, disappearances, torture, and political murder as means of spreading terrorism. More importantly, state violence results in far more deaths than nonstate terrorism.[15] Nevertheless, a more accurate comparison might result if we knew what nonstate terrorism was.

Defining Terrorism

In 1937, the League of Nations attempted to pass a treaty on terrorism, *The Convention for the Prevention and Punishment of Terrorism*. It managed to attract 24 state signatures, but only one state (India) ratified it.[16] The United Nations has 12 conventions dealing with terrorism[17], but none contains a clear definition of terrorism. It may seem that the international community has come a long way, to the point when now the United Nations has undertaken to draft a comprehensive treaty on terrorism.[18] In the interim, the international community has put into force over 20 thematic conventions on terrorism.[19] Yet, one fundamental flaw underlies these efforts.

There is nothing approaching a consensus on how to define terrorism. The US federal government defines terrorism as: "premeditated, politically motivated violence perpetrated against noncombatant targets by subnational groups or clandestine agents" while a terrorist group is defined as "any group, or which has significant subgroups which practice international terrorism (international terrorism being terrorism involving citizens or the territory of more than one country)."[20] The FBI defines it as: "the unlawful use of force or violence against persons or property to intimidate or coerce a government, the civilian population, or any segment thereof, in the furtherance of political or social objectives."[21] Unlike the federal definition, the FBI definition does not require intent and is limited to specific objectives on the part of the perpetrators. States within the United States also have their own definitions of terrorism. Arkansas law states that "a person commits the offense of terroristic threatening if, with the purpose of terrorizing another person, he threatens to cause death or serious physical injury or substantial property damage to another person."[22]

Pundits blame the lack of an international consensus on a rift between Arab and non-Arab states. Arab states exclude armed struggle for liberation and self-determination in their definitions of terrorism.[23] However, a flexible, open-ended sense of terrorism serves the interests of all nation-states, Arab and non-Arab.

The scholarly arena is just as definitionally muddied as the legal field.[24] A search of the literature quickly reveals scholars falling over one another in an attempt to carve out a place for terrorism among the worst global crimes. Yet, one survey found that 77 percent of scholars in leading journals in Political Science who focused on terrorism failed to define it.[25] Let us at least make an attempt to offer a definition, however abortive it will turn out to be.

Elements of Terrorism

Actus Reus. As proposed in Chapters 1 and 4, certain harms lie at the core of genocide and torture. For genocide, mass killing constitutes the central *actus reus*, and for torture, physical pain is the core ingredient of that crime. Without those elements, prosecutors would not be able to convict for those crimes. What is the core harm at stake in terrorist acts? Of the hundreds of definitions, legal and academic, not one of them fully captures the core harm. The US definitions do not even list terrorist acts beyond violence in general. The UK definition modifies that somewhat by requiring serious violence.[26] France lists specific terrorist acts, including murder.[27] This comes the closest to capturing the core harm of terrorism. The horrifying feature of so-called terrorist acts lies in a particular kind of violence, namely, killing. Otherwise, Palestinian youths throwing stones at Israeli soldiers could be construed as terrorist acts. Intuitively, however, it is the Palestinian suicide bomber killing and maiming innocent Israeli civilians riding a bus that symbolizes the abhorrent aspect of a terrorist act. The targeting and killing of innocent civilians seem to lie at the heart of terrorism.

Mens Rea. Many commentators, jurists, and legal documents treat terrorism as a special intent crime.[28] The intent to instill terror, that is, fear, in a population distinguishes terrorism from other crimes.[29] After all, terrorists intend that their acts instill terror, that is, fear, in their victims.

If instilling fear were so critical to terrorism, it is curious, indeed, that many of the thematic conventions on terrorism, which designate specific acts of terrorism, fail to even mention the production of fear as an aspect of the terrorist acts. For example, none of the conventions that cover terrorist acts relating to civil aviation mention this psychological component.[30] Further, it is notoriously difficult to use a vague concept like fear as a legal element of a crime.[31]

Other commentators hone in on the political motive that allegedly underlies terrorist acts.[32] Motive presents even more difficulties than intent. Domestic law, especially in the United States, does not include motive as an essential element underlying a criminal act.[33] The motive qualifier, "political" or even "ideological, religious, or ethnic," proves even more problematic.

If instilling fear (and not killing innocents) is the critical ingredient of the crime of terrorism, then a different set of acts other than killing innocents becomes central. Acts other than killing innocents can instill greater fears. These other acts include arbitrary detention, disappearances, torture, and political murder. In short, this makes up a list of acts used by states to conduct terrorist campaigns. A sinister message underlies this observation. Analysis comes to the aid of ideology. The singular analytic focus on killing innocents conveniently steers critics away from state terrorism. Nonstate actors engage primarily in killings. State agents, while not adverse to killings, have a much wider array of acts at their disposal. This holds true not only for state agents who directly do these acts but also for so-called state sponsors, that is, those states that indirectly undertake the acts through financial and other means of support. The focus on killing innocents facilitates a ready condemnation of nonstate actors and helps to immunize state agents from charges of terrorism. In short, al-Qaeda kills; the United States outsources torture. Further, al-Qaeda's killings of innocents then can be interpreted as nonjustifiable. Whereas the US killings of innocents through drone strikes becomes perhaps not justified but excusable since the primary targets are those who killed innocents.

If this to-and-fro analysis causes dizziness, then mission accomplished. If terrorism were a subject open to clear-cut analysis, then it conceptually would not serve the purposes of the states that have promoted terrorism as the number one international crime.

Comparisons of Terrorism to International Crimes

Terrorism does not rise to level of gravity and seriousness, especially when compared to recognized international crimes. When compared to genocide, the case is strong. The case regarding torture proves more complicated.

Genocide

Except for perhaps war crimes and state terrorism, no other international crime rises to the level of number of fatalities as genocide. However, there also is a fundamental difference between the two acts. The very randomness and seeming unpredictability of terrorism creates conditions ripe for the development of a general fear, which is most often more difficult to offset than a specific fear. Citizens of Israel never know when an act of terrorism will erupt. Yet, as argued in Chapter 1, intentional killing ranks as morally and legally worse than random killing. Terrorism is not genocide because the victims are not targeted solely because of their identity or status and the act is not carried out in order to annihilate all or significant portion of victims of the same type or identity. The notion of random killing associated with terrorism is seldom analyzed and can be misleading. A purely random act, by humans or even among elementary particles, turns out to be more difficult to define than one might expect. Obviously, individuals do not carry out terrorist acts on a purely random basis, if by that we mean without any planning or forethought. In international law, that element of planning is captured by the term "targeting," which is an element of crimes against humanity. The randomness associated with terrorism comes more from the perceptions of the actual and potential targets than from the mindset of the terrorists.

Torture

Torture makes for a more difficult case since it often involves inflicting pain on only one or, at most, a few individuals. However, torture as *jus cogens* crime, that is, a universal prohibition discussed further in Chapter 6, represents the position taken by the international community that that kind of treatment of one individual by another, namely, the infliction of pain, will not be tolerated. Unfortunately, the same cannot be said of killing innocent people. The laws of war, with some notable exceptions, tolerate the killing of innocents. So-called humanitarian law turns out to be far less humanitarian than many might think.

Perhaps the strongest argument against treating terrorism as an international crime is that instances of terrorism are justifiable if not justified. If the core element of terrorism is not some human rights violation, but, more specifically, the targeting and killing of innocent civilians, as argued earlier, then this may seem to provide fodder for those who find terrorism, in all its forms, unjustifiable. Indeed, the targeting and killing of innocents does seem to make terrorism a particularly reprehensible act. This would seem to make it even harder to justify.

However, certain forms of political violence may be justified, depending on what they are responses to. Some jurists and scholars have attempted to justify political violence, in general, and terrorism, in particular.[34] The philosopher Virginia Held, for example, proposed a nonconsequentialist justification for terrorism that makes a case for redistributing harms in the form of rights violations.[35] Again, this illustrates yet another example of an appeal to harms without an attendant ranking of those harms. For, surely, if one group merely systematically violates the rights (to housing, to free speech) of another group, that would not justify killing members of the first group who benefit from the violations. Held needs something stronger than rights violations.

Perhaps, that something stronger can be found in the analysis of Primoritz, who offers two conditions to justify terrorism.[36] First, it must be the only method available that is likely to succeed. Second, it must prevent a moral disaster. Fulfillment of these ("virtually but not absolutely nonexistent") conditions, supposedly, makes terrorism justifiable. To qualify as justifiable, there must be rationally and morally conceivable conditions. Genocide is unjustifiable. Within the bounds of rationality and morality, as argued in Chapter 1, we cannot even make-up a scenario wherein genocide would become justifiable. In contrast, terrorism may be justifiable, that is, justified in principle (and perhaps in practice).

Terrorism appears to qualify as justifiable, at least, in the manner set out by Primoritz. As examples of moral disasters Primoritz considers genocide and ethnic cleansing as two possible candidates. Yet, Primoritz needs to sort out and rank these types of moral disasters. If the forced removal of large portions of an ethnic community from their homes constitutes ethnic cleansing, then that would not justify killing innocent members of the removing group. Otherwise, the Kosovars would have been justified in killing innocent Serbs when the Serbs forced nearly one million Albanians from their homes in Kosovo.

Perhaps, if genocide was the moral disaster at stake, then killing innocent individuals within the same group as the *genocidaires* becomes justifiable if it could and would stop an ongoing genocide. However, it is difficult to imagine a situation where this might apply. If, during the 1994 Rwanda genocide, French military forces had turned on the Hutus and massacred segments of their population, that act most likely would have fueled rather than have halted further genocide. Still, Primoritz has at least made a prime facie case for the justifiability of terrorism.

Moreover, targeting civilians may not only be justifiable but also be historically justified. In fact, some of those cases are not those carried out by nonstate actors but by states—and by states not typically associated with terrorism. During World War II, the Allies, mainly the British, firebombed German cities such as Dresden, resulting in an estimated 25,000 deaths.[37] The United States issued objections to the early use of firebombing by the British but carried out its own version against Japan. Perhaps, the firebombing of Tokyo, resulting in 100,000 deaths, fits into the category of the unjustified. However, due to the power and lure of hindsight, many scholars and commentators tend to defend the nuclear devastation reaped on Hiroshima and Nagasaki. The atomic bombs obviously targeted innocent civilians, but, arguably, they also brought a quicker end to the war with perhaps fewer casualties. Finally, note that if instilling fear were the key component of the crime of terrorism, then there would be even stronger grounds for arguing for the justifications for the killing of innocents.

Genocide is neither conceivably justifiable nor historically justified. Torture, while conceivably justifiable, is not contingently justified. It is not justified because of the practically inconceivable nature of the assumptions that would have to be made to make it justified. The hypothetical ticking bomb scenarios designed to demonstrate the justifiability of torture assume that the subject knows the whereabouts of the ticking bomb and that the subject's information is accurate. In any realistic instantiation of this scenario, it is difficult to accept conditions under which the torturer knows that the suspect knows and knows that the information is accurate.

These same kinds of practical inconceivability do not plague the issue of finding justifications for terrorism. The problems are more of an empirical matter. Were there realistic alternatives to dropping atomic bombs on Japan? Did the dropping of the atomic bombs, in fact, save countless lives? These are empirical questions or at least more on the contingent end of the spectrum, whereas the case of torture raises those on the more conceptual end of the spectrum.

Assessments of Terrorism

This section poses three challenges to those who want to elevate the harm of terrorism. First, the actual, overall harm from so-called terrorism is highly exaggerated and, relative to other harms, rather minimal. Second, the slippery notion of terrorism all too easily overextends inappropriately to, for example, environmental protest activity. Finally, and legally most importantly, the many acts lumped under the terrorism label are already covered by domestic and international laws.

Exaggerated

Finding accurate statistics on terrorism proves difficult. Most analysts regard the Global Terrorism Database as the best source. However, caution needs to be exercised in examining the data. A sharp drop off of terrorism incidents in 1993 was due to the box of data falling off a truck while being transported, and the spike in 2012 represented a change in coding methods and not a dramatic increase in terrorist incidences. The database, as discussed later, is also over inclusive, especially in including eco-terrorist attacks, which are directed almost exclusively at property.

Statistically, terrorism does not cause very many deaths compared to other harmful things, including food poisoning.[38] "Until 9/11, no terrorist operation had ever killed more than 500 people."[39] The attack on 9/11 seems to have been *sui generis* (unique) in terms of the total number of deaths from a terrorist attack. There were 2,996 deaths from 9/11. Most people would have difficulty guessing the next two on the list: 796 fatalities from the 2007 bombings of Yazidi communities in Iraq and 774 deaths from a 1990 massacre of police in Sri Lanka.[40]

"At current rates, an American's chance of becoming a victim of terrorism in the U.S., even with 9/11 in the calculation, is about 1 in 3.5 million per year. In comparison, that same American stands a 1 in 22,000 yearly chance of becoming a homicide victim, a 1 in 8,000 chance of perishing in an auto accident, and a 1 in 500 chance of dying from cancer."[41] The National Consortium for the Study of Terrorism and Responses to Terrorism puts the odds higher, 1 in 20 million.[42] According to the *Economist*, the comparative risks of death in America are 1: 24,974 for assault by firearm; 1: 100,686 from choking; 1: 117,519 from postsurgery complications; 1: 150,681 from alcohol; 1: 157,300 from falling down staircases.[43] "Undoubtedly, terrorism commands disproportionate attention relative to the harm it causes, and other kinds of violence—particularly by States, and even by common criminals—cause greater harm."[44]

Overextended

Terrorism has a wide reach. It even grabs those dedicated to protecting the environment and animals. Many countries including the United Kingdom[45] and France[46] have extended their definitions of terrorism to include eco-terrorism. These activists now are labeled as eco-terrorists. In the United States, the Animal Enterprise Protection Act of 1992 first covered these "wrongs." Subsequent, more stringent legislation, the Animal Enterprise Terrorism Act of 2006 (AETA), included an interesting name change. The 2006 version of this act passed both houses of Congress by near-unanimous consensus. A year earlier, the FBI ranked eco-terrorism as the most serious of the many types of terrorist threats.[47]

In 2009, four activists were arrested in California for protesting. The prosecutor claimed that protesting instilled fear in others. Members of Stop Huntingdon Animal Cruelty (SHAC) tried to close down the animal testing facilities of Huntingdon Life Sciences, largely by coordinating actual and virtual civil disobedience through their website. In 2009, a US federal court upheld their convictions on conspiracy charges.[48] In 2010, William James Viehl was convicted under AETA (2006) for setting free 500 minks from a farm. Almost all of these cases involve, at worst, damage to property.[49] It is difficult to attribute any deaths to eco-terrorism.

Covered

Second, there is no need to have a separate crime of terrorism. To the extent that terrorism has a relatively clear-cut set of criminal elements, domestic or international law already covers those elements. In short, within international and domestic criminal law, there is no need for a new crime under the heading terrorism. Some might argue that terrorism does not fit in international law neatly under the crimes against humanity banner. Crimes against humanity must be widespread or systematic, whereas terrorist acts occur in isolated episodes. However, domestic laws should and do cover it as a single event. If it becomes widespread enough to cross borders, it may become a transnational crime or, if it becomes more serious, an international crime against humanity. If more systematic or widespread, then it would fit under the international criminal category of crimes against humanity, particularly if conducted in peacetime. If committed during armed conflict, then international humanitarian law would cover it.

Some of the debate over terrorism has centered on the status of terrorists within humanitarian law. However, humanitarian law only applies to armed conflict. There is an underlying assumption that humanitarian law is good and that not applying it is bad. However, even the word humanitarian is misleading, for humanitarian law is not very humanitarian. There is a great deal of harm that can be legally done under humanitarian law that cannot be done under human rights law.

Of course, the actual legal classification has many more obstacles than these descriptions might indicate. The important point for purposes of this analysis is that there should not be a separate crime called terrorism.

If the act is relatively small scale, then, generally, domestic criminal law should or does cover it. "87 states lack special terrorism offences and hence use ordinary offences; 46 states have simple generic terrorism offences; and 48 states have composite generic terrorism offences."[50] Those states that have a single and those that have multiple generic elements of terrorism do not agree about those elements. As one commentator notes, "even the basic element of an intent to create terror is not found in all definitions."[51]

The judiciaries throughout the world have tried numerous terrorist cases, with varying degrees of success.[52] Italy, for example, has combated domestic terrorism while still managing to maintain constitutional guarantees.[53] Yet, even after this success, Italy passed major antiterrorism legislation to deal with foreign terrorists. Researchers have found that maintaining a sound rule of law notably reduces the likelihood of terrorist attacks.[54] Strong armed tactics tend to strengthen rather than to deter terrorism.

A key question is whether to treat terrorism as a police or as a military matter. The key according to University of Notre Dame law professor Mary O'Connell is whether terrorism is an armed conflict, which, within international law, is carried out by organized armed groups engaged in intense intergroup fighting. The two key elements are the intensity of the violence and the level of organization. Terrorist acts are isolated and sporadic and not prolonged and intense. According to ICJ Judge Christopher Greenwood: "In the language of international law, there is no basis for speaking of a war on [al Qaeda] or any other terrorist group, for such a group cannot be a belligerent, it is merely a band of criminals, and to treat it as anything else risks distorting law while giving that group a status which to some implies a degree of legitimacy."[55]

The argument for making policing instead of the military the primary means of combating terrorism does not imply an endorsement of all policing techniques nor does it mean that terrorism should become the number one crime for police to combat. The same kind of comparative harm analysis helps to shed some light on this. Except for New York and Washington, DC, the focus on counterterrorism seems to have increased the crime rate in just about every other major American city.[56] The same diversionary problem exacerbates development efforts internationally. Resources devoted to counterterrorism divert much more needed resources for development.[57] In 2002, for example, over half of all humanitarian aid went disproportionately the Afghanistan way to fight terrorism.[58]

Further, the policing thesis does not imply that terrorism should even be considered as a new domestic crime. A good example of this is the Patriot Act, which does not provide a separate definition of terrorism. Instead, it lists a series of acts—hijacking, assassinations, bombings, etc.—that are already criminal acts within domestic law.[59]

Therefore, where there might arguably be a core harm or criminal element at stake for terrorism, as we have seen, other long-recognized international and domestic legal classifications cover that harm. However, as argued in the next section, there is something far more sinister at work with the War on Terrorism.

Fundamental Indeterminacy

There is something far more sinister at stake than a simple overlap and redundancy of legal classification. The vast array of different definitions of terrorism helps to undermine the previous analysis that made a case for a central harm at stake for terrorism. The inability to identify a central harm and to find an agreed upon definition of terrorism creates indeterminacy. There are various kinds of indeterminacy recognized by legal theorists, including normative and linguistic.[60] However, the indeterminacy at work in terrorism discourse plays a far more sinister role than any of these.[61] Indeterminacy in that case means that there is no clear-cut way for the law alone to decide what is a terrorist act and what is not. In case of some forms of indeterminacy, legal theorists argue that indeterminacy at one level, the legislative, merely creates an opportunity to resolve indeterminacy at a "higher" judicial level. In other words, the indeterminacy creates conditions for a delegation from one level to the next. In the case of terrorism, who delegates to whom? Those promoting the need to combat terrorism rely on the indeterminacy. It creates optimal conditions for politicians to delegate to themselves (typically the executive in complicity with the legislature). The judiciary came and comes late to these determinations.

This situation would be troublesome enough if it were not for one more component added to the mix—namely, fear. The seeming randomness, the ascribed devastation, and the indeterminacy create optimal conditions for fear. The vaguer the phenomena, the more openings there are for manipulation. Political leaders throughout the world do not want a clear definition of terrorism. Vagueness and uncertainty serve their interests all too well.

Discussions of Hobbes focus on the plight of individuals in the state of nature. The plight of individuals in the state, in Leviathan, however, is just as disturbing if not more so. Fear underlies both. Political fear is "a political tool, an instrument of elite rule or insurgent advance, created and sustained by political leaders and activists who stand to gain something from it."[62]

Fear proves difficult for people to locate when they are in its midst. Do Americans fear terrorism? In the United States, for example, terrorist fear has taken on a more distant cast since now its imminence in the form of a foreign attack does not appear close at hand. Even so, fear of terrorism still plays a role in the American political psyche.

A retrospective look at similar and related fears provides a needed analytical distance. The connection between past and current terrorist fears should not but does need an explanation. For some time, the attack of September 11, 2001, on the Twin Towers, held its place in isolation—a single, unique, solitary event. No official or scholar would admit to or discuss its connection with past events. However, now, after it is too late to have a calming effect on the American political psyche, most admit that a 1993 attack on the Twin Towers preceded the 2001 attack.

Terrorism fails the test of a legal analysis, in among others things, lacking basic criminal elements. The lack of contextual analysis surrounding 9/11 makes terrorism even more amorphous and mysterious. The 9/11 attacks literally came out-of-the-blue, at least that is what the pundits would have us believe. Contextual facts run counter to this picture. 9/11 was not the first time that terrorists attacked the United States or, more pointedly, attacked the World Trade Center (WTC). In fact, if the 1993 prior attack had gone as planned, it would have caused far more destruction to life and property than the 9/11 attack.

Yet, for many years, no one connected the dots. If they had, they would have found a direct link between the two attacks. Basically, roughly the same groups (with some complications) carried out both attacks. The history of the Egyptian Muslim Brethren provides the keys to these links.

In the 1950s, the Brethren had forged close links with Nasser, who had overthrown King Farouk. Nasser, in fact, reportedly asked Sayyid Qutb, a Brethren leader later known for giving intellectual sustenance to al Qaeda, to join his government. The alliance completely ruptured when Nasser, for internal political reasons, turned on the Brethren. He twice imprisoned, later executed, and ultimately martyred Qutb. Prison radicalized Qutb—as it typically does for so many terrorists.

Sadat, Nasser's successor, made peace with and even armed the Brethren. Despite these concessions, a disgruntled faction of the Brethren viewed this cooperation with disgust. Some of the breakaway faction's members assassinated Sadat in front of his future successor, Mubarak. Members of that faction immigrated to the United States and carried out the first WTC bombing in 1993. Soon thereafter, it formally allied with al Qaeda. The rest, as they say, is history.

This contextual indeterminacy when added to the legal indeterminacy creates an amorphous space ripe for political manipulation. It is time to put the smoke back into the bottle and put terrorism in its right-ful place on the lower shelves of injustice.

Conclusion

The unjustified elevation of terrorism by the War on Terrorism has had disastrous effects. It has diverted efforts and resources away from far worse global injustices. It is and will remain impervious to definition, making it easily subject to manipulation of state leaders. More impor-tantly, it diverts any efforts to cast the spotlight on the terrors most pernicious and vicious agents—states.

PART III

From Theory to Practice:
Humanitarian Intervention Revised

CHAPTER 6

Universal Wrongs

Jus Cogens

"It's a bird, It's a plane..." It's a sham; it's *jus cogens*.[1] Many jurists find peremptory norms[2] an empty concept—"at best useless and at worst harmful...."[3] Yet, the task of finding the highest or universal norms of international law has proponents as well as detractors. Among publicists, only a few deny the existence of *jus cogens*.[4] Yet, beyond an agreement that it exists, *jus cogens* remains clouded in mystery. This chapter blows away some of the mysterious fog by defending a single *jus cogens*, universal norm, namely, the prohibition against genocide. Armed with a defensible core concept of *jus cogens*, the more troublesome outer perimeters become more tractable.

The debate over *jus cogens* seldom goes beyond a few theoretically inspired disputes. This seemingly technical concept and related discussions have critical ramifications. First, *jus cogens* signals the reappearance of natural law in international law.[5] Fomenting at a subterranean level, natural law is due for a revival, and its quiet development has given it time to establish itself on much surer foundations than past formulations. Those in search of law's universal foundations look to natural rights as contained, for example, in the Universal Declaration of Rights. In the meantime, a less disputatious version of universal claims has arisen in the form of *jus cogens*. Whatever the status of first- (civil and political), second- (social and economic), and third-generation (cultural, environmental, and solidarity) rights, certain forms of harm warrant universal disapproval. Second, as demonstrated in the next chapter, the case for universal prohibitions provides the groundwork for making a case for humanitarian intervention.

Overall, this chapter, through a series of steps, makes a case for a natural law approach to *jus cogens*. The first section briefly recounts the history of *jus cogens* and its relation to the natural law tradition. Then, the second section turns to complicated legal analysis of the legal sources of *jus cogens*. It makes a case for general principles providing the initial ingredients for a full-fledged ethical foundation of *jus cogens*. Similarly, the third section illustrates how an ethical version of *jus cogens* sits atop a conception of a global legal order. These sections pave the way in the fourth section for interpreting *jus cogens* in terms of universal wrongs rather than in the classical natural law tradition as universal goods. Having established the foundation of *jus cogens*, the fifth section reveals the content of these universal wrongs with genocide as the prime candidate. The acceptance of universal wrongs should entail the acceptance of universal obligations (obligations *erge omnes*), discussed in the sixth section of this chapter and developed in the next chapter. The final section summarizes the case for ranking international crimes, leaving open an analysis and ranking of crimes against humanity, taken up in the final chapter.

History of *Jus Cogens*

Although it holds a place in a long philosophy of law/natural law tradition reaching back to Hugo Grotius[6] and carrying through De Vattel's 1758 treatise, *jus cogens* has a relatively brief legal history.[7] The systematic development of the legal concept began after World War I with an article by Alfred von Verdross, who proposed the idea of an immoral treaty, that is, a treaty voided by a judiciary on moral grounds (*contra bonos mores*).[8]

Today, those who want to undermine state sovereignty use *jus cogens* as a weapon. Interestingly, Vendross saw *jus cogens* as a way to protect state sovereignty, in contrast to Grotius who employed natural law as a means of taming unjust states. For Verdross, a treaty became *contra bonos mores* "if a state is prevented by an international treaty from fulfilling the universally recognized tasks of a civilized state."[9] Verdross wanted to protect Austria and other countries from treaties requiring them to reduce their armies and thereby rendering them defenceless against external attacks. Verdross declared treaties like these immoral since they seriously undermined state sovereignty. He interpreted *contra bono mores* as "against the public order of the international community."[10]

In 1953, Hersch Lauterpacht, special rapporteur of the prestigious Internal Law Commission (ILC), continued in the natural law vein set by Verdross.[11] Lauterpacht characterized *jus cogens* as "overriding principles of international law which may be regarded as constituting principles of international public policy (*ordre international public*)."[12] Verdross and Lauterpacht saw *jus cogens* as serving a judicial function. Some commentators interpret the ILC's 1966 action as symbolizing a move away from these natural law renditions of *jus cogens* and toward a more positivistic approach. As evidence of the positivists' turn they note that the ILC treats *jus cogens* as modifiable by states.[13] However, the ILC's positivistic turn amounted to no more than noting and acknowledging that many *jus cogens* norms had become codified into positive law.[14]

In the 1960s, the ILC launched a trial balloon calling for further development of *jus cogens*. With developments in international law and international relations (if the increasing numbers of genocide and mass atrocity cases can even be called "international relations"), the time has come to heed the call. The increasing recurrence of genocide, recounted in Part I, has made it imperative for the international community to recognize the universality of the prohibition of genocide. Rather than succumbing to positivistic impulses, international jurists should take the opportunity to turn *jus cogens* in a natural law direction, as we do in the following sections.

Sources of *Jus Cogens*

The concept of *jus cogens* (compelling law that binds all) as distinguished from *jus dispositivum* (agreed upon law that binds only the consenting parties) first appears formally codified in the 1969 text of the *Vienna Convention on the Law of Treaties*. Article 53 states:

> A treaty is void if, at the time of its conclusion, it conflicts with a peremptory norm of general international law. For the purposes of the present Convention, a peremptory norm of general international law is a norm accepted and recognized by the international community of States as a whole as a norm from which no derogation is permitted and which can be modified only by a subsequent norm of general international law having the same character.

Only eight states voted against this provision.[15] The Article reflects a common understanding of *jus cogens*, namely, for *jus cogens* to be effective, it must have a basis in customary law. In other words, to become fully operative a peremptory a norm must have become fully incorporated into state practice. This pragmatic understanding, however, should not be confused with the theoretical problem of finding a source and justification for *jus cogens*. While source and justification overlap, they remain distinct.

Article 38(1) of the Statute of the International Court of Justice specifies the following sources of international law:

> (a) international conventions, whether general or particular, establishing rules expressly recognized by the contesting states; (b) international custom, as evidence of general practice accepted as law; (c) the general principles of law recognized by civilized nations; (d) subject to the provisions of Article 59, judicial decisions and the teachings of the most highly qualified publicists of the various nations, as subsidiary means for the determination of rules of law.

Natural law theorists and positivists continually talk past one another, as the following example demonstrates. Mary Ellen O'Connell, a self-professed natural law theorist, maintains that *jus cogens* cannot be derived from any of these sources because, she assumes, that a positive rule cannot void another positive rule, which is just what *jus cogens* does.[16] Yet, that is far off the mark since positive constitutional principles can void positive statutory legislation. Further, if these sources are positive rules, they are not all the same type of positive rule. Customary law is far different from treaty law, which are both different from general principles.

Jus cogens can arise from the first source, multilateral treaties, such as the United Nations' Charter, but treaties cannot serve as a basis for *jus cogens* because peremptory norms can bind nonsignatories and even objectors, whereas treaties can bind only signatories to the treaty, except when treaties codify customary law or *jus cogens*. Exceptions, particularly those set forth in the United Nations' Charter, do exist for a treaty binding nonparties. Article 2(6) prescribes that non–member states act to maintain international peace and security. The exceptions show, at best, that peremptory norms gain strong support when embedded in treaties that have widespread state approval, but peremptory norms still need independent justification outside treaty mechanisms. *Jus cogens* must stand outside treaties to play an adjudicatory role regarding treaties.

Custom, the second source, consists of state practice and *opinio juris*, that is, the state's belief that it acts in a legally obligatory way. Once *jus cogens* is in place, even contrary widespread practices cannot overturn it. Article 64 of the Vienna Convention provides that, "If a new peremptory norm of general international law emerges, any existing treaty which is in conflict with that norm becomes void and terminates." Yet, basing *jus cogens* and human rights on custom creates other problems. State practices regarding group harms and human rights do not often live up to the principles and standards. Basing peremptory norms against genocide and other harms on custom would make them hostage to state practice when, similar to their relation to conventions, they should stand above state practice to guide and adjudicate state practice.[17] Ultimately, custom rests in state practice, and *jus cogens* challenges state practice. *Jus cogens* cannot simultaneously depend on and challenge state practice. Thus, custom fails as a source of *jus cogens* even though, like convention, it provides critical support for it.

General principles, the third source, seem to provide a more secure source for *jus cogens* as general principles do not have to be moored in state practice.[18] Justifying *jus cogens* in general principles avoids the problem of requiring prior state compliance for "in the development of human rights law principles have always preceded practice."[19] General principles derive from international as well as from domestic sources.

Advocates of general principles as sources of *jus cogens* think that they can avoid any reference to natural law by focusing on the demand that states must accept and recognize peremptory norms. The prohibition against genocide becomes an international law when states accept, for example, the *Genocide Convention* and recognize war crime tribunals. So, unlike natural law, *jus cogens*, grounded in principles, would depend not on state practice per se but on some form of state acquiescence to the principles.

A rationale for general principles poses the same conceptual problems as the convention and customary law arguments. On this approach, peremptory norms depend upon state consent. Yet, peremptory norms must stand outside states to serve as a basis for judging states. This problem of consent, embedded in the Vienna Convention, is reason enough for many prominent jurists to reject the Convention as setting forth a justification for *jus cogens*.[20]

Another reading of Article 53 of the Vienna Convention can overcome the problem of needing state action of some sort and still retain the general principles' framework, except that it means embracing rather than avoiding a natural law interpretation. The clause on acceptance-and-recognition should be read as part of the entire phrase "accepted and recognized by the international community as a whole (*actio popularis*)." "Acceptance and recognition by the *whole* international community" does not mean acceptance and recognition by any set number of states.[21] For purposes of the [Vienna] Convention, which included codifying treaty law, Article 53 made reference to "acceptance and recognition" in the sense that it described (not prescribed) the situation.[22] Indeed, by the time of the Vienna Conference, international law had progressed far enough where a multilateral forum could report on the acceptance and recognition by states of peremptory norms. The Vienna Conference tried to push *jus cogens* more onto the world stage but not by promoting majority rule or some other quantitative measure for the acceptance of a principle.

To further underscore the argument against a numeric test embedded in Article 53, we need to ask: what if a majority or a significant minority of states do not accept and recognize the prohibition against genocide? If *jus cogens* prohibitions supersede anything, they should supersede the tyranny of the majority of states (or the wrongful acts of a single state or a minority of states). The phrase "international community of states as a whole" refers to the universal boundaries of civilized states.[23] States, as Vattel recognized long ago, constitute moral persons "susceptible of obligations and rights."[24] "Civilized," in this context, serves as shorthand for a principle governing the moral persons called states.

Peremptory norms signify the boundary conditions that any nation must meet to qualify as civilized. Article 38(1) refers to "the general principles of law recognized by civilized nations." *Jus cogens does* not depend entirely on recognition by a nation-state. *Jus cogens* constitutes a moral principle of statehood, captured by the word "civilized."

Even though the concept of *jus cogens* becomes codified first in a convention on treaties, its power does not primarily lie in its effect on treaties. True, the Vienna Convention speaks of treaties becoming void when they conflict with *jus cogens* provisions. However, as discussed later, substantive *jus cogens* norms, for example, the prohibition against genocide, do not always lend themselves to treaty provisions. States will generally not devise treaty provisions to commit genocide. The arrangements among the Nazis and its satellite countries provide the closest historical examples; yet, the arrangements to ship Jews to extermination camps did not have treaty status.[25] Commercial contracts to produce the poison gas, Zyklon B, for the SS also fall outside public international law.[26]

Yet, if *jus cogens* provisions have practically nothing to do with treaty provisions, then Article 53 seems an exercise in futility. States do not generally parade their genocidal activities in treaty provisions. Despite the intuitive implausible connection between treaties and *jus cogens*, we can forge a closer link. First, those peremptory norms involving human rights do not exhaust the list of *jus cogens* norms. Treaty provisions in violation of non–human rights *jus cogens* have more plausibility. So, some *jus cogens* principles will have close links to treaties. Second, a treaty might be found in violation of the *jus cogens* norm prohibiting genocide if the treaty has an indirect link to the acts proscribed by *jus cogens*. For example, an arms treaty or even a trade agreement might violate *jus cogens* if the weapons or items became the main instrument by which a state carried out its genocide.

Whatever its links to treaties, the real power of *jus cogens* lays in its application to unilateral acts.[27] A state should be charged with violations of *jus cogens* even before and in the absence of treaty prohibitions against genocide. Ideally, outrage and legal sanctions against a crime of the magnitude of genocide should not depend upon agreements among states. If a state cannot violate a peremptory norm through a treaty, then it cannot violate it unilaterally.[28]

Practically, however, acceptance and successful implementation of *jus cogens* depend upon consent and compliance of states, manifested, inter alia, through treaty obligations.[29] A staunch critic of *jus cogens* accidentally linked treaties with *jus cogens*: "A treaty, per se, cannot create a universally binding norm of international law, except when it is so massively acceded to as, e.g., the UN Charter or the Geneva Conventions of 1949."[30] The universally acceded to *Genocide Convention* provides an even better example of *jus cogens* embedded in but not entirely dependent on a treaty. We need to separate the pragmatic issues regarding implementing *jus cogens* principles, which depend on state compliance, and the theoretical foundation of *jus cogens* provisions, which should not depend on state consent.

The picture of *jus cogens* that emerges so far can be summarized as follows. *Jus cogens* has many sources, but its justification does not depend on those sources, although the sources provide additional support for *jus cogens*. *Jus cogens* include those general moral principles that make up the prerequisites for a state to qualify as civilized. A state must not engage in certain activities if it wants to be part of the international community. The violations of certain prohibitions undermine the very idea of international community.

One problem remains. If the peremptory norms have such an exalted status, standing apart from and as a benchmark for the states, how can they ever be subject to reinterpretation? Article 53 also states that peremptory norms "can be modified only by subsequent norm of general international law." However, the modification provision only serves as recognition that our age might be wrong about a peremptory norm's formulation or that progress in international morality might necessitate a modification of peremptory norms. Peremptory norms, unlike some versions of natural law, can evolve. Whatever route the modification might take, it must be a product of something that has the same status as a peremptory norm. A majority of states cannot effect a modification, contrary to what some commentators have claimed.[31] A modification might come about through a refinement or an expansion of the definition of genocide to include, for example, rape. The Vienna Convention allows for moral progress (and, perhaps, for moral regress, as well).

Legal Order Arguments for *Jus Cogens*

The argument for substantive *jus cogens* ultimately depends on the acceptance of ethical principles. Arguments for certain substantive *jus cogens* cannot be separated from the ethical content of *jus cogens* principles. Take, for example, the argument that the nature of legal dispute resolution requires an appeal to *jus cogens*. Consider the basic hierarchical structure of a legal system. By its very nature, a legal system consists of some kind of a hierarchical decision making. If someone appeals to law as a means of adjudicating a dispute between individuals, that person invokes a hierarchy. The law, in a sense, stands above individuals. For consequential and other reasons, legal adjudication of a dispute ranks as superior to individuals taking the matter into their hands. By admitting the role of legal hierarchy in the resolution of disputes, the rule of law takes priority over the rule of people.

Just as law adjudicates individual disputes, an appeal to a higher-ordered law can resolve a conflict between lower-level ones. *Jus cogens* finds a natural perch at the top of this hierarchy partially because of the consequences of not having it. To retain the rule of law, some principles must take on the rank of the highest order. Otherwise, the dispute gets thrown back into the more political fray ruled by certain individuals and interests. A commitment to *jus cogens* preserves the idea of the rule of law.[32] *Jus dispositivum* cannot revoke a peremptory norm; this, then, serves as an argument for making peremptory law a separate hierarchical category.[33]

Although differences abound, *jus cogens* plays an analogous role regarding laws among states as law does to individual disputes. Legal adjudication of disputes reigns superior to states taking matters into their hands. Peace and stability take priority over war and disorder.

The argument from the appeal to public order (*ordre public*) in municipal systems rests on an analogy. As with any analogy, the one with municipal law contains similarities and dissimilarities to the international law system. Municipal legal systems have substantially more centralized control than the international legal regime. Further, jurisdiction in domestic systems does not depend on consensus, whereas the jurisdiction of almost every judicial international body rests on consent from the states involved. Commentators have latched onto the dissimilarities between municipal and international regimes as grounds for rejecting *jus cogens*.[34] Despite dissimilarities, compelling structural arguments justify appeals to *jus cogens*. Let us lay the groundwork.

Considerations of the structure of dispute resolution provide some support for the proposition:

> When law-by-agreement breaks down at Level 1, it creates a need to formulate decisions at a higher level, Level 2.

Yet, problems remain. Not every breakdown of treaties among states (or every instance of individual state behavior) creates a need to appeal to a higher level. The failure of a state to honor a treaty obligation need not undermine the international community. Only certain kinds of violations require an appeal to a higher level of dispute resolution, and only a subset of those justifies invoking the highest level, *jus cogens*. A ranking of ethical norms provides a means of determining those violations deserving the application of *jus cogens*. The justification for certain *jus cogens* norms depends on justifications for universal moral principles. Let us ease into the more controversial substantive proposal by first considering procedural analyses of *jus cogens*.

A distinction between municipal and international regimes that does make a difference lies in the former's reliance on *ordre public*. If *ordre public* means, as it did in late Roman law, any norms that would disturb the structure of public order, then *jus cogens* cannot fully embrace it. I say "not fully" because, to become more viable and acceptable, *jus cogens* cannot completely thwart the system of sovereign states. Yet, *jus cogens*, for the very same reasons of viability, cannot be entirely dependent on a system of state sovereignty. Therefore, commentators from Verdross to Lauterpacht to present-day analysts have continually shifted their interpretation of *jus cogens* from one that emphasizes public order to one that focuses on morality. Peremptory norms must challenge the public order without completely cutting off the ties upon which it depends.

The moral substantive sense of *jus cogens* holds firm in theory, but is fragile in practice.

Specific examples of jus *cogens* track the procedural and substantive justifications. For the proceduralists, "*jus cogens* would include those rules whose non-observance would affect the very essence of the legal system."[35] On a proceduralist account, Level 2 rules include procedural ones.[36] *Pacta sunt servanda* (treaties are binding on the parties) serves as an example of a procedural, nonderogable, Level 2 rule. In keeping with this analysis, a Level 2 rule prohibits two states from entering a treaty declaring all past and future treaties between them not binding. A Level 1 treaty of this nature would necessitate an appeal to Level 2 as it challenges the very nature of treaty making. However, procedural examples like these constitute "legal constructions driven to an absurd for the sake of academic purity."[37] Substantive *jus cogens* norms, discussed subsequently, however, are far from academic.

Before turning to the substantive content of *jus cogens*, we need to discharge one more aspect of the proposition within the municipal law analogy. In describing the hierarchical nature of law, the municipal law analogy led us to formulate the lower level as law-by-agreement, but this is not the only type of law needing a higher-level appeal. The breakdown of law at Level 1 can occur internally within a state. Certain breakdowns would be so egregious as to necessitate an appeal to a higher level external to the state.

So, the argument for *jus cogens* depends, in part, on justifying the idea of there being a hierarchy of norms and laws in international law. A hierarchical ordering, with ethically based principles at the top, of laws serves not simply as a desirable feature but rather as what makes international law lawful. Now that we have the hierarchical framework in place, we need to establish the content and foundations of the highest level. The apex of the hierarchy consists of *jus cogens* held together with the mortar of natural law.

Foundations of *Jus Cogens*

Natural law has a long, noble tradition, but it has a relatively small following among legal theorists today. The quest to justify *jus cogens* provides an opportunity to reestablish natural law, but with a slightly different twist. Instead of promoting universal goods, which typifies the natural law tradition, the concept of *jus cogens* requires a formulation in terms of universal wrongs, that is, universal prohibitions. To bring out the differences, let us compare the negative approach implicit in *jus cogens* with one of the most influential contemporary natural law theories, namely that proposed by John Finnis.

Finnis claimed the following as self-evident universal values: (1) concern for the value of human life; (2) procreation of human life; (3) sexual activity restrictions; (4) concern for truth; (5) values of cooperation; (6) friendship; (7) property rights; (8) value of play; (9) respect for the dead; and (10) concern for superhuman principles or powers.[38] While Finnis refused to place these in hierarchical order, let us concentrate on the first, because, without it, the others fall by the wayside. Finnis elaborated on the concern for life only briefly, noting that it permits the killing of other human beings only with some fairly definite justification.[39] Finnis found that this value, found in every culture, fits the self-evident basic good of life itself.[40] He justified the universal values as self-evident truths that all of us can discover.

Commentators criticize Finnis for not adequately justifying the universal principles and for resorting to general, nonspecific universal goods, which provide little specific guidance. *Jus cogens* can meet both challenges, but before showing this we need to differentiate the *jus cogens'* approach from Finnis's position. Like every other natural law theorist, Finnis describes the universal values in positive terms. *Jus cogens*, while coming in a variety of descriptions, almost invariably have negative descriptors. In short, natural law frameworks work with universal prescriptions (goods), while *jus cogens* posits universal prohibitions (bads).

Although the difference between goods and "bads" or wrongs may seem one of emphasis, it has critical ramifications. First, it proves easier to justify prohibitive bads than it does prescriptive goods. A construction analogy will help to make this point. Arguments over which materials make up the best foundation of a house seem interminable. However, while we may not agree on the sufficient conditions for a sturdy house, we can find consensus on the necessary components. Similarly, assessments on the morality of sexual activity vary across cultures, but certain prohibitions, for example, against rape, would remain culturally invariant.

Further, for prohibitive acts we do not need to resort to devices such as self-evidence to immunize the universal from attack. In fact, by proposing *jus cogens* prohibitions, we welcome attack; indeed, the claims are contestable. The case for the prohibitions relies on the fact that no successful attack has been launched thus far and that future attacks are unlikely. We can say this with confidence since the argument for the universal character of the prohibitions relies on the following. Without the prohibitions, moral discourse about law becomes jeopardized for the prohibitions define the necessary conditions needed for a civilized, that is, moral, society and for an ethical global community. If a nation violates *jus cogens* prohibitions, then it no longer qualifies as a member of the civilized world community.

The second ground for preferring the *jus cogens* approach over classical natural law construals, such as that proposed by Finnis, revolves around the specificity of the former in contrast to the elusive generality of the latter.[41] The concern-for-life and the associated valuing-of-life provide either too vague or excessively restrictive moral guides. It is difficult to determine how to act according to a concern-for-life. Does it mean that a person should at least consider the value of life in making a moral decision? If so, then it offers little guidance. Or does it entail opposition to euthanasia and abortion? If so, then we need more arguments than a simple appeal to the so-called universal value.

Finnis provided some guidance when he noted that concern-for-life prohibits unjustified killing. However, again, he did little to help us determine what constitutes unjustified killing. Finnis's theory does not aid in that determination, whereas *jus cogens* does. *Jus cogens* specifies the types of killings considered universally unjustified. The specific content of *jus cogens* illustrates this point, but before doing that, let us entertain one further consideration in favor of the universality of *jus cogens* prohibitions.

Finnis offered an epistemological defense of natural law; namely, that we know universal principles self-evidently. I offered a different defense, claiming that whatever defensible ordering we give to the moral underpinnings of law, certain prohibitions will be foundational, that is, without key prohibitions, the other ingredients collapse. An ontological approach offers a different track from these.

The ontological argument maintains the existence of a "normative natural order."[42] As Weinreb, another contemporary natural law theorist, notes, "in classical Greek culture, at the very center of natural law was an affirmation of the reality of moral experience."[43] Prohibitions against harm reside deeply embedded within human experience. We describe our reactions to the sufferings of others as natural. Those reactions have a normative component; our revulsion to the act and our sympathy with the victims have strong moral judgments associated with them. Responses to the Holocaust run rather uniformly across cultures, for acts of genocide undermine our status as ethical animals, challenging our humanity.

The idea of a normative natural order needs greater elaboration than I can give it here, but it provides a consideration that gives further weight to *jus cogens*. A single argument for *jus cogens* does not suffice. However, when taken together, the arguments provide a convincing case. First, we find a need for a hierarchical ordering of moral and legal authority. Second, we discover universal prohibitions, adequately specified, on top of the hierarchy. Third, we see these prohibitions as consonant with our moral experience.

Content of *Jus Cogens*

What qualifies as *jus cogens*? Leading commentators and jurists differ over their inventory of *jus cogens* provisions. Oscar Schacter lists slavery, genocide, torture, mass killings, prolonged arbitrary imprisonment, systematic racial discrimination, and any other gross violations of internationally recognized human rights.[44] The Commentary of the International Law Commission mentions "trade in slaves, piracy or genocide" as examples.[45] Other candidates include the prohibition upon the nongenocidal "crimes against humanity," the non-refoulement of refugees, the illegality of unequal or leonine treaties.[46] In the *Western Sahara* case, the International Court of Justice found the principles of self-determination as a peremptory norm in international law based on a series of General Assembly resolutions and state practice of decolonization. Despite the disagreement over what to include on the list, few disagree over the inclusion of two acts on the list. Genocide and slavery make most lists.[47]

As Thornberry notes, "the prohibition of genocide per se or as part of international criminal law seems to figure in practically every listing of principles of *jus cogens*."[48] Genocide is "the most fundamental denial of human dignity and equality, and its prohibition is fittingly *jus cogens*."[49] If anything qualifies as *jus cogens*, genocide should qualify. In the *Reservations* case, the International Court stated:

> The origins of the Convention [on the Prevention and Punishment of the Crimes of Genocide] show that it was the intention of the United Nations to condemn and punish genocide as "crime under international law" involving a denial of the right of existence of entire human groups, a denial which shocks the conscience of mankind and results in great losses to humanity, and which is contrary to moral law and the spirit and aims of the United Nations . . . The first consequence arising from this conception is that the principles underlying the Convention are principles which

are recognized by civilized nations as binding on States, even without any conventional obligation. A second consequence is the universal character both of the condemnation of genocide and the co-operating required in order to liberate mankind from such odious scourge. [50]

The prohibition against slavery is the only other relatively noncontentious peremptory rule.[51] Beyond that, we find little agreement. However, as demonstrated in Chapter 1,, genocide takes priority over slavery as the highest-ranking universal prohibition.

A comparative group harm approach, by grading group harms, can forge agreement over inclusion on the list. The stronger the case for group harm on the hierarchy, the stronger the case for treating that harm as *jus cogens*. The analogue here is to a sliding scale model for the US Supreme Court's Fourteenth Amendment equal protection analysis.[52] On that model, different characteristics trigger different levels of review, ranging from strict scrutiny (almost a per se rejection of a legislation) through intermediate to rational review (an acceptance of almost any rationale for the legislation). Just as matters of race trigger strict scrutiny for the US Supreme Court, so genocide and slavery should invoke the peremptory norms of international law.

The prohibition on derogation serves as a critical test for a peremptory norm. If states cannot find any justifiable excuse for derogating from a norm, then the norm qualifies as peremptory. Hannikainen analyzes derogation grounds that do not serve as excuses for violating peremptory norms: "derogation from peremptory norms on the ground of necessity, emergency, reprisal, or self-defense, all of them being situations which allow deliberation before the action is taken, is not permitted."[53] None of these would qualify as an excuse for violating the prohibition against genocide. If someone has the slightest time for reflection, that person, organization, or state has no excuse for choosing genocide.

However, Hannikainen, in one of the few books devoted solely to *jus cogens*, does find *force majeure* and distress acceptable grounds for derogation from peremptory norms. However, even these should not excuse outrageous harms like genocide. An irresistible force or unforeseen external event beyond the control of the state would not excuse a state from committing genocide. Rather than providing a narrow exception, *force majeure* provides an array of excuses including the state's inability to control perpetrators of the genocide or to protect victims from the elements.

Distress presents a different challenge to the prohibition of derogation. The idea of distress captures those extreme situations, if any truly exist, where a state has no real choice but to sacrifice individuals. Even if the weighted concerns include saved lives and group sacrifice under conditions of distress, saved lives never excuses group sacrifice. Hannikaeinen's analysis fails him here: "If a given peremptory norm is understood as prohibiting only severe and widespread violations, an act done in a situation of distress could be interpreted as not infringing such a peremptory norm, or could be interpreted as only a nominal derogation from such a peremptory norms." Genocide becomes particularly deplorable in its usual form of severe and widespread slaughter but should be just as inexcusable in its more nominal forms.

Situations might arise that would necessitate even the killing of group members due to irresistible forces or to distress. Conceivably, a state might hasten the inevitable deaths of those suffering from the deadly Ebola virus to prevent massive contagion. A situation such as this, however, does not provide grounds for derogation from a peremptory norm against genocide. Rather, assuming many other pieces of the picture, it would not qualify as violation of the peremptory norm in the first place. The state would not be killing people because of their group affiliation but because of their disease status.

Obligations *Erga Omnes*

Two other related concepts in international law—obligations *erga omnes* and international crimes—generally serve more to confuse than to illuminate *jus cogens*. However, clarifying these ideas helps to make more sense of *jus cogens*. They complement *jus cogens*. *Erga omnes* signify those obligations needed to uphold peremptory norms. International crimes include violations of *jus cogens*. So, *jus cogens* are the peremptory norms; *erga omnes*, the responsibilities regarding those norms; and international crimes, those violations, including *jus cogens* crimes, considered wrong by the international community.

A distinction drawn in the *obiter dicta* of the *Barcelona Traction* case between bilateral obligations and those obligations owed to the international community as a whole provides further support for the claim that international law recognizes a set of norms, higher than those governing interactions among states, governing the international community as a whole.[54] Obligations *erga omnes* refer to these latter obligations. It becomes a Herculean task to clarify exactly what legal commentators and courts mean by obligations *erga omnes*, but the following should clarify matters.[55]

Obligations *erga omnes* are the flip side of peremptory norms. The former represent those things a state must do to carry out effectively the prohibitions encompassed in the latter. *Barcelona Traction* makes clear not only that states cannot contract out of (derogate from) peremptory norms but also that states have a legal obligation to uphold the peremptory norms. So, states have a responsibility to comply with peremptory norms irrespective of their practice, acceptance, and recognition. States have the same responsibilities to enforce *jus cogens* provisions against other states as they do to comply with them within their borders.

A state cannot gloss over, ignore, or act against these responsibilities. For obligations, *erga omnes* help define an international community. To deny them is to deny that sense of community. A community consists, in part, of members mutually responsible to one another and to a sense of a greater good. Judge Mosler characterized this "public order of the international community" as "consist[ing] of principles and rules the enforcement of which is of such vital importance to the international community as a whole that any unilateral action or any agreement which contravenes these principles can have no legal force."[56]

At a minimum, obligations *erga omnes* may find vindication through instituting legal proceedings. Legal action of this nature can hardly constitute interference with state sovereignty. More ambitiously, obligations *erga omnes* pave the way for more direct intervention discussed more fully in the next chapter. The legal realm of action serves as a first step toward states taking concerted action in halting genocide.

Beyond those codified in treaties, international law presently does little to bind states. Few states accept the compulsory jurisdiction of the International Court of Justice (ICJ), and many that accept its jurisdiction restrict its scope. Further, under Articles 62 and 63 of the ICJ, third parties have limited rights to intervention. The idea of an obligation *erga omnes* provides one window through which to develop truly international actions beyond the limited means currently available. In short, it provides a critical step in making the case for humanitarian intervention, as set forth in the next chapter.

International Crimes

I shall go against the tide of commentators who think that the notion of international crimes unduly complicates matters. The International Law Commission (ILC) adopted the following definition in Article 19(2):

> An internationally wrongful act that results from the breach by a State of an international obligation so essential for the protection of

fundamental interests of the international community that its breach is recognized as a crime by that community as a whole constitutes an international crime.

Article 19 gives examples of acts rising to the level of international crimes: aggression, the establishment or maintenance by force of colonial domination, slavery, genocide, apartheid, and massive pollution of the atmosphere or of the seas. The confusion comes from the list of examples that does not include a hierarchical ranking, and from the commentary, which mistakenly interprets *jus cogens* as broader than the category of international crimes when the latter should be seen as including the former.

The list would make more sense if it more systematically incorporated the distinction between peremptory and nonperemptory norms made in the Vienna Convention. International crimes include, minimally, those acts that violate the peremptory norms. At least two acts, genocide and slavery, clearly violate international community interests as a whole. The Draft Statute did grant genocide special treatment since it is the only crime where the then-proposed International Criminal Court would have compulsory or inherent jurisdiction.[57] However, unfortunately, the final Rome statute dropped this special provision. Nevertheless, it is also clear, as argued in Chapter 5, that certain candidate crimes such as terrorism do not qualify as universal prohibitions. For one thing, it is difficult to make the case for terrorism when there is no consensus over how to define terrorism.[58] In contrast, as argued in Chapter 4, torture clearly qualifies as a *jus cogens* crime.

The ILC assigns legal interests to states not directly injured in those cases involving international crimes. To assign a legal interest does not open the gate to some states acting as police officers of the world. The ILC opens the door for states to act judicially and "not to act entirely unilaterally in the vindication of a public interest."[59] Further support for this interpretation comes from the ILC's Statute for an International Criminal Court, Article 25(1), which allows any state party to the Genocide Convention to lodge a complaint with the Prosecutor alleging the commission of genocide.

Christopher Ford argued that the ICJ can already adequately adjudicate *jus cogens* claims.[60] While I am sympathetic to his arguments, he bypasses one critical problem with ICJ jurisprudence.[61] Neither individuals nor groups and their representatives have standing before the Court. Only state parties to the Statute of the Court have recourse to the Court. Since states, for the most part, instigate harms against groups, the groups (or harmed individuals) constitute the most reasonable adversaries against the state.

While individuals have duties and responsibilities under international law, the case for individuals to have access to international courts and tribunals has not been made fully. The pendulum had shifted from giving individuals some standing in the 1920s to keeping individuals out completely. Now, a discernible movement exists to give individuals standing. Individuals could apply directly to international courts under the minority protection provisions of the 1919 Peace Treaties. The Permanent Court of International Justice accepted individual complaints in the 1928 *Danzig Railway Officials* case.

A strong case exists for granting individuals the right to bring charges of genocide before an international court or tribunal. The failure to place the Cambodian case on the international agenda in any sustained way illustrates the need for opening up the complaint process more to individuals. Because of their assessments of the political costs and benefits, the international community at first refused to charge Pol Pot and others with genocide. An international judicial glitch helped to delay an investigation into a serious case of mass killings.

Peremptory international crimes do not only harm individuals. Although they may not injure a specific state, they, in an important sense, injure all states, that is, the international community.[62] In the *Genocide* case, the ICJ stated the following about the Genocide Convention: "In such a convention the contracting States do not have any interests of their own; they merely have, one and all, a common interest, namely, the accomplishment of those high purposes which are the raison d'être of the convention." Genocide injures individuals; it also injures all states, that is, the international community. Genocide constitutes an international crime.

So, *jus cogens* encompasses a sliding scale of peremptory norms that states have obligations to prohibit, and states have (whereas groups and individuals should have) legal standing and responsibility to seek judicial redress even if the state bringing the action is not directly injured.

Conclusion

The international crime of the prohibition against genocide constitutes a peremptory norm, a natural law, binding on all states and creating an obligation on states to enforce it against one another. The concept of *jus cogens* offers hope for international law. If a prohibition of genocide does not give full force to *jus cogens*, then we have little hope of creating an international community. *Jus cogens*, universal prohibitions, form the foundation stone of an international community. Far from a sham, *jus cogens* symbolize the dove of moral sanity, a form of sanity that should lead to taking action, as proposed in the next chapter.

CHAPTER 7

Duty to Act

Beyond Responsibility to Protect

> If humanitarian intervention is, indeed, an unacceptable assault on sovereignty, how should we respond to a Rwanda to a Srebrenica, how should we respond to a Rwanda, to a Srebrenica—gross and systematic violations of human rights that offend every precept of our common humanity.[1]

The project of this book, the distinguishing among and ranking international crimes provides an analytic framework for formulating a defensible policy on when other countries and organizations should intervene in another country's internal affairs. A brief survey of recent humanitarian interventions does not reveal any defensible set of intervention standards. The humanitarian reach of international law has extended considerably, especially since the early days, and by the "early days" we do not have to look back very far. States dominate the United Nations, effectively blocking voices outside the nation-state. In 1968, Resolution 1296 even threatened to expel nongovernmental organizations (NGOs) from their role as consultants to UN agencies, seeing them as a threat to state domination over international law. Now, NGOs play a critical role in the United Nations.

The dominant view has been that what states did to their own population was their business and not the business of other states or of international bodies. State sovereignty held supreme. Nonintervention dominated the policy choices. In 1969, UN Secretary General U Thant voiced concern on behalf of the UN over the public execution of Jews in Baghdad, but cautioned that it was purely an internal affair of the sovereign state of Iraq. The 1990s began a shift toward intervention. After the UN authorized intervention in Bosnia, the failure to intervene in Rwanda, where far more extensive atrocities had taken place, raised serious concerns about the ethics of intervention. In 1995, a number of countries (Austria, Canada, Denmark, The Netherlands, Norway, Poland, and Sweden) attempted to establish a UN humanitarian military force, The United Nations Multilateral Standing High Readiness Brigade (SHIRBRIG). Sadly, SHIRBRIG was dissolved in 2009.

Cases of humanitarian intervention have been legally mixed. Some of the more successful interventions have involved state consent. The successful intervention by the UK in Sierra Leone came with the consent of the government. The Indonesian government was cajoled into consenting to intervention in 1999.

A survey of humanitarian intervention cases, however, does uncover one clear-cut international consensus that has emerged. Forceful, military humanitarian intervention to halt the crime of genocide has overwhelming international support. This proves extremely important—an insight lost on the international legal community. Genocide has come to the forefront as a scourge of humanity, as *the* crime to confront. Yet, its horrifying role in the world has not been matched by a comparable jurisprudential reaction to it. Genocide has faded into the background of legal debates.

The diminishing role of genocide in formulating international standards is no more evident than in the conceptual shift away from humanitarian intervention to the novel formulation of a duty to protect. Like the history of successive actions that have gone under the heading of humanitarian intervention, the conceptual development of its kin, a responsibility to protect (R2P), yields nothing short of an analytic mess. Worse yet, genocide has lost its central conceptual place, being lumped together with other mass atrocities, namely, crimes against humanity, war crimes, and ethnic cleansing. Genocide, then, gets treated as one more example of a mass atrocity, one among many. Yet, as previously argued, genocide ranks above, if that is a proper word for it, other crimes of mass atrocity. Everyone seems to agree to this ranking, but no one seems to act or think accordingly. "Never again" has become a lost and plaintive cry in a political world where genocide has, at least on some accounts, happened again, again, and again. Similarly, the consequences of fully accepting and adhering to this admonition have not been fully digested and integrated into the body of the international legal system.

The background story to the R2P shows how other concerns became intermingled with a desire to make "Never again" an effective command. The story began with Professor Francis Deng's efforts to find a way to convince states to take responsibility for internally displaced peoples. He saw the idea of sovereignty as the primary obstacle. States treated internally displaced peoples as an internal matter, immune from outside intervention. Deng cleverly led a movement to rethink sovereignty. He saw it not solely as a right of nations but also as a duty of states. The International Commission on Intervention and State Sovereignty (ICISS), sponsored by Canada, took up the gauntlet. Then, in 2005, the World Summit adopted R2P. Accordingly, the right to sovereignty became conditioned on the responsibility of states to protect their own population. By the logic of R2P, when states fail to live up to this duty, they forfeit their sovereignty rights. On this reconfiguration of the idea of sovereignty, genocide, unfortunately, became just one more example of a state's failure to protect its own people.

A positive feature of this new responsibility to protect formulation is its focus on mass atrocities. This sets off a specific type of human rights abuse. As Gareth Evan, the cochair of the Secretary General's 2004 High Level Panel, said,

> to use the responsibility to protect too broadly, in non-mass-atrocity contexts, is to delete to the point of uselessness its role as a mobilizer of instinctive, universal action in cases of conscious-shocking killing, ethnic cleansing, and other such crimes against humanity. . . . if R2P is about protecting everybody from everything, it will end up protecting nobody from anything.[2]

R2P proponents did not want to water down the concept by overextending its reach to all human rights violations. However, they, in turn, have watered down the concept of mass atrocities by not differentiating among them.

However noble the R2P movement, the resulting new view of genocide borders on, with all due respect, the absurd. Genocide is not about the failure of a state to protect. To the contrary, it, most often, is about the state doing harm. The state does not typically sit back and neglect its protective duty while the forces of genocide gain strength within its border. The state is not just a background player that is negligent in its duties to protect its dear population or perhaps complicit in the crime undertaken by others. Historically, the state is the primary actor in the crime of genocide. In fact, as discussed in Chapter 1, it is difficult to conceive of genocide occurring without the organizational power of the state, a level of force that few if any other nonstate organization could even dream of mustering.

Among the international crime, sovereignty should not stand as an obstacle to intervention in cases of genocide. Genocide ranks as *the* crime (but, as discussed earlier later, not *the only* international crime) where the international community, in the end, has and should regard morality as trumping politics, including and most notably the restrictions of the UN Charter. Kofi Annan's challenge, quoted at the beginning of this chapter, bears repeating here.

> If humanitarian intervention is, indeed, an unacceptable assault on sovereignty, how should we respond to a Rwanda to a Srebrenica, how should we respond to a Rwanda, to a Srebrenica—gross and systematic violations of human rights that offend every precept of our common humanity?[3]

The inference and reference in this statement is clear. If international law permits another Rwandan genocide, if international law prohibits humanitarian intervention, if international law does not facilitate military intervention in cases like Rwanda, then there is something terribly wrong with international law. Unfortunately, Annan does not explicitly reference genocide, in general, and the Rwandan genocide, in particular. Setting the bar at the level of human rights abuses places it far too low. It leaves us with the problem of sorting out what constitutes "gross violations of human rights" when a way of differentiating and ranking international crimes is readily within reach.

If we cannot forge a consensus over what action to take in clear-cut cases of genocide, then we should abandon all hope. Fortunately, we need not take the resignation route. A consensus about genocide has emerged within the international community. It is unimaginable that it could not. Otherwise, a state would have to adopt the entirely indefensible position that some cases of genocide might be justifiable. That, as shown before in Parts I and II, is completely untenable.

A criticism of the moral position promoted here is that it does not address the problem of who or what is to make a determination that genocide is taking place. But this seems to be a version of one person's terrorist is another person's freedom fighter. That formulation has a highly offensive ring to it if applied to genocide. I am not even sure how to formulate it. "One person's genocide is . . . "—what? Of course, the problem of determination remains. Indeed, there are dangers in having these moral judgments made outside the framework of the Charter. Some have argued that a moral position taken on humanitarian intervention in Syria opens the way for Russia, for example, to argue for humanitarian intervention in the Ukraine.[4]

First of all, the cases are hardly comparable. If the harms at stake in the humanitarian intervention argument are something nebulous like human rights abuses, then the above realist position, where pragmatic policy considerations take precedence, has merit. However, genocide, unlike human rights violations, has, as demonstrated in Chapter 1, a relatively exact and specific definition. Second, the moral position does not advocate an automatic bypassing of a determination made by the Security Council or any other body. Every effort should be made to comply fully with the Charter. Failure of Security Council action, however, creates a serious problem. A possible but still problematic procedure is an appeal to the General Assembly's Uniting for Peace Resolution 377, which states that,

> if the Security Council, because of lack of unanimity of the permanent members, fails to exercise its primary responsibility for the maintenance of international peace and security in any case where there appears to be a threat to the peace, breach of the peace, or act of aggression, the General Assembly shall consider the matter immediately with a view to making appropriate recommendations to Members for collective measures, including in the case of a breach of the peace or act of aggression the use of armed force when necessary, to maintain or restore international peace and security.[5]

Short of this procedural route, which overrides a Security Council inaction or veto[6], or some other procedural maneuver, Kofi Annan's challenge remains unaddressed.

Two legal concepts, developed in the previous chapter, show ways out of these difficulties. If anything constitutes *jus cogens*, a universal prohibition, it is genocide. If anything triggers obligations *erga omnes*, it is genocide. These obligations are not among obligations of a state to protect its own population. Obligations *erga omnes* extend to all peoples. Nations and organizations do not simply have a right to intervene in cases of genocide; they have an obligation to intervene.

This case can be put quite explicitly. History, unfortunately, provides at least two clear cases of genocide, the Holocaust and Rwanda. Morality has progressed enough that it is difficult to find any rational position that would not recognize these two cases as examples of genocide and that would not posit a need to intervene in both cases.

Contrary to the R2P, the strategy should be to obtain explicit and clear-cut commitments of the international community to condemn, universally and in no uncertain terms, genocide. That seems a doable task. If problems ensue with this strategy, the fallback position is that the universal prohibition of genocide is a matter of treaty law and of international customary law. Treaty law, surprisingly, has only limited use in confronting the scourge of genocide. Although the *Genocide Convention* has 146 state ratifications to date, it seems only to prohibit a state to carry out genocide internally, that is, within its borders. However, a good case, which we presented in the previous chapter, can be made that state practice and *opinio juris* of states provides a basis for treating the prohibition against genocide as customary law.

The next part of the strategy involves building on that consensus by seeing how far to extend the reach of genocide to other mass atrocities. For then, states and organizations would have a similar duty to act, that is, to intervene, as it had for genocide. This approach piggybacks the case for intervention in mass atrocity crimes that come close to genocide onto the case for genocide intervention.

Cambodia under the Khmer Rouge provides a stark example of a mass atrocity approaching genocide, narrowly interpreted. The Cambodian case has long perplexed scholars, who cannot agree about whether to label the mass killings of over two million Cambodians by the Khmer Rouge as genocide. Part of the problem lies in the definition of genocide that restricts victim groups to four types: racial, ethnic, national, and religious. Disproportionate numbers of Buddhist, Chinese, Vietnamese, and other groups met with brutal ends at the hands of the Khmer Rouge. However, the Khmer Rouge also disproportionately slaughtered people from their own ethnic, Cambodian group. Although the analysis becomes difficult and nuanced, the following serves as an outline of a way out of this classificatory morass. While the Khmer Rouge targeted ethnic and religious groups, its primary target, which encompasses the ethnic and religious groups, were political enemies. This helps explain the targeting of Eastern Khmers, whom the Khmer Rouge became suspicious of because of their close proximity to Cambodia's then archenemy, Vietnam.

The Cambodian case led some scholars to call for expanding the list of victim groups within the definition of genocide to include political groups. However, good historical and theoretical reasons exist for keeping the list of victim groups restricted to racial, ethnic, national, and religious groups. For one thing, the nonjustifiablity of genocide and its consequent highest ranking among international crimes depends, in part, on the relative immutability of the target groups. Political groups are simply too malleable, too permeable. More importantly, some circumstances might justify targeting political groups. Terrorists (assuming, as discussed in Chapter 5, we had a clear way to distinguish terrorism), for example, constitute an obvious political group for this dubious distinction. This does not justify actions taken by the Khmer Rouge against political groups, including those with the same ethnicity. The argument is that the mass atrocity committed by the Khmer Rouge did not rise to the level of genocide but that, as a type of crime against humanity, their acts were so much like genocide so as to have them perhaps qualify for military, humanitarian intervention.

Many developing countries fear that opening the door to some humanitarian intervention opens the door to almost any humanitarian intervention, especially those actions motivated by imperialist concerns and by other interests of the most powerful nations. The position set forth here addresses these worries. The foundation for this interventionist model lies firmly embedded in a firm commitment to combat the international crime of genocide. Genocide is indefensible and completely unjustified. It would be difficult, indeed, for a nation *not* to reaffirm its staunch opposition to genocide and thereby its support of military intervention to halt genocide. In a rational world, any attempt to extend the case of genocide to genocide-like cases should meet little or no opposition. Of course, in the topsy-turvy world of, at times, highly irrational politics, reasonable expectations can be and are easily dashed. Yet, vulnerability to irrational political forces depends, in part, on the rational strength of the proposal.

The question arises as to whether the case for military intervention in cases of genocide and genocide-like harms can be extended down the scale to other nonlethal crimes against humanity. The answer is affirmative, but it is based on a far different analysis from what an R2P approach and its kin provide. I shall focus my critique on a philosophical position closely akin to the R2P formulation.

Larry May, a philosopher, defends a right of one country to cross the border of another country when the latter country has a right to cross the border of the former on the basis, in part, of what he calls the security principle:

If a State deprives its subject of physical security or subsistence, or is unable or unwilling to protect its subjects from harms to security or subsistence,

a) then that State has no right to prevent international bodies from "crossing its borders" in order to protect those subjects or remedy their harms;

b) and then international bodies may be justified in "crossing borders" of a sovereign State when genuinely acting to protect those subjects.[7]

Fortunately, May does not allow that any harm to security or subsistence would suffice, for that would surely make the grounds for intervention extremely broad. He, then, couples the security principle with a harm principle.

However, he commits two mistakes. First, he makes the security principle grounds for intervention and the harm principle grounds for prosecution. Second, his notion of harms is far too vague and weak. He starts down the right track by limiting harms to serious ones and further narrowing those to group harms. Things then become obscure especially when, with sleight of hand, he resorts to a metaphorical reference to harms against humanity: "One interest of humanity is that its members, as members, not be harmed."[8] Further, the critical notion of harm gets watered down when May construes it as "a serious setback to an important interest."[9] In response, we need only refer back to earlier chapters to appreciate the analysis of harms that simply and directly emphasizes that harms hurt (torture, Chapter 4) and/or kill (genocide, Chapter 2). The idea of interests adds little or nothing more to the concept of harms.

Crimes against humanity are part of a "widespread or systematic attack on a civilian population." Perhaps, this reveals an important factor about crimes against humanity overlooked by commentators such as May. There is something particularly heinous about targeting civilians, particularly outside the context of an armed conflict, wherein their innocence can more safely be presumed than in contexts of armed conflict. Genocide targets specific groups; crimes against humanity involve targeting civilians.

However, there are a number of problems with building a case for intervention around crimes against humanity. Genocide has a firm international legal foundation in treaty law and war crimes in international humanitarian law. Crimes against humanity are rooted largely in human rights law, which provides weak grounds for violating a state's sovereignty.[10] More importantly, the problem with crimes against humanity is not the victim group but the notion of an attack.

Codifications of crimes against humanity include an undifferentiated potpourri of acts:

1. For the purpose of this Statute, "crime against humanity" means any of the following acts when committed as part of a widespread or systematic attack directed against any civilian population, with knowledge of the attack:

(a) Murder;

(b) Extermination;

(c) Enslavement;

(d) Deportation or forcible transfer of population;

(e) Imprisonment or other severe deprivation of physical liberty in violation of fundamental rules of international law;

(f) Torture;

(g) Rape, sexual slavery, enforced prostitution, forced pregnancy, enforced sterilization, or any other form of sexual violence of comparable gravity;

(h) Persecution against any identifiable group or collectivity on political, racial, national, ethnic, cultural, religious, gender as defined in paragraph 3, or other grounds that are universally recognized as impermissible under international law, in connection with any act referred to in this paragraph or any crime within the jurisdiction of the Court;

(i) Enforced disappearance of persons;

(j) The crime of apartheid;

(k) Other inhumane acts of a similar character intentionally causing great suffering, or serious injury to body or to mental or physical health.

Admittedly, these acts must be widespread or systematic. However, beyond these restrictions, almost anything goes. NGOs such as Amnesty International and Human Rights Watch have alleged the carrying out of forced disappearances in over 25 countries, including acts by the United States against terrorists. However deplorable these acts, their commission surely would and should not justify military intervention by other states or organizations.

Some may find hope in a proposed draft of a Convention for Crimes Against Humanity.[11] In 2014, the International Law Commission voted to add drafting the Convention to its agenda. However, the draft contains little to get excited about. It basically copies provisions from other treaties, particularly the Rome statute.[12] The most important shortcoming is that it simply copies the same list of crimes found in Article 7 of the Rome Statute, which established the International Criminal Court. It makes no attempt to rank the crimes according to their seriousness. Moreover, it adopts the R2P framework of prevention, punishment, and punishment. So, it makes no attempt to make any contribution to the issue of humanitarian intervention.

The way to confront the problems that crimes against humanity creates for prointerventionists is not to codify what already exists or even to device a clever alternative approach. Instead, there is a crying need for conceptual clarity regarding the many different kinds of crimes that fit under crimes against humanity. The same thing that this book has done for the broad categories of international crimes needs to be done for the many acts falling under crimes against humanity. I have argued in previous chapters that mass killing constitutes the primary *actus reus* of genocide and that inflicting pain is at the heart of the act of torture. A similar *actus reus* for crimes against humanity also can be developed.

A full-blown classification, ordering, and ranking of the acts of crimes against humanity would take another book. A sketch, however, can be offered here. The acts listed as crimes against humanity fall into three groups. The first group of acts finds parallels in the acts of genocide. Instead of killing, the Rome Statute lists murder. Murder for crimes against humanity has the same relationship to extermination and "deportation or forcible transfer" as killing for genocide has to the following related acts:

- (b) Causing serious bodily or mental harm to members of the group;
- (c) Deliberately inflicting on the group conditions of life calculated to bring about its physical destruction in whole or in part;
- (d) Imposing measures intended to prevent births within the group;
- (e) Forcibly transferring children of the group to another group.

When the related acts are connected to murder, these crimes against humanity become particularly odious. Another set of acts under crimes against humanity involves, like torture, the infliction of pain.

The many acts listed under crimes against humanity fall into three broad categories: Lethal Violence (murder), Nonlethal Violence, and Liberty Deprivation. Using the original sequence of letters from Article 7 of the Rome Statute, these categories yield the following classificatory scheme:

Lethal Violence

(a) murder
(b) extermination

(d) deportation
(h) persecution
(i) disappearance

Nonlethal Violence

(f) torture
(g) sexual violence
(j) inhumane acts

Deprivation of Liberty

(c) enslavement
(e) imprisonment
(j) apartheid

The acts listed under Lethal Violence parallel the listing of acts listed under genocide. Chapter 1 argued that the acts (e.g., "imposing measures intended to prevent births") listed after killing, for genocide often occur as preludes to or as means to killing. In short, the gravity of these acts comes not so much from the crimes themselves but from the role they typically play in bringing about murder or killing. (Some of the acts under the other main headings, particularly sexual violence, can also be means to murder.) Murder and extermination are obviously per se lethal acts. Deportation, persecution, and disappearance are not, but they are often preliminaries or preludes to per se lethal acts.[13]

The acts under the next main category, Nonlethal Violence, are, unlike all those except murder and extermination in the first category, grave acts in themselves (and not because of their contingent connection to other crimes). The final set of acts, under Deprivation of Liberties, are, arguably, less severe than those connected to and under the two violence categories.

Sorting out the acts that fall under the label crimes against humanity has a number of advantages. First, it contributes some conceptual clarity by making some sense of how these acts relate. Second, it demonstrates the need for much more nuanced and detailed discussions about crimes against humanity. Third, it serves as a template for thinking about the different levels of seriousness of each act and how this might impact in thinking about different degrees of punishment. Fourth and most importantly for purposes of this analysis, the classificatory scheme provides a framework for analyzing and justifying humanitarian intervention.

The acts included under Lethal Violence overlap considerably with those listed under the acts of genocide. That observation provides a springboard for making a case for humanitarian intervention in genocide and in genocide-like cases. Previously, I argued for extending the case for military intervention in genocide cases like Rwanda to genocide-like cases like Cambodia. This argument might be further extended to cases of crimes against humanity that have considerable overlap with the genocide and genocide-like cases. In other words, are there cases of actual or impending murder through deportation and other acts related to the Lethal Violence category of crimes against violence?

A candidate case might surprise many. The military intervention in Kosovo has long been regarded as legally illegitimate. On the model proposed here, the question turns on whether the actual persecution and deportation of Albanians by the Serbs indicated a likelihood of murder of those Albanians in Kosovo. A strong case that can be made for an affirmative answer to that question lays the groundwork for justifying military intervention.

While genocide anchors the case for intervention, terrorism, on this analysis, does not qualify as a ground for intervention. Indeed, as the International Bar Association Task Force on Terrorism notes, "The duty to prevent and repress terrorism is found in a patchwork of 15 subject-specific multilateral conventions or protocols, seven regional treaties, and a range of UN Security Council and General Assembly Resolutions."[14] However, as the Report goes on to conclude, these laws impose duties on States to deal with terrorism. They do not create a new international crime of terrorism.

Responding to terrorism with military intervention has little or no moral or legal justification. On the day after the September 11, 2001, attack on the World Trade Center, the United Nations Security Council treated the attack as a "threat against peace" rather than as an "armed attack."[15] Most Council members correctly characterized the attack as a criminal act rather than as an act of war.[16]

Conclusion

Humanitarian intervention, after gaining considerable momentum in the 1990s, has suffered some serious drawbacks since the beginning of this century. The Responsibility to Protect represents a deplorable backing away by the international community from a commitment to intervene even in cases of genocide. The way forward is not to take cautious steps backwards but giant steps forward. These giant steps should not be toward intervention against terrorism. Those tracks should be avoided at all costs.

The steps recommended here are easier to take than they might seem. Jurists can begin by doing what is required of any criminal code, including an international one, that is, classifying, categorizing, and ranking the potpourri of crimes included in the overall category of crimes against humanity. In short, it is time to adopt a principle of a duty to act. Anything short of this is shirking our responsibility as a civilized international community.

Conclusion

D omestic criminal codes rank crimes in terms of their seriousness. Different crimes receive different penalties and punishments depending on their seriousness. Why should international criminal law be the exception, the outlier? The problem at the international level is more a matter of political will and practical politics than anything else. There are no good reasons other than pragmatic obstacles for not establishing a hierarchy of crimes at the international level.

Not all harms are equal; some harms are worse than the others. Two candidate moral wrongs are killing and inflicting pain. Prohibitions against each of these should serve as a basis for constructing any defensible individual and social ethic. Of course, these need to be refined. Massive killing lies at the core of genocide, as does inflicting pain with torture. However, there is something particularly odious about genocide and torture. That something has to do with the status of the victims for both of these crimes. The core wrong of genocide consists of killing individuals because of their perceived vulnerable group status. Torture consists of inflicting pain on victims because of their knowledge. In short, both crimes do not simply tangentially involve the status of the victim. Victim status lies at the core of these crimes. In short, they target victims explicitly, primarily, and solely because of their status. Genocide has nothing to do with what the victims have done but only with what group status the victims have or are perceived to have. The torture victim may have some connection to an actual or potential wrong action. However, the perpetrator inflicts pain solely because of the victim's assumed knowledge. Torture is generally not punishment per se but is a means of extracting information.

Genocide and torture both have clear definitions. However, nuanced distinctions have entered the torture debate, resulting in a diminution of it as a *jus cogens* crime. Iconography, the use of iconic images, helps cure this malady. The medieval rack should serve as an icon of torture. If the rack serves as the paradigm, then "cruel, degrading, and inhuman" acts become no different in kind from the act of the medieval rack. Waterboarding and unbearably loud noises become only different degrees of inflicting pain and not different kinds, such as mental suffering.

While genocide like torture has a clear definitional base, iconic images serve more to distort than illuminate debates over genocide. Instances of genocide, like any harm, are amenable to comparisons. The Holocaust was not unique, but it does rank, historically, as the worst genocide. Unfortunately, Holocaust images have been used to compare other mass atrocities and mostly, thereby, to dismiss them. Using the definition rather than images as a basis of comparison proves highly beneficial. It helps to explain why the killing fields of Cambodia did not fully qualify as genocide and why Darfur was also found wanting as genocide.

As status crimes, genocide and torture stand apart from most other international crimes, which, under certain circumstances, can take place because of what the victim did. In short, genocide and, for most part, torture stand unique among international crimes, as nonjustifiable in principle. That qualifies them as *jus cogens* crimes, that is, as universal prohibitions from which there can be no derogation.

Terrorism does not fit into this scheme. Genocide and torture have clear definitions. Terrorism, quite conveniently, does not. Terrorism should be cast out of the international crime club. International law and domestic criminal law already cover any of the acts of terrorism that the many definitions use. The definition framework for terrorism is so elastic that acts to protect the environment and to protest the abuse of animals are quite unjustifiably brought under the terrorism label.

Concerted efforts must be taken against the overinflating or even interpreting terrorism as an international crime. Similarly, concerted efforts should be made to bolster the status of the Rwandan genocide. Moral relativism has played a pernicious role in discussions about Rwanda.

A consensus has already formed around the *jus cogens* status of genocide, including the Holocaust and the Rwandan genocide. The international community should take advantage of that agreement and use it as a basis for formulating a justifiable measure for humanitarian intervention instead of retreating to weak, vague, and probably useless Responsibility to Protect. Using genocide, as narrowly interpreted, as a basis for determining the justifications for humanitarian intervention paves a more promising road. Further, paving that road opens up the discussion for extending the grounds for humanitarian intervention to genocide-like crimes against humanity. That road, however, requires doing the same ranking exercise to sort out the many crimes included under crimes against humanity.

The ranking exercise pays high dividends. The most important is to recognize that certain crimes undercut the very idea of a civilized, moral community.

Appendix A

Genocide, Torture, and Terrorism Compared

	NONJUSTIFIABILITY	NONJUSTIFIED
Genocide	X	X
Torture	X	X
Terrorism		

	DEFINED ACT	ICONOGRAPHY
Torture	X	X
Genocide	X	
Terrorism		X

Appendix B

International Crimes Compared

CRIME	TYPE	RANK	CRIMINAL ACT	VICTIM STATUS
GENOCIDE	1	1	Killings, Massive	Vulnerable Groups
TORTURE	1	2	Pain, Infliction of	Knowledge Victim
SLAVERY	1	3	Liberty, Deprivation of	Racial Groups
CRIMES AGAINST HUMANITY	2	4	Violence, Lethal	Identifiable Groups
CRIMES AGAINST HUMANITY	2	5	Widespread or Systematic	Civilians
CRIMES AGAINST HUMANITY	2	6	Widespread or Systematic	Civilians, Armed Conflict
CRIMES AGAINST HUMANITY	2	7	Violence, Nonlethal	Civilians
CRIMES AGAINST HUMANITY	2	8	Liberty, Deprivation of	Civilians
WAR CRIMES		2	Violence, Lethal and Non	POWs, Combatants, Etc.

Listed in Rank Order

Type 1 = *Jus Cogens* Crime and International Crime

Type 2 = International Crime

Notes

Introduction

1. R. St. J. MacDonald, "Fundamental Norms in Contemporary International Law," *Canadian Yearbook of International Law* 25 (1987): 134.
2. David Luban, "A Theory of Crimes against Humanity," *Yale Journal of International Law* 29 (2004): 85–167.
3. Win-chiat Lee, "International Crimes and Universal Jurisdiction," in *International Criminal Law and Philosophy*, eds. Larry May and Zachary Hoskins (New York: Cambridge University Press, 2010).
4. Jiewuh Song, "Pirates and Torture: Universal Jurisdiction as Enforcement Gap," *Journal of Political Philosophy* (2014): 1–20.
5. Andrew Ashworth, *Principles of International Criminal Law*, 3rd ed. (Oxford: Oxford University Press, 1999), 37.
6. Antonio Cassese, *International Criminal Law* (Oxford: Oxford University Press, 2003), 157.
7. I owe this point to Richard Falk.
8. They are more than "crimes against the peace and security of mankind." Freda Adler, Gerhard Mueller, and William Laufer, *Criminal Justice*, 5th ed. (New York: McGraw-Hill, 2009). This misleading definition is the type typically adopted in the social sciences. See Harry R. Dammer and Jay S. Albanese, *Comparative Criminal Justice Systems* (Belmont, CA: Wadsworth, 2014), 2. International crimes undermine global morality.

1 Comparing Wrongs

1. Convention on the Prevention and Punishment of the Crime of Genocide, 78 U.N.T.S. 277, Res. 2670, GAOR 3rd Sess., Pt. 1, U.N. Doc. A/810, p. 174, adopted by the General Assembly 9 December 1948, entered into force 12 January 1951. [hereinafter, Genocide Convention.]
2. Rome Statute of the International Criminal Court, 17 July 1998, 2187 UNTS 90, UN Doc., A/CONF 183/9, 37 ILM 1002 (1998).
3. William Schabas, *Genocide in International Law: The Crimes of Crimes* (Cambridge: Cambridge University Press, 2000), 452.
4. See Alison Palmer, "Ethnocide" in *Genocide in Our Time*, eds. Michael N. Dobkowski and Isidor Walliman, chap. 1 (Ann Arbor, MI: Pierian Press, 1992).

5. Thomas W. Simon, *The Laws of Genocide: Prescription for a Just World* (Westport, CT: Praeger Security International, 2007): 56.
6. Convention Against Torture and Other Cruel, Inhuman or Degrading Treatment or Punishment, 1465 UNTS 113 (10 December 1984).
7. Etymology provides a further important clue for finding the basics of a genocide act. Given the word's derivation from the Latin *caedere* ("to kill"), whatever else genocide encompasses, it should include the act of killing. Adam Jones, *Genocide: A Comprehensive Introduction* (New York: Routledge, 2006): 8.
8. James Alan Fox and Jack Levin, *Overkill: Mass Murder and Serial Killing Exposed* (New York: Plenum Press, 1994), 201–206.
9. Ibid., 225.
10. Thomas. W. Simon, "Defining Genocide," *Wisconsin International Law Journal* 15 (1996): 248.
11. Nina H.B. Jorgensen, *The Responsibility Of States For International Crimes*,(New York: Oxford University Press, 2000), 112.
12. Philip L. Reichel, *Comparative Criminal Justice Systems*(Engelwood Cliffs, NJ: Prentice Hall, 2012), 72.
13. Simon, *The Laws of Genocide*, 136.
14. William A. Schabas, "State Policy as an Element of International Crimes," *Journal of Criminal Law and Criminology* 98 (2008): 966–67.
15. Alexander K. A. Greenwalt, "Rethinking Genocidal Intent: The Case for Knowledge-Based Interpretation," *Columbia Law Review* 99 (1999): 2284–88.
16. Ibid.
17. *Prosecutor v. Akayesu*, Case No. ICTR-96-4-T, Judgment, ¶ 520 (Int'l Crim. Trib. for Rwanda Sept. 2, 1998), http://www.unictr.org/Portals/0/Case/English/Akayesu/judgement/akay001.pdf.
18. Ibid., ¶ 541.
19. Simon, *The Laws of Genocide*, 73.
20. Kai Ambos, "What Does "Intent to Destroy" in Genocide Mean?" *International Review of Red Cross* 91 (2009): 834–35.
21. Simon, *The Laws of Genocide*, 73–74.
22. Cruse's acts are analogous to lethal acts against innocents, which constitute a crime against humanity. The test there is whether the perpetrator had knowledge and whether the acts were widespread or systematic. Lépine's acts are analogous to genocide in that he intentionally targeted not simply innocents but a particular type of innocents. I owe this to David Lea.
23. See Thomas W. Simon, "A Theory of Disadvantaged Groups," in *Democracy and Social Injustice* (Lanham, MD: Rowman & Littlefield, 1995), 71–107.
24. I owe this point to Jeffrey Reiman.
25. If we take the position that a successful defense (justification) to a charge of homicide or regicide renders the original charge incorrect, then at least regicide, as a status crime, may look more like genocide. However, this only

complicates the argument since we would then have to show that genocide ranks as a worse status crime than regicide. Further, even as a status crime, we could at least entertain a defense based on the claim that a monarchy is an immoral form of government. The comparable and indefensible claim would be that the group identity designation could conceivably be entertained as an immoral grouping.

26. As quoted in Merle Hoffman, "I Am Against Fanatics," in *On Prejudice: A Global Perspective*, ed. Daniela Gioseffi (New York: Anchor, 1993), 549.

27. George J. Andreopoulos, "Introduction: The Calculus of Genocide," *Genocide: Conceptual and Historical Dimensions*, ed. George J. Andreopoulos (Philadelphia: University of Pennsylvania Press, 1994), 1.

28. Richard Rorty, *Philosophy and Social Hope* (New York: Penguin Books, 1999), 83.

29. This includes: Armenia (1915–23: 1 m), Holocaust (5.7 m), Cambodia (1975–78: 1.6 m), Bosnia (1992–95: .3 m), and Rwanda (1994: 1 m).

30. Jones, *Genocide*, 39.

31. I owe this point to Jeffrey Reiman.

32. Stanley M. Elkins, *Slavery: A Problem in American Institutional and Intellectual Life*, 2nd ed. (Chicago: The University of Chicago Press, 1968), 56.

33. George Fitzhugh, *Cannibals All! Or Slaves Without Masters*, ed. C. Vann Woodward (Cambridge, MA: The Belknap Press of Harvard University, 1960, 1988).

34. Laurence Thomas, "Characterizing the Evil of American Slavery and the Holocaust," in *Jewish Identity*, eds. David Theo Goldberg and Michael Krausz (Philadelphia, PA: Temple University Press, 1993), 153–76, 172.

35. R. J. Rummel, "The Holocaust in Comparative and Historical Perspective," Paper delivered to the Conference on "The 'Other' as a Threat: Demonization and Antisemistism," June 12–15, 1995 at Hebrew University of Jerusalem.

36. Ronald Gossop, *Confronting War: An Examination of Humanity's Most Pressing Problem*, 2nd ed. (Jefferson, NC: MacFarland, 1987), 7.

37. Eric Markusen, "Genocide and Modern War," in *Genocide in Our Time*, eds. Michael N. Dobkowski and Isidor Walliman (Ann Arbor, MI: Pierian Press, 1992), 122.

38. Irving Louis Horowitz, *Taking Lives: Genocide and State Power*, 3nd ed. (New Brunswick, NJ: Transaction Books, 1982), 1–2.

39. See Markusen, "Genocide and Modern War," 123.

40. The issue of racism against the Japanese resurfaced in a controversy over a proposed exhibit of the Enola Gay, which dropped a nuclear bomb on Hiroshima, at the Smithsonian Institute.

41. Cf. "I cannot accept the view that... the bombing, in time of war, of such civilian enemy populations as those of Hiroshima, Nagasaki, Hamburg, and Dresden does not constitute genocide within the terms of the [UN]

convention." Leo Kuper, *Genocide: Its Political Use in the Twentieth Century* (New York: Penguin Books, 1981). Kuper cites the following estimates of deaths from Allied pattern bombings: In Dresden at least 40,000 people were killed; in Hamburg 40,000; and in Tokyo as many as 130,000 were victims. Leo Kuper, "Theoretical Issues Relating to Genocide: Uses and Abuses," in *Genocide: Conceptual and Historical Dimensions*, ed. George J. Andreopoulos (Philadelphia: University of Pennsylvania Press, 1994), 35.

42. Michael Walzer, *Just and Unjust Wars* (New York: Basic Books, 1977), 160.

43. As quoted in Walzer, *Just and Unjust Wars*, 264.

44. Walzer, *Just and Unjust Wars*, 268.

45. Report of the International Law Commission on the work of its forty-sixth session, UN GAOR, 49th Sess., Supp. No. 10, at 76, UN Doc. A/49/10 (1994). Also, see Chapter 7 on the definition of crimes against humanity for the International Criminal Court.

46. Genocide Convention.

47. Raul Hilberg, *The Destruction of the European Jews* (New York: Holmes & Meier, 1985), 171, 264.

48. "CRIMES AGAINST HUMANITY: namely, murder, extermination, enslavement, deportation, and other inhumane acts committed against any civilian population, before or during the war, or persecutions on political, racial, or religious grounds in execution of or in connection with any crime within the jurisdiction of the Tribunal, whether or not in violation of domestic law of the country where perpetrated." Texts of the Agreement for the Establishment of an International Military Tribunal and Annexed Charter, 5 U. N. T. S. 251.

49. A narrow definition of genocide distinguishes genocide from civilian war deaths. Unfortunately, space does not permit a defense of this important distinction.

50. Genocide Convention, art. I.

2 Comparing Genocides

1. Robert D. Kaplan, *Balkan Ghosts: A Journey Through History* (New York: Vintage, 1993), p. xviii.

2. Alan S. Rosenbaum, ed., *Is the Holocaust Unique?* (Boulder, CO: Westview Press, 1996).

3. Steven T. Katz, "The Uniqueness of the Holocaust: The Historical Dimension," in Rosenbaum, *Is the Holocaust Unique?* 32–37.

4. David E. Stannard, "Uniqueness as Denial: The Politics of Genocide Scholarship," in Rosenbaum, *Is the Holocaust Unique?* 163–208.

5. For arguments against comparing harms in this way, see Kenneth Seeskin, "What Philosophy Can and Cannot Say about Evil," in *Echoes from the Holocaust: Philosophical Reflections on a Dark Time*, eds. Alan Rosenberg

and Gerald E. Myers (Philadelphia, PA: Temple University Press, 1988), 91–104.

6. Alan Rosenberg and Evelyn Silverman, "The Issue of the Holocaust as a Unique Event," in *Genocide In Our Time*, eds. Michael N. Dobkowski and Isidor Wallimann (Ann Arbor, MI: Pierian Press, 1992), 47.

7. For a similar attack on this dilemma see, Alan Rosenberg, "The Crisis in Knowing and Understanding the Holocaust," in *Echoes from the Holocaust: Philosophical Reflections on a Dark Time*, eds. Alan Rosenberg and Gerald E. Myers (Philadelphia, PA: Temple University Press, 1988), 379–95.

8. George M. Kern and Leon H. Rappoport, "Discussion: Of Pierre Papazian's a Unique Uniqueness?" *Midstream* 30, no. 4 (April 1984): 22.

9. Primo Levi, *The Drowned and the Saved* (New York: Summit Books, 1988), 125.

10. Piers Paul Read, *Alive: Sixteen Men, Seventy-Two Days, and Insurmountable Odds—The Classical Adventure of Survival in the Andes* (New York: Harper, 2005, 1974).

11. Richard Posner, *The Problems of Jurisprudence* (Cambridge, MA: Harvard University Press, 1990), 10.

12. Vzhakn N. Dadrian, "The Comparative Aspects of the Armenian and Jewish Cases of Genocide: A Sociohistorical Perspective," in Rosenbaum, *Is the Holocaust Unique?* 105.

13. Israel W. Charny, "Forward," in Rosenbaum, *Is the Holocaust Unique?* x.

14. Ernst Nolte, "A Past Will Not Pass away—A Speech it was Possible to Write, but not to Present," *Yad Vashem Studies* 19 (1988): 65–73.

15. Jürgen Habermas, "A Kind of Indemnification: The Tendencies toward Apologia in German Research on Current History," *Yad Vashem Studies* 19 (1988): 75–92.

16. Steven T. Katz, *The Holocaust in Historical Perspective* (New York: Oxford University Press, 1944) 1: 28.

17. Katz, *The Holocaust*, 58.

18. Nolte, "A Past Will Not Pass Away," 65–73.

19. Katz, *The Holocaust*, 34.

20. Ibid.

21. William Schabas, *Genocide in International Law: The Crimes of Crimes* (Cambridge: Cambridge University Press, 2000), 91.

22. Alvin H. Rosenfeld, *The End of the Holocaust* (Bloomington, IN: University of Indiana Press, 2011), 167.

23. Raphael Lemkin, *Axis Rule in Occupied Europe: Laws of Occupation, Analysis of Government, Proposals for Redress* (Washington, DC: Carnegie Endowment for International Peace, 1944), 79.

24. Photo: Young survivors behind a barbed wire fence in Buchenwald Concentration Camp (on file with author with permission from Dodge-Chrome, Inc.).

25. Christian Axboe Nielsen, "Surmounting the Myopic Focus on Genocide: The Case of War in Bosnia and Herzegovina," *Journal of Genocide Research* 15, no. 1 (2013): 21, 24.

26. See Roy Gutman, *A Witness to Genocide: The 1993 Pulitzer Prize-Winning Dispatches on the "Ethnic Cleansing" of Bosnia* (New York: Macmillan, 1993), 126.

27. Thomas Deichmann, "The Picture that Fooled the World," *Living Marxism* 97 (1997): 24–31, available at http://www.slobodan-milosevic.org/fooled.htm.

28. David Campbell, "Atrocity, Memory, Photography: Imaging the Concentration Camps of Bosnia—the Case of ITN versus Living Marxism, Part 1," *Journal of Human Rights* 1, no. 1 (2002): 1.

29. Photo: Bosnian genocide (Patrick Robert/Corbis Sygma August 1992) (on file with author with email permission from Patrick Robert, June 18, 2014, 18:44 EDT) The iconic photo appeared on cover of *Time* on August 17, 1992. I was unable to pay the $621.00 to reprint that one.

30. Roland Paris, "Kosovo and the Metaphor War," *Political Science Quarterly* 117, no. 3 (2002): 423, 423–50.

31. Marc Weller, "The Crisis in Kosovo, 1989–1999: From the Dissolution of Yugoslavia to Rambouillet and the Outbreak of Hostilities," *International Documents & Analysis* 1 (1999): 333–35.

32. Kosovo Assault, "Was Not Genocide," BBC News (September 7, 2001), http://news.bbc.co.uk/2/hi/europe/1530781.htm.
    The U.N. Sponsored Supreme Court Of Kosovo Found:[There] had been a "systematic campaign of terror, including murders, rapes, arsons and severe multreatments." Crimes against humanity and war crimes did take place, it said, but "the executions committed by Milosevic's regime cannot be qualified as criminal acts of genocide, since their purpose was not the destruction of the Albanian ethnic group . . . but its forceful departure from Kosovo."

33. Richard G. Hovannislan, "Etiology and Sequalae of the Armenian Genocide," in *Genocide: Conceptual and Historical Dimensions*, eds. George J. Andreopoulos (Philadelphia: University of Pennsylvania Press, 1994), 113.

34. Pierre Papazian, "A 'Unique Uniqueness'?" *Midstream* 30, no. 4 (April 1984): 16.

35. David E. Stannard, "Uniqueness as Denial: The Politics of Genocide Scholarship," in Rosenbaum, *Is the Holocaust Unique?* 163–208.

36. Katz, "The Uniqueness of the Holocaust," 32–37.

37. Vahakn N. Dadrian, "The Comparative Aspects of the Armenian and Jewish Cases of Genocide: A Sociological Perspective," in Rosenbaum, *Is the Holocaust Unique?* 101–136.

38. Dadrian, "The Comparative Aspects," 129.

39. Katz, "The Uniqueness of the Holocaust," 33.

40. Dadrian, "The Comparative Aspects," 129.

41. "I believe that the nation as such should be annihilated, or, if this was not possible by tactical measures, have to be expelled from the country...this will be possible if the water-holes from grootfontein to gobabis are occupied. The constant movement of our troops will enable us to find the small groups of nation who have moved backwards and destroy them gradually." Mahmood Mandami, *A People Betrayed: The Role of the West in Rwanda's Genocide* (New York: Zed Books, 2000): 11.

42. Lyman H. Letgers, "The Soviet Gulag: Is it Genocide?" in *Toward the Understanding and Prevention of Genocide*, ed. Israel W. Chaney (Boulder, CO: Westview Press, 1984); Robert Conquest, *The Harvest of Sorrow: Soviet Collectivization and the Terror-Famine* (New York: Oxford University Press, 1986).

43. Hearing of The Senate Foreign Relations Committee, Testimony Of Secretary Of State Colin Powell; US Department of State, Documenting Atrocities in Darfur (September 2004).

44. Report of the International Commission of Inquiry on Violations of International Humanitarian Law and Human Rights Law in Darfur, UN Doc. S/2005/60, Para's. 491, 4.

45. Avishai Margalit and Gabriel Motzkin, "The Uniqueness of the Holocaust," *Philosophy And Public Affairs* (Winter 1996): 65–83.

46. Margalit and Motzkin, "The Uniqueness of the Holocaust," 79.

47. Helen Fein, *Accounting for Genocide* (New York: The Free Press, 1979), 29

48. Ian Hancock, "Responses to the Porrajmos: The Romany Holocaust," in Rosenbaum, *Is the Holocaust Unique?* 54.

49. Margalit and Motzkin, "The Uniqueness of the Holocaust," 79.

50. See Thomas W. Simon, "Defining Genocide," *Wisconsin International Law Review* (Fall 1996).

51. Mahmood Mamdami, *Saviors and Survivors: Darfur, Politics, and The War on Terror* (Three Rivers Press, 2010).

52. Nanjing also erected a memorial museum to the rape of Nanjing and modelled it after memorials to the Holocaust.

3   Rwanda: Undervalued Injustice

1. Raul Hilberg, *The Destruction of the European Jews*, Student Edition (New York: Holmes & Meier, 1985).

2. UN SC Res. 2150 (April 2014) SC/11356.

3. *Prosecutor v. Akayesu*, ICTR-96–4-T (1998).

4. Jurists have turned to a slightly more sensible but still problematic designation of these groups in terms of different ethnicities.

5. A great deal of my historical information about Rwanda and the genocide comes from Alison Des Forges, *Leave None to Tell the Story: Genocide in Rwanda* (New York: Human Rights Watch, 1999). Des Forges wrote one the definitive works on Rwanda and, on February 12, 2009, tragically

and ironically, died in a plane crash in my hometown of Clarence Center, New York. For an annotated survey of research on Rwanda, see Rene Lemarchand, *Rwanda: The State of Research*. Online Encyclopedia of Mass Violence (2013). http://www.massviolence.org/rwanda-the-state-of-research, 742.

6. Smaller minorities such as the Twa in Rwanda and the Roma in the Balkans seldom receive mention.
7. John H. Speke, *Journal of the Discovery of the Source of the Nile* (London: Blackwoods, 1863).
8. Rene Lemarchand, *The Dynamics of Violence in Central Africa* (Philadelphia, PA: University of Pennsylvania Press, 2009).
9. John T. Bowen, "The Myth of Global Ethnic Conflict," *Journal of Democracy* 7, no. 4 (1996): 13–14.
10. Rene Lemarchand, *Rwanda and Burundi* (London: Pall Mall, 1970), 18.
11. Philip Gourevitch, *We Wish to Inform You that by Tomorrow My Family and I will be Dead* (New York: Farrar, Straus and Giroux, 1998).
12. Mahmood Mamdani, *When Victims Become Killers: Colonialism, Nativism, and the Genocide in Rwanda* (Princeton: Princeton University Press, 2002), 38.
13. Ibid.
14. Gerard Prunier, *The Rwanda Crisis: History of Genocide* (New York: Columbia University Press, 1995), 224.
15. Report of the Independent Inquiry into the Actions of the United Nations During the 1994 Genocide on Rwanda, UN Doc. S/1999/1257 (1999).
16. John Cory, "A Formula for Genocide," *American Spectator* 31, no. 9 (1998): 22–27.
17. Mamdani, *When Victims Become Killers*, 219–20.
18. The ICTY found that genocide was not committed in Bosnia except in Srebrenica. *Prosecutor v. Radislav Kristic*, IT-98–33-T, Trial Judgment (August 2, 2001).
19. Ethnic cleansing is the forced population transfers within a state's borders. See Michael P. Roch, "Forced Displacement in Former Yugoslavia: A Crime Under International Law?" *Dickinson Journal of International Law* 14 (1995): 1. It is not per se a criminal offence. It was not included in ICTY or ICTR Statutes but was included in ICC.
20. Gourevitch, *We Wish to Inform You*, 219.
21. Africa Rights, *Rwanda: Death, Despair and Defiance* (1995), 1126.
22. *International Herald Tribune* (June 13, 1994).
23. "Discussion Paper: Rwanda," Office of the Assistant Secretary of Defense for the Middle East/Africa Region, Department of Defense.
24. Edward S. Herman and David Peterson, *The Politics of Genocide* (Monthly Review Press, 2010).
25. Rene Lemarchand, "Disconnecting the Threads: Rwanda and the Holocaust Reconsidered," *Journal of Genocide Research* 4, no. 4 (2002): 48–70.

26. Ravi Bhavnani and David Backer, "Localized Ethnic Conflict and Genocide: Accounting for Differences in Rwanda and Burundi," *Journal of Conflict Resolution* 44, no. 3 (June 2000): 283–306.

27. Astri Suhke and Bruce Jones, "Preventative Diplomacy in Rwanda: Failure to Act or Failure of Actions?" In *Opportunities Missed. Opportunities Seized: Preventive Diplomacy in Post–Cold War World*, ed. Bruce W. Jentleson (Lanham, MD: Rowman & Littlefield, 2000), 256.

28. As cited in Gourevitch, *We Wish to Inform You*, 219.

29. R. J. Rummel, *Statistics on Democide: Genocide and Mass Murder Since 1900* (New Brunswick, NJ: Transaction Publishers, 1997), chap. 9.

30. Philip Verwimp, "Testing the Double-Genocide Thesis for Central and Southern Rwanda," *The Journal of Conflict Resolution* 47, no. 4 (2003): 423–42.

31. Lemarchand, "Disconnecting the Threads." 13–14.

32. Gerard Prunier, From Genocide to Continental Wars: The Congolese Conflict and the Crisis of Contemporary Africa (C. Hurst, 2009).

33. *Prosecutor v. Zeljko Raznjatovic* (Arkan), IT-97–27, Indictment (September 23, 1997).

34. Timothy Longman, *Christianity and Genocide in Rwanda* (New York: Cambridge University Press, 2010).

35. Gourevitch, *We Wish to Inform You.*

36. *The State of Israel v. Ivan (John) Demjanjuk*, Crm. Case No. 373/86 (Jerusalem, July 29, 1999).

37. *Demjanjuk v. Israel*, Crm. App. No. 347/88 (Supreme Court, July 29, 1993).

38. *In the Matter of Surrender of Elizaphan Ntakirutimana*, US Dist. Ct. Southern Dist. Of TX.Laredo Div., Misc. No L-96–5 (December 17, 1997).

39. *Elizaphan Ntakirutimana v. Janet Reno et al.*, 184 F.3d 419 (United States Court of Appeals Fifth Circuit, August 5, 1999); and 528 U.S. 1135 (2000), certiorari denied.

40. *Prosecutor v. Elizaphan Ntakirutimana and Gerard Ntakirutimana*, ICTR-96–10-T (February 21, 2003). The Appeals Chamber upheld his conviction for aiding and abetting genocide by helping to transport the attackers to the killing site. ICTR-96–17-T (December 14, 2004). He was sentenced to ten years in prison.

41. Ibid.

42. Norman G. Finkelstein, *The Holocaust Industry: Reflections on the Exploitation of Jewish Suffering* (New York: Verso, 2000).

4 Torture: Undervalued Injustice

1. Franz Kafka, "In the Penal Colony," in *Kafka's Selected Stories*, ed. Stanley Corngold (New York: W.W. Norton, 2007), 44.

2. Convention Against Torture and Other Cruel, Inhuman or Degrading Treatment or Punishment, Dec. 10, 1984, 1465 U.N.T.S. 85 [hereinafter Torture Convention], art. 1.

3. See, for example, Office of the High Commissioner on Human Rights, "Interpretation of Torture in the Light of the Practice and Jurisprudence of International Bodies," 2011, http://www.ohchr.org/Documents/Issues/Torture/UNVFVT/Interpretation_torture_2011_EN.pdf. This interpretation provides the following analysis:

> Many acts, conducts or events may be viewed as torture in certain circumstances, while they will not be viewed as torture in some other situations. In fact, there is no single definition [of torture] existing under international law...It should be recalled that usually in legal dispositions, torture is linked with cruel, inhuman and degrading treatment or punishment or ill-treatment. Torture is not an act in itself, or specific type of acts, but it is the legal qualification of an event or behaviour, based on the comprehensive assessment of this event or behaviour. Therefore, the difference between these different qualifications, torture, cruel, inhuman and degrading treatment or punishment or ill-treatment depends on the specific circumstances of each case and is not always obvious (Ibid., 2).

4. William Schabas, *Unimaginable Atrocities: Justice, Politics, and Rights at the War Crimes Tribunals* (New York: Oxford University Press, 2012).

5. Photo: Sanford Levinson, ed. *Torture: A Collection* (Oxford University Press, 2006), 4. Photo originally an engraving appended to the Austrian Empire's 1769 Criminal Procedure Code.

6. Clifford Geertz, *Local Knowledge: Further Essays in Interpretive Anthropology*, 3rd ed. (New York: Basic Books, 1983), 84. (Promoting symbolic anthropology, which examines the interpretation of symbols).

7. Laura Perini, "The Truth in Pictures," *Philosophy of Science* 72 (2005): 262, 274.

8. See generally, Thomas Kuhn, *The Structure of Scientific Revolutions* 3rd ed. (University of Chicago Press, 1962); Mary Hesse, *Models and Analogies in Science* revised ed. (Notre Dame, IN: University of Notre Dame, 1966). Michael Weisberg, *Simulation and Similarity: Using Models To Understand The World* (New York: Oxford, 2013).

9. See Theo van Leeuwen and Carey Jewitt, eds. *Handbook of Visual Analysis* (London: SAGE Publications, 2001), 73.

10. See Thomas W. Simon, *Democracy and Social Injustice: Law, Politics, and Philosophy* (Lanham, MD: Rowman & Littlefield, 1995), 21.

11. Ronald Dworkin, *Law's Empire* (Cambridge, MA: Harvard University Press, 1986), 72.

12. Denise Chong, *The Girl in The Picture: The Story of Kim Phuc, the Photograph, and the Vietnam War* (New York: Viking, 2000), 76.

13. Eamonn Carrabine, "Just Images: Aesthetics, Ethics, and Visual Criminology," *British Journal of Criminology* 52 (2012): 463.

14. Susan Sontag, *On Photography* (New York: St Martin's Press, 1977), 20.

15. Susan Sontag, *Regarding The Pain Of Others* (New York: Penguin, 2004), 105.

16. Adam L. Rosman, "Visualizing the Law: Using Chats, Diagrams, and Other Images to Improve Legal Briefs," *Journal of Legal Education* 63 (2013): 70.

17. See Alfred W. McCoy, "Beyond Susan Sontag: The Seduction of Psychological Torture," in *Screening Torture: Media Representations of State Terror and Political Domination*, eds. Michael Flynn and Fabiola F. Salek (New York: Columbia University Press, 2012), 109, 115. Stating the Inquisition also may have marked a theological shift from the life to the death of Jesus.

18. Photo: Medieval Rack (Public Domain), *available at* http://en.wikipedia.org/wiki/Torture#mediaviewer/File:Streckbett.jpg.

19. Henry Charles Lea, *A History of the Inquisition of the Middle Ages* (1887), 1: 82.

20. Ibid., 337.

21. Ibid.

22. Benjamin D. Wicker, *Status: Inquisition in the Catholic Church*, Catholic Education Resource Center, http://www.catholiceducation.org/articles/history/world/wh0029.html.

23. Claudia Card, *The Atrocity Paradigm: A Theory of Evil* (New York: Oxford University Press, 2002).

24. John H. Langbein, *Torture and the Law of Proof: Europe and England in the Ancien Régime* (Chicago: University of Chicago Press, 2012).

25. Henry Kamen, *The Spanish Inquisition: A Historical Revision* (New Haven, CT: Yale University Press, 1998).

26. Photo: Medieval Torture Devices (Public Domain), *available at* http://en.wikipedia.org/wiki/Torture.

27. Cullen Murphy, *God's Jury: The Inquisition and the Making of the Modern World* (New York: Houghton Mifflin Harcourt, 2012), 90.

28. See Father Angelo Clareno (1304 A.D) *A Catholic Inquisition Torture Session*, http://www.corvalliscommunitypages.com/Europe/jesuits_saints_inquisition_reformation/an_inquisition_torture_session.htm (last visited September 16, 2012).

The torturer entered with his assistants and tied the prisoner's hands behind his back. Then he had him raised up by means of a pulley attached to the roof of the house, which was very high. After the prisoner had hung there for an hour the rope was released suddenly. The idea was that, broken by the intense pain, he would be defeated and confess that he had once been a heretic. After he had been raised and suddenly dropped many times they asked whether he would confess that he was or had been a heretic. He replied, I'm a faithful and catholic Christian, always have been, and always will be. If I said anything else to you shouldn't believe me, because I would only have said it to escape the torture. Let this be my perpetual confession to you, because it's the truth. Anything else would be a lie extorted by torture.

29. See Jerome H. Skolnick and James J. Fyfe, *Above the Law: Police and the Excessive Use of Force* (New York: Free Press, 1993), 43. This may have something to do with the origin of the phrase "the third degree," a euphemism for brutal police interrogation techniques.
30. Murphy, *God's Jury*, 93.
31. Ibid.
32. Ibid.
33. Ibid.
34. Photo: *Toca* or waterboarding (Public Domain), *available at* http://www.npr.org/templates/story/story.php?storyId=15917081.
35. *In re Kemmler* 136 U.S. 436, 446 (1890).
36. *Brown v. Mississippi*, 297 U.S. 278, 285–86 (1936).
37. *Ashcraft v. Tennessee*, 332 U.S. 143, n.8 (1944) ("State and federal courts, textbook writers, legal commentators, and governmental commissions consistently have applied the name of 'inquisition' to prolonged examination of suspects conducted as was the examination of Ashcraft"). See, for example, Cuthbert W. Pound, *"Inquisitorial Confessions,"* *Cornell Law Quarterly* 1, no. 2 (1916): 77; *Chambers v. Florida*, 309 U. S. 227 (1940); *Bram v. United States*, 168 U. S. 532, 544 (1897); *Brown v. Walker*, 161 U. S. 591, 596 (1896); *Counselman v. Hitchcock*, 142 U. S. 547, 573 (1892); cf. *Cooper v. State*, 86 Ala. 610 (1889), 611. In a case where no physical violence was inflicted or threatened, the Supreme Court of Virginia expressly approved the statement of the trial judge that the manner and methods used in obtaining the confession read "like a chapter from the history of the inquisition of the Middle Ages." *Enoch v. Commonwealth*, 126 S.E. 222, 225(Va. 1925); and see *Cross v. State*, 221 S.W. 489 (Tenn. 1920). The analogy, of course, was in the fact that old inquisition practices included questioning suspects in secret places, away from friends and counsel, with notaries waiting to take down "confessions," and with arrangements to have the suspect later affirm the truth of his confession in the presence of witnesses who took no part in the inquisition. See *Inquisition Definition,* Encyclopaedia Britannica, http://www.britannica.com/EBchecked/topic/288915/inquisition (last visited November 19, 2014).

In the more serious offenses the party suspected is arrested, he is placed on his inquisition before the chief of police, and a statement is obtained.... Where the office of the district attorney is in political harmony with the police system, the district attorney is generally invited to be present as an inquisitor. *Wharton's Criminal Evidence*, 11th ed. (1935) 2:1021–22.

38. *Chambers v. Florida*, 309 U.S. 227, 237–38 (1940).
39. *Blackburn v. Alabama*, 361 U.S. 199, 206 (1960).
40. *Pennsylvania v. Muniz*, 496 U.S. 582, 596 (1990) (quoting *Ullmann v. United States*, 350 U.S. 422, 428 (1956).
41. Seth F. Kreimer, "Too Close to the Rack and the Screw: Constitutional Constraints on Torture in the War on Terror," *University of Pennsylvania Journal of Constitutional Law* 6 (2003): 278, 289.
42. See Jeremy Waldron, "Torture and Positive Law: Jurisprudence for the White House" 105 *Columbia Law Review* (2005): 1681, 1703, critiquing the analysis of torture on a continuum.
43. Memorandum from Jay S. Bybee, Assistant Attorney Gen., U.S. Department. of Justice, to Alberto R. Gonzales, Counsel to the President, Standards of Conduct for Interrogation under 18 U.S.C. § § 2340–2340A (Aug. 1, 2002), *reprinted* in Mark Danner, Torture and Truth: America, Abu Ghraib, and the War on Terror 115 (2004).
44. Memorandum from Jay S. Bybee, Assistant Attorney Gen., U.S. Dep't of Justice, to John Rizze, Acting General Counsel of the Central Intelligence Agency, Interrogation of al Qaeda Operative (August 1, 2002).
45. Elizabeth Swanson Goldberg, *Beyond Terror: Gender, Narrative, Human rights* (New Brunswick, NJ: Rutgers University Press, 2007), 213.
46. Murphy, *God's Jury*, 87.
47. Jane Mayer, *The Dark Side: The Inside Story of How the War on Terror Turned into a War on American Ideals* (New York: Knopf Doubleday Publishing Group, 2008), 171.
48. Jane Mayer, "A Deadly Interrogation. Can the CIA Legally Kill a Prisoner?" *New Yorker*, November 14, 2005, 44, http://www.newyorker.com/magazine/2005/11/14/a-deadly-interrogation.
49. Randall Mikkelson, "CIA Says Used Waterboarding on Three Suspects," *Reuters*, February 5, 2008, 6:13pm EST, http://www.reuters.com/article/2008/02/05/us-security-usa-waterboarding-idUSN0517815120080205.
50. Case of Husayn (Abu Zubaydah) v. Poland, Application No. 7511/13, Judgment (Eur. Ct. H.R. July 24, 2014), http://hudoc.echr.coe.int/sites/eng/pages/search.aspx?i=001-146047.
51. Timothy Brook, Jérôme Bourgon, Gregory Blue *Death by a Thousand Cuts* (Cambridge, MA: Harvard University Press, 2008), 2.
52. Ibid., 1.
53. Photo: The Lingchi of "Pseudo-Fuzhuli" (name and date unknown), *reprinted in* Georges Bataille, Les Larmes D'Eros X (2004).
54. James Elkins, *The Object Stares Back: On the Nature of Seeing* (New York: Mariner Books, 1996), 110.
55. Brook et al., *A Thousand Cuts*, 2.
56. Elkins, *Object Stares Back*.
57. Brook et al., *A Thousand Cuts*, 1.

58. Ibid., 2.
59. Ibid., 3–4.
60. Ibid., 2.
61. Ibid., 28.
62. Sir Henry Norman, *The People and Politics of the Far East* (London: T. F. Unwin, 1895), 224–25.
63. Brook et al, *A Thousand Cuts*.
64. Ibid., 204.
65. Ibid.
66. Brook et al., *A Thousand Cuts*, 211.
67. Ibid.
68. Ibid., 210.
69. Ibid., 207.
70. Ibid., 220.
71. Ibid., 9.
72. Ibid., 2.
73. Ibid., 43.
74. Ibid.
75. Photo: Ming Dynasty torture implements: wooden manacles, finger press, ankle press, fetters, "box-bed," interrogation baton, light and heavy flogging sticks, cangue, prisoner's card, restraining board, Wang Qi, ed., *Sancai Tuhui, reprinted in* Brook et al., *A Thousand Cuts*, 45.
76. Brook et al., *A Thousand Cuts*, 47.
77. Ibid.
78. Maria Antónia Lima, "The Dark Side of the Mediterranean—Expressions of Fear from the Inquisition to the Present," *Babilónia* no. 8/9 (2010), 141, 143, describing an exhibition of torture instruments presented in Evora in 1994.
79. Brook et al., *A Thousand Cuts*, 172.
80. Ibid., 48.
81. Ibid., 211–13.
82. Chris Berry, "Lust, Caution: Torture, Sex, and Passion in Chinese Cinema," in *Screening Torture: Media Representations of State Terror and Political Domination*, eds. Michael Flynn and Fabiola F. Salek (New York: Columbia University Press, 2012), 71, 79.
83. Ibid., 80–81.
84. Jérôme Bourgon, "Obscene Vignettes of Truth. Construing Photographs of Chinese Executions as Historical Documents," in *Visualizing China: 1845–1965*, eds. Christian Henriot and Wen-hsin Yeh (Boston, MA: Brill, 2013), 39, 89–90.
85. Melinda Smith and Jeanne Segal, *Child Abuse & Neglect,* Helpguide.org, http://www.helpguide.org/mental/child_abuse_physical_emotional_sexual_neglect.htm (last updated July 2014).

86. John E.B. Myers, "A Short History of Child Protection in America," *Family Law Quarterly* 42 (2008–2009), 449–50.

87. Child Welfare Training Institute, "Evolution of Federal Child Welfare Legislation" (2007), http://php.ipsiconnect.org/CWTI/Law/textOnly-Law.html.

88. Ibid.

89. Ibid.

90. Myers, "History of Child Protection," 451.

91. Child Welfare Training Institute, "Child Welfare Legislation."

92. John E.B. Myers, *Child Protection in America: Past, Present, and Future* (New York: Oxford University Press, 2006), 30.

93. Ibid.

94. Ibid., 33.

95. Ibid.

96. Ibid., 35.

97. Ibid.

98. Myers, "History of Child Protection," 452.

99. Thomas Hove et al., "Newspaper Portrayals of Child Abuse: Frequency of Coverage and Frames of the Issue," *Mass Communication and Society* 16 (2013): 89, 91.

100. Children's Bureau of U.S. Department of Health and Human Services, "Child Maltreatment 2012," (2013), xi, http://www.acf.hhs.gov/sites/default/files/cb/cm2012.pdf; Childhelp, "Child Abuse Statistics & Facts," http://www.childhelp.org/pages/statistics (last visited July 29, 2014), stating that the year 2012 saw 78.3% neglect, 18.3% physical abuse, and 9.3% sexual abuse.

101. David Finkelhor et al., *Updated Trends in Child Maltreatment, 2012* (University of Nebraska Press, 2013), 2.

102. National Academy of Sciences, "Rates of Physical and Sexual Abuse Have Declined, But Not Child Neglect," *Science Daily*, Sept. 12, 2013, http://www.sciencedaily.com/releases/2013/09/130912143940.htm.

103. See UN Committee against Torture, *Consideration of Reports Submitted by States Parties under Article 19 of the Convention: Convention against Torture and Other Cruel, Inhuman or Degrading Treatment or Punishment: Initial Reports of States Parties Due in 2003: The Holy*, March 8, 2013, CAT/C/VAT/1; See Convention against Torture and Other Cruel, Inhuman or Degrading Treatment or Punishment, UN document CAT/C/VAT/1, Dec. 7, 2012.

104. Center for Constitutional Rights, "Shadow Report," April 2014 [hereinafter The Shadow Report] (prepared for the 52nd Session of the UN Committee Against Torture in Connection with its Review of the Holy See), 2.

105. UN Committee Against Torture, Convention Against Torture and Other Cruel, Inhuman or Degrading Treatment or Punishment, General

Comment 2, ¶ 22, UN Doc. CAT/C/GC/2, Jan. 24, 2008. [Hereinafter, Torture Convention].

106. See Torture Convention.

[A]ny act by which severe pain or suffering, whether physical or mental, is intentionally inflicted on a person *for such purposes as obtaining from him or a third person information or a confession, punishing him for an act he or a third person has committed or is suspected of having committed, or intimidating or coercing him or a third person, or for any reason based on discrimination of any kind*....(emphasis by author).

107. *Prosecutor v. Jean-Paul Akayesu*, Case No. ICTR-96-4-T, Judgment, ¶ 688 (Int'l Crim. Trib. for Rwanda Sept. 2, 1998), http://www.unictr.org/Portals/0/Case/English/Akayesu/judgement/akay001.pdf, *adopted in* Prosecutor v. Delalić, Case No. IT-96-21-T, Judgment, ¶¶ 478–79 (Int'l Crim. Trib. for the Former Yugoslavia Nov. 16, 1998), http://www.icty.org/x/cases/mucic/tjug/en/981116_judg_en.pdf. The Trial Chamber in the *Akayesu* case (the first to successfully prosecute an individual for rape) defined sexual violence as "any act of a sexual nature, which [sic] is committed on a person under circumstances which [sic] are coercive. Sexual violence is not limited to physical invasion of the human body and may include acts which [sic] do not involve penetration or even physical contact."

108. See David Pimentel, "Criminal Child Neglect and the 'Free Range Kid': Is Overprotective Parenting the New Standard of Care?" *Utah Law Review* no. 2 (2012): 947. Unfortunately, Pimentel concludes an otherwise insightful article with lame recommendations to have the law provide guiding factors for parents in raising their children.

109. *Make Sure You Know the Cases of Child Abuse*, Laws.com, http://children-laws.laws.com/child-abuse/cases-of-child-abuse (last visited September 29, 2014).

110. *McKune v. Lile*, 536 U.S. 24, 41 (2002).

111. See also 705 Ill. Comp. Stat. 405/2–3(1)(d)(2013) (Illinois law defines a neglected minor, in part, as "any minor under the age of 14 years whose parent or other person responsible for the minor's welfare leaves the minor without supervision for an unreasonable period of time without regard for the mental or physical health, safety, or welfare of that minor."). See also *Md. Code Ann., Fam. Law* § 5–801(a) (LexisNexis 2014).

A person who is charged with the care of a child under the age of 8 years may not allow the child to be locked or confined in a dwelling, building, enclosure, or motor vehicle while the person charged is absent and the dwelling, building, enclosure, or motor vehicle is out of the sight of the person charged unless the person charged provides a reliable person at least 13 years old to remain with the child to protect the child.

112. Robin Estrin, "Don't Let Sleeping Tots Lie, Parent Learns" *Los Angeles Times*, Apr. 6, 1997, http://articles.latimes.com/1997-04-06/news/mn-45952_1_parent-learns.

113. Ibid.

114. Ibid.

115. Ibid.

116. *Gross v. State*, 817 N.E.2d 306, 307 (Ind. Ct. App. 2004).

117. Judith Warner, "Dangerous Resentment," *New York Times*, July 9, 2009, 9:00pm, http://opinionator.blogs.nytimes.com/2009/07/09/dont-hate-her-because-shes-educated/?_php=true&_type=blogs&_r=0.

118. Admittedly, recent cases of children dying in locked cars have come to light, but, on closer examination, these cases look like the case of Mary Ellen. See Deborah Hastings, "22 Month-Old Georgia Boy Left to Die in Hot Car had Scratches on Face and Head," *New York Daily News*, July 5, 2014, 12:00pm, http://www.nydailynews.com/news/national/22-month-old-ga-boy-died-hot-car-scratches-head-article-1.1855937. Explaining how Cooper Harris, who died of hypothermia after his father locked him in the car, had abrasions over his body.

119. *Wilson v. Seiter*, 501 U.S. 294, 296 (1991).

120. Ibid., 306.

121. See generally Philip E. Carlan, Lisa S. Nord, and Ragan A. Downey, *An Introduction to Criminal Law* (Jones & Bartlett, 2011), 5. In New York State, First Degree Grand Larceny is the stealing of property that exceeds one million dollars and carries a sentence not to exceed 25 years, whereas Fourth Degree Grand Larceny consists of stealing property that exceeds one thousand dollars with a sentence not to exceed four years imprisonment.

122. Ibid., 77.

123. See Rome Statute of the International Criminal Court art. 6, *opened for signature* July 17,1988, 2187 U.N.T.S. 3 (entered into force July 1, 2002) [hereinafter Rome Statute].

124. See Carlan et al., *Introduction to Criminal Law*, 77.

125. Guyora Binder, "The Origins of American Felony Murder Rules" *Stanford Law Review* 57 (2004): 120–21. Giving the example that only some common law jurisdictions such as California recognize the felony murder rule, making participants in a felony liable for murder even if unintentional.

126. Rome Statute, art. 6(a).

127. Convention on the Prevention and Punishment of the Crime of Genocide art. II, *adopted* Dec. 9, 1948, S. Treaty Doc. No. 81–15, 78 U.N.T.S. 277 (entered into force Jan. 12, 1951) [hereinafter Genocide Convention].

128. John T. Parry, "What Is Torture, Are We Doing It, and What If We Are?" *University of Pittsburgh Law Review* 64 (2003): 249. For Parry, torture occurs "against a background of total control and potential escalation

that asserts the state's dominance and unsettles or destroys the victim's normative world."

129. J. Jeremy Wisnewski, *Understanding Torture* (Edinburgh University Press, 2010), 10.

130. Henry Shue, "Torture," *Philosophy & Public Affairs* 7, no. 2 (1978): 124.

131. Michael Davis, "The Moral Justifiability of Torture and Other Cruel, Inhuman, or Degrading Treatment," *International Journal of Applied Philosophy* 19 (2005): 167.

132. David Sussman, "What's Wrong with Torture?" *Philosophy & Public Affairs* 33, no. 1 (2005): 4.

133. Harvey M. Weinstein, "Victims, Transitional Justice and Social Reconstruction: Who Is Setting the Agenda?" in *Justice For Victims: Perspectives on Rights, Transition and Reconciliation*, ed. Inge Vanfraechem, Antony Pemberton and Felix Mukwiza Ndahinda (2014), 161, 169.

134. David Luban and Henry Shue, "Mental Torture: A Critique of Erasures in U.S. Law," *Georgetown Law Journal* 100, no. 3 (2012): 823, 860.

135. See, for example, Anthony Cullen, "Defining Torture in International Law: A Critique of the Concept Employed by The European Court of Human Rights," *California Western International Law Journal* 34, no. 1 (2003): 29, 33. "The experience of the victim is of primary consideration in determining acts that constitute torture."

136. Torture Convention, art. 16, ¶ 1, at 116 ("Each State Party shall undertake to prevent in any territory under its jurisdiction other acts of cruel, inhuman or degrading treatment or punishment which do not amount to torture as defined."); Convention for the Protection of Human Rights and Fundamental Freedoms, art. 3, Nov. 4, 1950, 513 U.N.T.S. 222 ("No one shall be subject to torture or to inhuman or degrading treatment or punishment"); S. Afr. Const., § 12(1), 1996 ("Everyone has a right to freedom and security of the person, which includes the right...not to be tortured in any way; and...not to be treated or punished in a cruel, inhuman or degrading way."); New Zealand Bill of Rights Act 1990, cl. 9 ("Everyone has the right not to be subjected to torture or to cruel, degrading, or disproportionately severe treatment or punishment.").

137. See, for example, *Ireland v. United Kingdom*, 25 Eur. Ct. H.R. (ser. A), 110–11, 111 n.12 (1978).

138. Jeremy Waldron, "The Coxford Lecture, Inhuman and Degrading Treatment: The Words Themselves," *Canadian Journal of Law & Jurisprudence* 23 (2010): 269.

139. Ibid., 280.

140. Ibid., 282. Citing a case where degrading treatment is found even where the victim is not aware of it; see also *R v. Gen. Med. Council* [2004] EWHC (Admin) 1879, [2005] Q.B. 424, at ¶ 178.

141. Cf. Bernhard Schlink, "The Problem with Torture Lite," *Cardozo Law Review* 29 (2007): 85, 86 ("Whatever the wording, the distinction

between torture and cruel, inhuman and degrading treatment is one of intensity. Intensity is also the crucial factor in the book's second distinction, the one between cruel, inhuman, and degrading treatment or treatment that shocks the conscience, and highly coercive interrogation techniques deemed acceptable.").

142. Metin Başoğlu et al., "Torture vs. Other Cruel, Inhuman, and Degrading Treatment: Is the Distinction Real or Apparent?" *Arch Gen Psychiatry* 64 (2007): 284. ("[A]lthough there is evidence that torture leads to PTSD in some cases, many people survive extremely severe torture in relatively good psychological health and never develop PTSD. Conversely, some survivors develop PTSD after ostensibly milder forms of ill treatment or psychological stressors that do not involve physical torture.")

143. Jessica Wolfendale, "The Myth of 'Torture Lite'," *Ethics & International Affairs* 23 (2009): 56.

144. Jeremy Waldron, *Torture, Terror, and Trade-Offs: Philosophy for the White House* (New York: Oxford University Press, 2010), 277, 278.

145. Andrew Mumford, "Minimum Force Meets Brutality: Detention, Interrogation and Torture in British Counter-Insurgency Campaigns," *Journal of Military Ethics* 11, no. 1 (2012): 17.

146. *Ireland v. United Kingdom*, App. No. 5310/71, 512 Y.B. Eur. Conv. On H.R., 378 (Eur. Comm'n on H.R.).

147. *Ireland v. United Kingdom*, 25 Eur. Ct. H.R. (ser. A) ¶ 165 (1978). Recently, however, the European Court of Human Rights found that waterboarding constituted torture. See *Case of Husayn v. Poland*, App. No. 7511/13, Eur. Ct. H.R. (July 24, 2014), available at http://hudoc. echr.coe.int/sites/eng/pages/search.aspx?i=001-146047.

148. Joseph Lelyveld, "Interrogating Ourselves," *New York Times*, June 12, 2005, http://www.nytimes.com/2005/06/12/magazine/12TORTURE. html?pagewanted=all&_r=0 ("[I]n which the detainee was hooded and placed on a low chair with a seat tilting down, pitching him forward while his arms were tightly handcuffed behind him in an unnatural, contorted way so that they had to support his weight, for two or three hours at a stretch.").

149. HCJ 5100/94 The Public Committee Against Torture in Israel v. The Government of Israel, 53(4) P.D. 817 (1999).

150. Amanda C. Pustilnik, "Pain as Fact and Heuristic: How Pain Neuroimaging Illuminates Moral Dimensions of Law," *Cornell Law Review* 97 (2012): 825.

151. Dan Jones, "Beyond Waterboarding: The Science of Interrogation," *New Scientist* 205 (2010): 40.

152. Luban and Shue, "Mental Torture," 829.

153. Cf. Pustilnik, "Pain as Fact and Heuristic," 825. Citing John T. Parry, "Escalation and Necessity: Defining Torture at Home and Abroad" in *Torture: A Collection*, ed. Sanford Levinson (2004), 147–48. See Aage

R. Møller, "Similarities between Chronic Pain and Tinnitus," *American Journal of Otolaryngology* 18 (1997): 577–88.

154. See Alan Lockwood et al., "Tinnitus," *New England Journal of Medicine* 347 (2002): 904.

155. Luban and Shue, "Mental Torture," 828.

156. *Pain Receptor*, Psychologycs, http://www.psychologycs.com/pain-receptor.htm (last visited Sept. 19, 2014) ("Any of the free nerve endings located throughout the body that function as sensory receptors, transmitting sensations of pain in response to noxious stimulation, one type (the monomodal nociceptor) being a thinly myelinated delta fibre that responds to severe mechanical deformation, the other (the polymodal nociceptor) being a C fibre that responds to mechanical deformation, excessive heat or cold, and irritant chemical stimulation, and is responsible for the axon reflex.").

157. Ibid.

158. Yoshio Takashima et al., "Diversity in the Neural Circuitry of Cold Sensing Revealed by Genetic Axonal Labeling of Transient Receptor Potential Melastatin 8 Neurons," *Journal of Neuroscience* 27 (2007): 14148.

159. A Google search for images of pain pathways will yield countless numbers of diagrams of simple physical pain pathways.

160. See Møller, "Similarities between Chronic Pain and Tinnitus," 118, 199. Showing an example of the diagrams.

161. Cullen, "Defining Torture in International Law" ("The experience of the victim is of primary consideration in determining acts that constitute torture.").

162. Amnesty International, *Amnesty International Report 1984*, at 286, AI Index POL 10/004/1984 (May 1, 1984) (the 1984 Second Amnesty Report (at 10) was and remains one of the few that describes the training of torturers, in this case, in Greece).

163. Convention Against Torture And Other Cruel, Inhuman, Or Degrading Treatment Or Punishment, S. Exec. Rep. 101–30, at 9 (1990) (the Convention Against Torture ("CAT") was adopted into US law through the Foreign Affairs Reform and Restructuring Act, Pub. L. No. 105–277, § 2242, 112 Stat. 2681. The implementing regulations are at 8 C.F.R. §§ 208.16–208.18 (2014)).

164. Oona Hathaway et al., "Tortured Reasoning: The Intent to Torture under International and Domestic Law," *Virginia Journal of International Law* 52 (2012): 795.

165. Torture Convention, art. 1, p. 114.

166. Alexander K. A. Greenwalt, "Rethinking Genocidal Intent: The Case for Knowledge-Based Interpretation," *Columbia Law Review* 99 (1999): 2264.

167. See Torture Convention, art. 1, ¶ 1, p. 114 ("[A]ny act by which severe pain or suffering, whether physical or mental, is intentionally inflicted

on a person *for such purposes* as obtaining from him or a third person information or a confession, punishing him for an act he or a third person has committed or is suspected of having committed, or intimidating or coercing him or a third person, or for any reason based on discrimination of any kind." (emphasis added)).

168. See ibid ("[W]hen such pain or suffering is inflicted by or at the instigation of or with the consent or acquiescence of a *public official* or other person acting in an *official capacity*." (emphasis added)).

169. *Zubeda v. Ashcroft*, 333 F.3d 463, 473 (3rd Cir. 2003).

170. Ibid.

171. Abraham D. Sofaer, Legal Adviser, Department of State, " Convention Against Torture: Hearing Before the S. Comm. on Foreign Relations" *101st Congress* 9 (1990) (Prepared Statement).

172. Manfred Nowak, "What Practices Constitute Torture?: US and UN Standards," *Human Rights Quarterly* 28 (2006): 821.

173. S. Exec. Rep. 101–30.

174. Special Rapporteur on Torture and Other Cruel, Inhuman or Degrading Treatment or Punishment, *Report on Torture and Other Cruel, Inhuman or Degrading Treatment or Punishment*, Human Rights Council, ¶ 34, U.N. Doc. A/HRC/13/39/Add.5 (Feb. 5, 2010) (by Manfred Nowak) [hereinafter Special Rapporteur Report]. This would indeed exclude the following hypothetical case offered by the U. N. Special Rapporteur: "A detainee who is forgotten by the prison officials and suffers from severe pain due to the lack of food is without doubt the victim of a severe human rights violation. However, this treatment does not amount to torture given the lack of intent by the authorities."

175. See generally Paul H. Robinson and Jane A. Grall, "Element Analysis in Defining Criminal Liability: The Model Penal Code and Beyond," *Stanford Law Review* 35 (1983): 681. Discussing the changes between common law criminal elements and the 1981 Model Penal Code.

176. *Matter of J-E-*, 23 I & N Dec. 291, 300–01 (B.I.A. 2002).

177. Mary Holper, "Specific Intent and the Purposeful Narrowing of Victim Protection Under the Convention Against Torture," *Oregon Law Review* 88 (2009): 779. Noting the US Reservation "shifted the focus in [Torture Convention] protection cases off the victim and onto the alleged torturer." (alteration in original).

178. Ibid.

179. Hitomi Takemura, "Big Fish and Small Fish Debate: An Examination of Prosecutorial Discretion," *International Criminal Law Review* 7 (2007): 680.

180. Thomas W. Simon, *The Laws of Genocide: Prescription for a Just World* (Westport, CT: Praeger Security International, 2007), 62.

181. Philip L. Reichel, *Comparative Criminal Justice Systems* (Engelwood Cliffs. NJ: Prentice Hall, 1994), 72.

182. Ibid.
183. Simon, *The Laws of Genocide*, 68.
184. Reichel, *Comparative Criminal Justice Systems*, 72.
185. Simon, *The Laws of Genocide*, 63–64.
186. Takemura, "Examination of Prosecutorial Discretion," 684.
187. Simon, *The Laws of Genocide*, 64.
188. *State Policy as an Element of International Crimes*, 971.

> [If] there exists a State policy... then the inquiry shifts to the individual, with the central question being not the individual's intent, but rather the individual's knowledge of the policy. Individual intent arises, in any event, because the specific acts of genocide, such as killing, have their own mental element, but as far as the plan or policy is concerned, knowledge is the key to criminality.

189. Waldron, "The Coxford Lecture," 270, n.6.
190. See Aditi Bagchi, "Intention, Torture, and the Concept of State Crime," *Penn State Law Review* 114 (2009): 4. Advocating to abandon the intent requirement altogether for holding states responsible for the crime of torture.
191. Lisa Yarwood, "Defining Torture: The Potential for Abuse," *Journal of the Institute of Justice & International Studies* 2008 (2008): 328.
192. Matthew H. Kramer, *Torture And Moral Integrity: A Philosophical Enquiry* (2014), 243.
193. See Universal Declaration of Human Rights, art. 5, G.A. Res. 217 (III) A, U.N. Doc. A/RES/217(III) (Dec. 10, 1948); Geneva Convention Relative to the Treatment of Prisoners of War, art. 3, Aug 12, 1949, 75 U.N.T.S. 135; European Convention on Human Rights, art. 3, Nov. 4, 1950, 213 U.N.T.S. 222; International Covenant on Civil and Political Rights, art. 7, Dec. 16, 1966, 999 U.N.T.S. 171; Inter-American Convention on Human Rights, art. 5, Nov. 22, 1969, 1144 U.N.T.S. 123; African Charter on Human and People's Rights, art. 5, Jun. 27, 1981, 1520 U.N.T.S. 217; Committee on Civil and Political Rights, General Comment 20, ¶ 3, U.N. Doc HRI/GEN/1/Rev. 1 at 30 (1992); First U.N. Congress on the Prevention of Crime and the Treatment of Offenders, Standard Minimum Rules for the Treatment of Prisoners, art. 31–34, 1955.
194. See generally Mathew Lippman, "The Development and Drafting of the United Nations Convention Against Torture and Other Cruel, Inhuman, or Degrading Treatment or Punishment," *Boston College International and Comparative Law Review* 17 (1994): 275. Unfortunately, this article is not a very revealing piece.
195. Amnesty International, *Report on Torture*, at 21, AI Index ACT 40/001/1973 (Jan. 1, 1973).
196. Torture Convention, art. 2.
197. Iveta Cherneva, "The Drafting History of Article 2 of the Convention Against Torture," *9 Essex Human Rights Review* 9 (2012): 7–8.

198. Rosemary Foot, "Torture: The Struggle over a Peremptory Norm," *International Relations* 20 (2008): 132.

199. See Omer Ze'ev Bekerman, "Torture: The Absolute Prohibition of a Relative Term: Does Anyone Know What is in Room 101?" *American Journal of Criminal Law* 53 (2005): 743.

200. Elie Wiesel and Merle Hoffman, "I am against Fanatics," in *On Prejudice: A Global Perspective*, ed. Daniela Gioseffi (New York: Anchor Books, 1993), 549–50.

201. Torture Convention, art. 2, ¶ 2, at 114.

202. Torture Convention, art. 16, ¶1, at 116.

Each State Party shall undertake to prevent in any territory under its jurisdiction other acts of cruel, inhuman or degrading treatment or punishment which do not amount to torture as defined in article I, when such acts are committed by or at the instigation of or with the consent or acquiescence of a public official or other person acting in an official capacity.

203. See J. Herman Burgers and Hans Danelius, *The United Nations Convention Against Torture* (1988), 124.

204. Thomas W. Simon, "Genocide, Evil, and Injustice: Competing Hells" in *Genocide and Human Rights, A Philosophical Guide*, ed. John K. Roth (New York: Palgrave Macmillan, 2005), 65.

205. Ibid.

206. See Simon, *The Laws of Genocide*, 84.

207. *Defusing the Ticking Bomb Scenario: Why we must say No to torture, Always*, Ass'n For Prevention Torture (2007), http://www.apt.ch/content/files_res/tickingbombscenario.pdf ("Suppose that a perpetrator of an imminent terrorist attack, that will kill many people, is in the hands of the authorities and that he will disclose the information needed to prevent the attack only if he is tortured. Should he be tortured?").

208. Henry Shue, "Torture in Dreamland: Disposing of the Ticking Bomb," *Case Western Reserve Journal of International Law* 37 (2006): 231.

209. Lucette. M. Lagnado, *Children of the Flames: Dr. Josef Mengele and the Untold Story of the Twins of Auschwitz* (1992). Explaining that Mengele would perform massive blood transfusions from one twin to another.

210. Brook et al., *A Thousand Cuts*, 249.

211. Michael Dorf, "Renouncing Torture," in *The Torture Debate in America*, ed. Karen J. Greenberg (New York: Cambridge University Press, 2006), 247, 250.

212. Ibid.

213. Waldron, "Torture and Positive Law," 1726.

5 Terrorism: Overvalued Injustice

1. A phrase made famous by Justice Potter Stewart when trying to define pornography in *Jacobellis v. Ohio*, 378 U.S. 184, p. 197 (Stewart concurring).

2. Henry Dammer and Jay Albanese, *Comparative Criminal Justice Systems* (Belmont. CA: Wadsworth, 2014).

3. Mia Bloom, *Dying to Kill: The Allure of Suicide Terror* (New York: Columbia University Press, 2005).

4. Bernard Lewis, *The Assassins* (New York: Basic Books, 2003).

5. Truth and Reconciliation Commission, Amnesty Committee, "Application in Terms of Section 18 of the Promotion of National Unit and Reconciliation Act, No. 34 of 1995," AC/2001/003. http://www.justice.gov.za/trc/decisions/2001/ac21003.htm

6. Bruce Hoffman, *Inside Terrorism* (New York: Columbia University Press, 2013).

7. Timothy Shanahan, *The Provisional Irish Republican Army and the Morality of Terrorism* (Edinburgh University Press, 2007).

8. Pamala L. Griset and Sue Maltan, *Terrorism in Perspective* (Thousand Oaks, CA: Sage, 2007), 4.

9. Ibid.

10. Hoffman, *Inside Terrorism*. See also Louise Richardson, *What Terrorists Want: Understanding the Enemy, Containing the Threat* (New York: Random House, 2006); Walter Lacquer, *A History of Terrorism* (New Brunswick, NJ: Transaction Publishing, 2001), *Voices of Terror: Manifestos, Writings and Manuals of Al Qaeda, Hamas, and Other Terrorists from Around the World and throughout the Ages* (Sourcebooks, 2004), *No End to war: Terrorism in the Twenty-first Century* (Continuum Publishing Group, 2004).

11. Ruth Blakeley, *State Terrorism and Neoliberalism: The North in the South* (New York: Routledge, 2011), 10.

12. Noam Chomsky and Edward S. Herman, *Washington Connection and Third World Fascism* (Boston, MA: South End Press, 1979).

13. Igor Primoratz, *Terrorism: A Philosophical Investigation* (Polity, 2013).

14. Jeffrey A. Sluka, *Death Squad: The Anthropology of State Terror* (University of Pennsylvania Press, 1999), 2.

15. Blakeley, *State Terrorism*, 1.

16. Ben Saul, "The Legal Response of the League of Nations to Terrorism," *Journal of International Criminal Justice* 4, no. 1 (2011): 78–102.

17. Convention on Offences and Certain Other Acts Committed on Board Aircraft, signed at Tokyo on September 14, 1963; Convention for the Suppression of Unlawful Seizure of Aircraft, signed at the Hague on December 16, 1970; Convention for the Suppression of Unlawful Acts against the Safety of Civil Aviation, signed at Montreal on September 23, 1971; Convention on the Prevention and Punishment of Crimes against Internationally Protected Persons, including Diplomatic Agents, adopted by the General Assembly of the United Nations on December 14, 1973; International Convention against the Taking of Hostages, adopted by the General Assembly of the United Nations on December 17, 1979; Protocol on the Suppression of Unlawful Acts of Violence at Airports Serving Convention on the Physical Protection

of Nuclear Material, signed at Vienna on March 3, 1980; Protocol on the Suppression of Unlawful Acts of Violence at Airports Serving International Civil Aviation, supplementary to the Convention for the Suppression of Unlawful Acts against the Safety of Civil Aviation, signed at Montreal on February 24, 1988; Convention for the Suppression of Unlawful Acts against the Safety of Maritime Navigation, done at Rome on March 10, 1988; Protocol for the Suppression of Unlawful Acts against the Safety of Fixed Platforms Located on the Continental Shelf, done at Rome on March 10, 1988; Convention on the Marking of Plastic Explosives for the Purpose of Detection, signed at Montreal on March 1, 1991; International Convention for the Suppression of Terrorist Bombings, adopted by the General Assembly of the United Nations on December 15, 1997; International Convention for the Suppression of the Financing of Terrorism, adopted by the General Assembly of the United Nations on December 9, 1999; International Convention for the Suppression of Acts of Nuclear Terrorism New York, adopted by the General Assembly of the United Nations on April 13, 2005; Convention on the Suppression of Unlawful Acts Relating to International Civil Aviation (Beijing 2010); Protocol Supplementary to the Convention on the Suppression of Unlawful Seizure of Aircraft (Beijing 2010).

18. Comprehensive Convention on International Terrorism contains the following draft:1. Any person commits an offence within the meaning of this Convention if that person, by any means, unlawfully and intentionally, causes:

(a) Death or serious bodily injury to any person; or

(b) Serious damage to public or private property, including a place of public use, a State or government facility, a public transportation system, an infrastructure facility or the environment; or

(c) Damage to property, places, facilities, or systems referred to in paragraph 1 (b) of this article, resulting or likely to result in major economic loss,

when the purpose of the conduct, by its nature or context, is to intimidate a population, or to compel a Government or an international organization to do or abstain from doing any act.

19. For example, the theme of Offenses Against Civil Aviation includes the following: Tokyo Convention on Offenses and Certain Other Acts Committed on Board Aircraft (1963), Hague Convention for the Suppression of Unlawful Seizure of Aircraft (1970, to cover "in flight" acts not covered by the 1963 Convention), Montreal Convention for Suppression of Unlawful Acts against the Safety of Civil Aviation (1971).

20. U.S. Code Title 22, Ch.38, Para. 2656f (d).

21. U.S. Department of Justice, FBI, *Terrorism in the United States*, 1988 (Terrorist Research and Analytic Center, Counter-Terrorism Section, Criminal Investigative Division, Dec. 31, 1988) at 34.

22. ARK. CODE ANN ¶ 5–13–301 (Michie 2002).

23. Arab Convention on Suppression of Terrorism (Cairo 1998) and Terrorism Convention of the Organization of the Islamic Conference (Ouagadougou, 1999).
24. Bassiouni, for example, makes no distinction between targeting innocent civilians and targeting combatants: "Terrorism is an ideologically-motivated strategy of internationally proscribed violence designed to inspire terror within a particular segment of society in order to achieve a prior-outcome or to propagandize a claim of grievance, irrespective of whether its perpetuators are acting for and on behalf of themselves, or on behalf of states." M. Cherif Bassiouni, *International Terrorism: Multilateral Conventions, 1937–2001* (2001), 16–17.
25. George Fletcher, "The Indefinable Concept of Terrorism," *Journal of Criminal Justice* 4, no. 5 (2006).
26. "Acts involving serious violence against a person, serious damage to property, acts that endanger a person's life, other than that of the person committing the action; acts that create a serious risk to the health or safety of the public or a section of the public, or acts designed seriously to interfere with or disrupt an electronic system." United Kingdom Terrorism Act of 2000, Ch. 11 Sect. 1(2).
27. "Attempted murder, assault, kidnapping, hostage-taking on airplanes, ships, all means of transport, theft, extortion, destructions, and crimes committed during group combat, the production or ownership of weapons of destruction and explosives including the production, sale, import and export of explosives, the acquisition, ownership, transport of illegal explosive substances, the production, ownership, storage, or acquisition of biological or chemical weapons, and money laundering." Article 421–1, French Criminal Code.
28. Ben Saul, *Defining Terrorism in International Law* (Oxford: Oxford University Press, 2006), 25.
29. Anthony Richards, "Conceptualizing Terrorism," *Studies in Conflict & Terrorism* 37, no. 3 (2014).
30. Tokyo Convention on Offenses and Certain Other Acts Committed on board Aircraft (1963); Hague Convention for Suppression of Unlawful Seizure of Aircraft (1970); Montreal Convention for Suppression of Unlawful Acts Against the Safety of Civil Aviation (1971). The problem that made the reach of these treaties so limited was that the treaties covered only nonstate actors, and the Lockerbie case involved state terrorist acts.
31. Saul, *Defining Terrorism*, 304.
32. Ibid., 25.
33. Kriangsak Kittichaisaree, *International Criminal Law* (Oxford: Oxford University Press, 2001), 92.
34. Garrett O'Boyle, "Theories of Justification and Political Violence: Examples of Four Groups [Provisional IRA, Red Army, al-Qaeda, anti-abortion]," *Terrorism and Political Violence* 14, no. 2 (2002): 23–46. Good

descriptions of how these groups justify violence with a mixture of deon-tology and consequentialism but short on analysis.

35. Virginia Held, "Terrorism and War," *Journal of Ethics* 8 (2004).

36. Igor Primoratz, "Philosopher Looks at Contemporary Terrorism," *Cardozo Law Review* 29 (2007–8): 132–52.

37. Walzer defends these early ariel bombing campaigns as the only means available for the British to avoid Nazi evil. Michael Walzer *Just and Unjust Wars*, 3rd ed. (New York: Basic Books, 2000), 261–68.

38. Conor Friedesdorf, "The Irrationality of Giving Up this Much Liberty to Fight Terror," *Atlantic* (June 10, 2013).

39. Hoffman, *Inside Terrorism*, 19

40. http://en.wikipedia.org/wiki/List_of_battles_and_other_violent_events_by_death_toll#Terrorist_attacks

41. John Mueller, "Has the Threat from Terrorism Been Exaggerated?" *Commentator* (January 8, 2014).

42. Global Terrorism Database www.start.umd.edu

43. "Danger of Death!" *Economist* (February 14, 2013).

44. Ben Saul, *Defining Terrorism in International Law* (Oxford: Oxford University Press, 2008): 314.

45. Prevention of Terrorism Bill (1999).

46. Art. 421–22, French Criminal Code.

47. Jennifer Varriale Carson, Gary LaFree, and Laura Dugan, "Terrorist and Non-Terrorist Criminal Attacks by Radical Environmental and Animal Rights Groups in the United States," *Terrorism and Violence* 24, no. 2 (2012): 295–319. Also see Will Potter, *Green Is the New Red: An Insider's Account of a Social Movement Under Siege* (City Lights Publishers, 2011); Donald R. Liddick, *Eco-Terrorism and Radical Environmental and Animal Liberation Movements* (New York: Praeger, 2006).

48. *United States v. Fullmer*, 584 F.3d 139 (3d Circuit 2009). See Michael Hill, "*United States v. Fullmer* and the Animal Enterprise Terrorism Act: 'True Threats' to Advocacy," *Case Western Reserve Law Review* 61, no. 3 (2011).

49. *United States v. Viehl*, 2:09-CR-19 (US District Ct., D Utah, Central Div. 2010).

50. Saul, *Defining Terrorism*, 264.

51. Ibid., 268.

52. Mary L. Volcansek and John F. Sack, Jr., eds., *Courts and Terrorism: Nine Nations Balance Rights and Security* (New York: Cambridge University Press, 2011).

53. Carolo Guarnieri, "Preserving Rights and Protecting the Public: The Italian Experience," in eds. Mary L. Volcansek and John F. Sack, Jr., *Courts and Terrorism: Nine Nations Balance Rights and Security* (New York: Cambridge University Press, 2011), 169–80.

54. Seung-Whan Choi Jr., "Fighting Terrorism through the Rule of Law," *Journal of Conflict Resolution* (2010), online.

55. Christopher Greenwood, "War, Terrorism, and International Law," *Current Legal Problems* 56 (2004): 529.
56. Petula Dvorak and Jamie Stockwell, "D.C. Homicides, Violent Crimes Fall: Slayings Jump 65 Percent in Pr. George's, Rise in Many U.S. Cities," *The Washington Post* (January 1, 2002), A01. As quoted in Mathieu Deflem, *The Policing of Terrorism: Organizational and Global Perspectives* (New York: Routledge, 2010), 59.
57. Saul, *Defining Terrorism*, 237.
58. Ibid., 315.
59. Mathieu Deflem, *The Policing of Terrorism: Organizational and Global Perspectives* (New York: Routledge, 2010), 66.
60. Mark Tushnet, "Critical Legal Theory (without Modifiers) in the United States," *Journal of Political Philosophy* 13, no. 1 (2005): 99.
61. "Semantic instability, irreducible trouble spots on the borders between concepts, indecision in the very concept of the border: all this must not only be analyzed as a speculative disorder, a conceptual chaos or zone of passing turbulence in public or political language. We must also recognize here strategies and relations of force. The dominant power is the one that manages to impose and thus, to legitimate, indeed to legalize (for it is always a question of law) on a national and world stage, the terminology and thus the interpretation that best suits it in a given situation." Jacques Derrida, as quoted in G. Borradori, *Philosophy in the Time of Terror: Dialogues with Jürgen Habermas and Jacques Derrida* (Chicago: University of Chicago Press, 2003), 105.
62. Corey Robin, *Fear: a History of a Political Idea* (Oxford, Oxford University Press, 2008).

6 Universal Wrongs: *Jus Cogens*

1. Anthony D'Amato, "It's a Bird, It's a Plane, It's Jus Cogens!" *Connecticut Journal of International Law* 6, no. 1 (1990); Prosper Weil, "Towards Relative Normativity in International Law," *American Journal of International Law* 77 (1983): 413.
2. Sztucki does not find the terms interchangeable. See Jerzy Sztucki, *Jus Cogens and the Vienna Convention on the Law of Treaties: A Critical Appraisal* (New York: Springer-Verlag, 1974), 103–106. I shall use the terms interchangeably with the understanding that we are not talking about peremptory norms invoked only for a particular purpose but rather those peremptory norms considered universal.
3. A. Mark Weisburd, "The Emptiness of the Concept of *Jus Cogens*, as Illustrated by the War in Bosnia-Herzegovina," *Michigan Journal of International Law* 17, no. 1 (Fall 1995): 10–20.
4. For an inventory of publicists, see George D. Haimbaugh Jr., "Jus Cogens: Root & Branch (An Inventory)," *Touro Law Review*, 3 (1987): 203.

5. Jonathan I. Charney, "Universal International Law," *American Journal of International Law* 87, no. 4 (1993): 541.

6. For Grotius, even God could not change natural law. Hugo Grotius, "What Is War? What Is Law?" Chap. 1 in *On the Law of War and Peace*, ed. J. B. Scott (London: Carnegie Endowment for International Peace, 1925), *vol.* 1.

7. Weisburd, "Emptiness of the Concept of *Jus Cogens*," 10–20.

8. Alfred von Verdross, "Forbidden Treaties in International Law," *American Journal of International Law* 31 (1937): 571.

9. Verdross, "Forbidden Treaties," 577.

10. Alfred von Verdoss, "*Jus Dispositivum* and *Jus Cogens* in International Law," *American Journal of International Law* 60 (1966): 56.

11. Hersch Lauterpacht, Report on the Law of Treaties, U.N. Doc. A.CN.4/63 (1953).

12. Lauterpacht, Report, p. 155.

13. Weisburd, "Emptiness of the Concept of Jus Cogens."

14. As Sir Humphrey Waldock remarked, "[The ILC] has based its approach to the question of *jus cogens* on positive law much more than on natural law because it had been convinced that there existed at the present time a number of principles of international law which were of a peremptory character." "United Nations Conference on the Law of Treaties," Official Records, First Session (Vienna, March 26 to May 24, 1968), New York 1969, 327–28 (as quoted in Haimbaugh, "*Jus Cogens*: Root & Branch," 203).

15. France refused to sign and ratify the entire treaty allegedly because of this one article. Hélène R. Fabri, "Enhancing the Rhetoric of Jus Cogens," *European Journal of International Law* 23, no. 4 (2012): 1049–58, 1050.

16. Mary Ellen O'Connell, "*Jus Cogens*: International Law's Higher Ethical Norms," in *The Role of Ethics in International Law*, ed. Donald Earl Childress III (Cambridge: Cambridge University Press, 2012).

17. Jonathan I. Charney, "Universal International Law," *American Journal of International Law* 87 (1993): 529. Charney proposes the use of multilateral forums as a more explicit way of developing general international law, but multilateral forums have not addressed genocide.

18. Proposed by the Committee on the Formation of Customary International Law, American Branch of the International Law Association: "The Role of State Practice in the Formation of Customary and Jus Cogens Norms of International Law," January 19, 1989. For an excellent discussion see Bruno Simma and Philip Alston, "The Sources of Human Rights Law: Custom, *Jus Cogens*, and General Principles," *Australian Yearbook of International Law* 12 (1988–1989): 82–108.

19. Simma and Alston, "Sources of Human Rights Law," 107.

20. In his last published article, Ronald Dworkin voiced his concern over the Convention's consent requirement. Ronald Dworkin, "A New Philosophy

of International Law," *Philosophy & Public Affairs* 41, no. 1 (2013). Dworkin also pokes fun at the last source of international law as perhaps recognizing the NYU law group as philosopher kings, ignoring the fact that the statute clearly designates this last source as subsidiary.

21. Members of the Vienna Conference had difficulty with this numerical test. See Sztucki, *Jus Cogens and the Vienna Convention*, 99–100. To avoid this conundrum the initial moral justification for substantive *jus cogens* should be kept distinct from the issue of further support for *jus cogens* through the acceptance and recognition of a number of states.

22. Larry May also mistakenly interprets this article of the Convention. Larry May, "Habeas Corpus as Jus Cogens in International Law," *Criminal Law and Philosophy* 4 (2010): 249–265.

23. Given the universal quality of *jus cogens*, it would be difficult to accept the idea of regional *jus cogens* as proposed by Boutros-Ghali and others. See Sztucki, *Jus Cogens and the Vienna Convention*, 107–8.

24. Emmerich De Vattel, *The Law of Nations*, trans. Joseph Chitty (Philadelphia, PA: T. & J. W. Johnson & Co.), (1863): lv.

25. Sztucki, *Jus Cogens and the Vienna Convention*, 21, fn. 67.

26. A British military court executed Bruno Tesch, a chemist and businessman, for his role in developing and selling Zyklon B to the Nazis.

27. See ILC Commentary, ILC Report (1966), UN Doc A/6309/Rev. 1, p. 89. Laura Hannikainen, *Peremptory Norms in International Law: Historical Development, Criteria, Present Status* (Lakimiesliiton Kustannus, Finnish Lawyers' Publishing Company, 1988), 6.

28. Hannikainen, *Peremptory Norms*, 6–8.

29. There are other ways *jus cogens* may tie into state action. *Jus cogens*, for example, connects more closely with aspiration state claims than other facets of international law. So, in determining the soundness of a peremptory norm claim so-called soft law, such as UN resolutions, takes on a new significance. When countries vote in favor of resolutions in the General Assembly that support or further refine *jus cogens*, those proclamations lend even more support to the viability of a *jus cogens* provision. Further, the international dimension plays another critical role to bolster *jus cogens* through the practice of organs of the UN.

30. Sztucki, *Jus Cogens and the Vienna Convention*, 75.

31. Michael Akehurst, "The Hierarchy of Sources of International Law," *British Yearbook of International Law* 47, no. 1 (1975): 273.

32. *Jus cogens* is, to use H. L. A. Hart's distinction, both a secondary rule (serving as the basis for determining what rules qualify as primary rules) and a primary rule (applying to acts). Harry D. Gould, *The Legacy of Punishment in International Law* (New York: Palgrave/Macmillan, 2010).

33. Cf. Hannikainen, *Peremptory Norms*, 10–13.

34. Gordon A. Christenson, "*Jus Cogens*: Guarding Interests Fundamental to International Society," *Virginia Journal of International Law* 28 (1988): 598–602; Weisburd, "Emptiness of the Concept of *Jus Cogens*," 25–27.
35. Sztucki, *Jus Cogens and the Vienna Convention*, 117.
36. See Lon Fuller, *The Morality of Law* (New Haven, CT.: Yale University Press, 1969). A proceduralist natural law theory.
37. Sztucki, *Jus Cogens and the Vienna Convention*, 72.
38. John Finnis, *Natural Law and Natural Rights* (Oxford: Clarendon Press, 1980), 83–84.
39. Ibid., 83.
40. Ibid., 86.
41. Jeremy Waldron criticizes natural law for not having the characteristics of law. Jeremy Waldron, "What Is Natural Law Like?" In *Reason, Morality, and Law: The Philosophy of John Finnis,* ed. John Keown and Robert P. George (New York: Oxford University Press, 2013), 73.
42. Lloyd L. Weinreb, *Law and Justice* (Cambridge, Ma.: Harvard University Press, 1987), 100. While I use Weinreb's phrase, I offer a different interpretation of it.
43. Lloyd L. Weinreb, "Natural Law and Rights," in *Natural Law Theory: Contemporary Essays*, ed. Robert P. George (Oxford: Clarendon Press, 1992), 298.
44. Oscar Schachter, "International Law in Theory and Practice: General Course in Public International Law," *Recueil des cours* 178, no. 21 (1982): 336.
45. Cited by Patrick Thornberry, *International Law and the Rights of Minorities* (Oxford: Clarendon Press, 1991), 95. Except for the prohibition against force as contrary to the UN Charter, the prohibition against genocide received more votes (13 out of 26 delegates) as an example of *jus cogens* at the meetings of the Vienna Conference. See, Sztucki, *Jus Cogens and the Vienna Convention*, 114–23.
46. Christopher A. Ford, "Adjudicating *Jus Cogens*," *Wisconsin International Law Journal* 13 (1994): 144–81, 164–65.
47. Hannikainen does not explicitly include prohibitions against genocide and slavery in his list except in so far as these concern respect for basic human rights. Hannikainen. *Peremptory Norms*, chap. 7.
48. Thornberry, *International Law*, 97.
49. Ibid., 100.
50. Reservations to the Convention on Prevention and Punishment of the Crime of Genocide, Advisory opinion, 1951 I.C.J. 23.
51. Ford, "Adjudicating *Jus Cogens*," 164.
52. See Thomas W. Simon, *Democracy and Social Injustice* (Lanham, MD: Rowman and Littlefield, 1995).
53. Hannikainen, *Peremptory Norms*, 265.

54. *Barcelona Traction, Light and Power Company, Limited* (Belgium v. Spain), Judgment, ICJ Reports 1970, p. 3, at 32.

    33. When a State admits into its territory foreign investments or foreign nationals, whether natural or juristic persons, it is bound to extend to them the protection of law and assumes obligations concerning the treatment to be afforded them. These obligations, however, are neither absolute nor unqualified. In particular, an essential distinction should be drawn between the obligation of a State towards the international community as a whole, and those arising vis-à-vis another State in the field of diplomatic protection. By their very nature the former are the concern of all States. In view of the importance of the rights involved, all States can be held to have a legal interest in their protection; they are obligations *ergo omnes.*

    34. Such obligations derive, for example, in contemporary international law, from the outlawing of acts of aggression, and of genocide, as also from the principles and rules concerning the basic rights of the human person, including protection from slavery and racial discrimination. Some of the corresponding rights of protection have entered into the body of international law . . . ; others are conferred by international instruments of a universal or quasi-universal character.

55. Admittedly, before and since *Barcelona Traction*, the ICJ has missed a number of opportunities to explicitly adopt obligations erge omnes. *South-West Africa* (Liberia v. South Africa, Ethiopia v. South Africa), ICJ (1966); *Case Concerning East Timor* (Portugal v. Australia) ICJ (1995).

56. Hermann Mosler, *The International Society as a Legal Community* (Springer, 1980), 18.

57. 1994 ILC Report, UN GAOR, 49th Sess., Supp. No. 10, 29–40, UN Doc. A/49/10 (1994), 67–68, Article 20.

58. Ben Saul, "The Legal Response of the League of Nations to Terrorism," *Journal of International Criminal Justice* 4, no. 1 (2011): 269.

59. A. J. J. deHoogh, "The Relationship between Jus Cogens, Obligations Erga Omnes and International Crimes: Peremptory Norms in Perspective," *Austrian Journal of Public International Law* 42 (1991): 183–214, 213.

60. Ford, "Adjudicating *Jus Cogens*," 168–81.

61. There are other problems as well. For example, only one-third of the states that are parties to the Statute of the Court have consented to the compulsory jurisdiction of the Court.

62. Hannikainen, *Peremptory Norms*, 289–92.

7   Duty to Act: Beyond Responsibility to Protect

1. Kofi Annan, "We the Peoples—The Role of the United Nations in the 21st Century" (known as "Millennium Report"), March 2000.

2. Gareth Evans, "The Responsibility to Protect," Fifth Committee of the General Assembly, GA/AB/3837 (March 4, 2008), 64–65.
3. Annan, Millennium Report.
4. Shane Reeves, "To Russia with Love: How Moral Arguments for a Humanitarian Intervention in Syria Opened the Door for an Invasion of the Ukraine," *Michigan State Law Review* 22, no. 1 (Fall 2014). ("reliance on morality as the basis for determining legal obligations . . . injects subjectivity, arbitrariness, and unpredictability into the determination," 12–13).
5. United Nations General Assembly, A/RES/377 (V). This was first implemented, in 1950, by the United States to bypass the Soviet Union, which had boycotted the Security Council, to get United Nations backing for waging the Korean War.
6. Andrew J. Carswell, "Unblocking the United Nations Security Council: The Uniting for Peace Resolution," *Journal of Conflict and Security Law* 18, no. 3 (Winter 2013): 453–80.
7. Larry May, *Crimes against Humanity: A Normative Account* (Cambridge, UK: Cambridge University Press, 2005), 68.
8. Ibid., 82.
9. Ibid., 81.
10. Antonio Cassese et al., *International Criminal Law: Cases & Commentaries* (Oxford University Press, 2011), 155.
11. William Schabas, *Unimaginable Atrocities: Justice, Politics, and Rights at the War Crimes Tribunals* (New York: Oxford University Press, 2012).
12. Leila Nadyra Sadat, ed., *Forging a Convention for Crimes against Humanity* (New York: Cambridge University Press, 2011).
13. I owe this distinction to David Duffee.
14. Elizabeth Stubbins Bates, *Terrorism and International Law: Accountability, Remedies, and Reform, A Report of the IBA Task Force on Terrorism* (New York: Oxford University Press, 2011), 1–2.
15. UNSC 56th Sess, 4370th mtg, Verbatim Report, September 12, 2001, UN Doc S/PV.4370.
16. Saul, *Defining Terrorism*, 233.

Bibliography

Articles / Books / Reports

Adler, Freda, Gerhard Mueller, and William Laufer. *Criminal Justice*. 5th edition. New York: McGraw-Hill, 2009.

Africa Rights. *Rwanda: Death, Despair and Defiance*. African Rights, 1995.

Akehurst, Michael. "The Hierarchy of Sources of International Law." *British Yearbook of International Law* 47, no. 1 (1975).

Ambos, Kai. "What Does 'Intent to Destroy' in Genocide Mean?" *International Review of Red Cross* 91 (2009).

Andreopoulos, George J. "Introduction: The Calculus of Genocide." In *Genocide: Conceptual and Historical Dimensions*, edited by George J. Andreopoulos. 1. Philadelphia: University of Pennsylvania Press, 1994.

Ashworth, Andrew. *Principles of International Criminal Law*. 3rd edition. Oxford: Oxford University Press, 1999.

Bagchi, Aditi. "Intention, Torture, and the Concept of State Crime." *Penn State Law Review* 114 (2009).

Bassiouni, M. Cherif. *International Terrorism: Multilateral Conventions. 1937–2001*. Ardsley, NY: Transnational Press, 2001.

Başoğlu, Metin, Maria Livanou, and Cvetana Crnobarić. "Torture vs. Other Cruel, Inhuman, and Degrading Treatment: Is the Distinction Real or Apparent?" *Arch Gen Psychiatry* 64 (2007).

Bekerman, Omer Ze'ev. "Torture: The Absolute Prohibition of a Relative Term: Does Anyone Know What is in Room 101?" *American Journal of Criminal Law* 53 (2005).

Berry, Chris. "Lust, Caution: Torture, Sex, and Passion in Chinese Cinema." In *Screening Torture: Media Representations of State Terror and Political Domination*, edited by Michael Flynn and Fabiola F. Salek. New York: Columbia University Press, 2012.

Bhavnani, Ravi and David Backer, "Localized Ethnic Conflict and Genocide: Accounting for Differences in Rwanda and Burundi," *Journal of Conflict Resolution* 44, no. 3 (June 2000).

Binder, Guyora. "The Origins of American Felony Murder Rules." *Stanford Law Review* 57 (2004).

Blakeley, Ruth. *State Terrorism and Neoliberalism: The North in the South.* New York: Routledge, 2011.

Bloom, Mia. *Dying to Kill: The Allure of Suicide Terror.* New York: Columbia University Press, 2005.

Borradori, G. ed. *Philosophy in the Time of Terror: Dialogues with Jürgen Habermas and Jacques Derrida.* Chicago: University of Chicago Press, 2003.

Bourgon, Jérôme. "Obscene Vignettes of Truth, Construing Photographs of Chinese Executions as Historical Documents." In *Visualizing China: 1845–1965,* edited by Christian Henriot and Wen-hsin Yeh. Boston: Brill, 2013.

Bowen, John T. "The Myth of Global Ethnic Conflict." *Journal of Democracy* 7, no. 4 (1996).

Brook, Timothy, Jérôme Bourgon and Gregory Blue. *Death by a Thousand Cuts.* Cambridge. MA: Harvard University Press, 2008.

Burgers, J. Herman and Hans Danelius. *The United Nations Convention Against Torture.* Leiden: Martinus Nihoff, 1988.

Campbell, David. "Atrocity, Memory, Photography: Imaging the Concentration Camps of Bosnia—the Case of ITN versus Living Marxism. Part 1." *Journal of Human Rights* 1, no.1 (2002).

Card, Claudia. *The Atrocity Paradigm: A Theory of Evil.* New York: Oxford University Press, 2002.

Carlan, Philip E., Lisa S. Nord and Ragan A. Downey. *An Introduction to Criminal Law.* Jones & Bartlett, 2011.

Carrabine, Eamonn. "Just Images: Aesthetics, Ethics, and Visual Criminology." *British Journal of Criminology* 52 (2012).

Carson, Jennifer Varriale, Gary LaFree, and Laura Dugan. "Terrorist and Non-Terrorist Criminal Attacks by Radical Environmental and Animal Rights Groups in the United States." *Terrorism and Violence* 24, no. 2 (2012).

Carswell, Andrew J. "Unblocking the United Nations Security Council: The Uniting for Peace Resolution." *Journal of Conflict and Security Law* 18, no. 3 (Winter 2013).

Cassese, Antonio, Guido Acquaviva, Mary Fan, and Alex Whiting. *International Criminal Law: Cases and Commentaries.* Oxford: Oxford University Press, 2011.

Charney, Jonathan I. "Universal International Law." *American Journal of International Law* 87, no. 4 (1993).

Cherneva, Iveta. "The Drafting History of Article 2 of the Convention Against Torture." *Essex Human Rights Review* 9 (2012).

Choi Jr., Seung-Whan. "Fighting Terrorism through the Rule of Law." *Journal of Conflict Resolution* (2010). online.

Chomsky, Noam, and Edward S. Herman. *The Washington Connection and Third World Fascism.* Boston: South End Press, 979.

Chong, Denise. *The Girl in the Picture: The Story of Kim Phuc, the Photograph and the Vietnam War.* New York: Viking, 2000.

Christenson, Gordon A. "*Jus Cogens*: Guarding Interests Fundamental to International Society." *Virginia Journal of International Law* 28 (1988).

Conquest, Robert. *The Harvest of Sorrow: Soviet Collectivization and the Terror-Famine.* New York: Oxford University Press, 1986.

Cory, John. "A Formula for Genocide." *American Spectator* 3, no. 9 (1998).

Cullen, Anthony. "Defining Torture in International Law: A Critique of the Concept Employed by The European Court of Human Rights." *California Western International Law Journal* 34, no. 1 (2003).

D'Amato, Anthony. "It's a Bird. It's a Plane. It's Jus Cogens!" *Connecticut Journal of International Law* 6, no. 1 (1990).

Dadrian, Vahakn N. "The Comparative Aspects of the Armenian and Jewish Cases of Genocide: A Sociological Perspective." In *Is the Holocaust Unique?*, edited by Alan S. Rosenbaum. Boulder. CO: Westview Press, 1996, 101–136.

Dammer, Harry R. and Jay S. Albanese. *Comparative Criminal Justice Systems.* Belmont. CA: Wadsworth, 2014.

Davis, Michael. "The Moral Justifiability of Torture and Other Cruel, Inhuman, or Degrading Treatment." *International Journal of Applied Philosophy* 19 (2005).

De Hoogh, A. J. J. "The Relationship between *Jus Cogens*, Obligations *Erga Omnes* and International Crimes: Peremptory Norms in Perspective." *Austrian Journal of Public International Law* 42 (1991).

De Vattel, Emmerich. *The Law of Nations*, translated by Joseph Chitty. Vol. lv. Philadelphia: T. & J. W. Johnson & Co, 1863.

Deflem, Mathieu. *The Policing of Terrorism: Organizational and Global Perspectives.* New York: Routledge, 2010.

Deichmann, Thomas. "The Picture that Fooled the World." *Living Marxism* 97 (1997).

Des Forges, Alison. *Leave None to Tell the Story: Genocide in Rwanda.* New York: Human Rights Watch, 1999.

Dorf, Michael. "Renouncing Torture." In *The Torture Debate in America*, edited by Karen J. Greenberg. New York: Cambridge University Press, 2006.

Dworkin, Ronald. *Law's Empire.* Cambridge, MA: Harvard University Press, 1986.

———. "A New Philosophy of International Law." *Philosophy & Public Affairs* 41, no. 1 (2013).

Elkins, Stanley M. *Slavery: A Problem in American Institutional and Intellectual Life.* 2nd edition. Chicago: The University of Chicago Press, 1968.

Elkins, James. *The Object Stares Back: On the Nature of Seeing.* New York: Mariner Books, 1996.

Fabri, Hélène R. "Enhancing the Rhetoric of Jus Cogens." *European Journal of International Law* 23, no. 4 (2012): 1049–58.

Farmer, Paul. "On Suffering and Structural Violence: A View from Below." *Daedalus* 125 (1996).

Fein, Helen. *Accounting for Genocide.* New York: The Free Press, 1979.

Finkelhor, David, Lisa M. Jones, Anne Shattuck and Kei Saito. *Updated Trends in Child Maltreatment, 2012*. University of Nebraska Press, 2013.

Finkelstein, Norman G. *The Holocaust Industry: Reflections on the Exploitation of Jewish Suffering*. New York: Verso, 2000.

Finnis, John. *Natural Law and Natural Rights*. Oxford: Clarendon Press, 1980.

Fitzhugh, George. *Cannibals All! Or Slaves Without Masters,* edited by C. Vann Woodward. Cambridge. MA: The Belknap Press of Harvard University, 1960.

Fletcher, George. "The Indefinable Concept of Terrorism." *Journal of Criminal Justice* 4. no. 5 (2006).

Foot, Rosemary. "Torture: The Struggle over a Peremptory Norm." *International Relations* 20 (2008).

Ford, Christopher A. "Adjudicating *Jus Cogens.*" *Wisconsin International Law Journal* 13 (1994).

Fox, James Alan and Jack Levin. *Overkill: Mass Murder and Serial Killing Exposed*. New York: Plenum Press, 1994.

Friedesdorf, Conor. "The Irrationality of Giving Up this Much Liberty to Fight Terror." *Atlantic* (June 10. 2013).

Fuller, Lon. *The Morality of Law*. New Haven, CT: Yale University Press, 1969.

Geertz, Clifford. *Local Knowledge: Further Essays In Interpretive Anthropology*. 3rd edition. New York: Basic Books, 1983.

Goldberg, Elizabeth Swanson. *Beyond Terror: Gender. Narrative. Human Rights*. New Brunswick. NJ: Rutgers University Press, 2007.

Gossop, Ronald. *Confronting War: An Examination of Humanity's Most Pressing Problem*. 2nd edition. Jefferson. NC: MacFarland, 1987.

Gould, Harry D. *The Legacy of Punishment in International Law.* New York: Palgrave/Macmillan, 2010.

Gourevitch, Philip. *We Wish to Inform You that by Tomorrow My Family and I will be Dead*. New York: Farrar, Straus and Giroux, 1998.

Greenwalt, Alexander K. A. "Rethinking Genocidal Intent: The Case for Knowledge-Based Interpretation." *Columbia Law Review* 99 (1999).

Greenwood, Christopher. "War, Terrorism, and International Law." *Current Legal Problems* 56 (2004).

Griset, Pamala L. and Sue Maltan. *Terrorism in Perspective*. Thousand Oaks, CA: Sage, 2007.

Grotius, Hugo. "What Is War? What Is Law?" In *On the Law of War and Peace,* edited by J. B. Scott. Vol. 1. London: Carnegie Endowment for International Peace, 1925.

Guarnieri, Carolo. "Preserving Rights and Protecting the Public: The Italian Experience." In *Courts and Terrorism: Nine Nations Balance Rights and Security,* edited by Mary L. Volcansek and John F. Sack. Jr. New York: Cambridge University Press, 2011.

Gutman, Roy. *A Witness to Genocide: The 1993 Pulitzer Prize-Winning Dispatches on the "Ethnic Cleansing" of Bosnia*. New York: Macmillan, 1993.

Habermas, Jürgen. "A Kind of Indemnification: The Tendencies toward Apologia in German Research on Current History." *Yad Vashem Studies* 19 (1988).

Haimbaugh Jr., George D. "Jus Cogens: Root & Branch (An Inventory)." *Touro Law Review*. 3 (1987).

Hannikainen, Laura. *Peremptory Norms in International Law: Historical Development. Criteria. Present Status*. Lakimiesliiton Kustannus, Finnish Lawyers' Publishing Company, 1988.

Hathaway, Oona A., Aileen Nowlan and Julia Spiegel. "Tortured Reasoning: The Intent to Torture Under International and Domestic Law." *Virginia Journal of International Law* 52 (2012).

Held, Virginia. "Terrorism and War." *The Journal of Ethics* 8 (2004).

Herman, Edward S. and David Peterson. *The Politics of Genocide*. Monthly Review Press, 2010.

Hesse, Mary. *Models and Analogies in Science* revised ed. Notre Dame, IN: University of Notre Dame, 1966.

Hilberg, Raul. *The Destruction of the European Jews*. New York: Holmes & Meier, 1985.

Hill, Michael. "*United States v. Fullmer* and the Animal Enterprise Terrorism Act: 'True Threats' to Advocacy." *Case Western Reserve Law Review* 61, no. 3 (2011).

Hoffman, Merle. "I Am Against Fanatics." In *On Prejudice: A Global Perspective*, edited by Daniela Gioseffi. New York: Anchor, 1993.

Hoffman, Bruce. *Inside Terrorism*. New York: Columbia University Press, 2013.

Holper, Mary. "Specific Intent and the Purposeful Narrowing of Victim Protection under the Convention against Torture." *Oregon Law Review* 88 (2009): 779.

Horowitz, Irving Louis. *Taking Lives: Genocide and State Power*. 3rd edition. New Brunswick. NJ: Transaction Books, 1982.

Hovannislan, Richard G. "Etiology and Sequalae of the Armenian Genocide." In *Genocide: Conceptual and Historical Dimensions*, edited by George J. Andreopoulos. Philadelphia: University of Pennsylvania Press, 1994.

Hove, Thomas, Hye-Jin Paek, Thomas Isaacson, and Richard T. Cole. "Newspaper Portrayals of Child Abuse: Frequency of Coverage and Frames of the Issue." *Mass Communication and Society* 16 (2013).

Jones, Adam. *Genocide: A Comprehensive Introduction*. New York: Routledge, 2006.

Jones, Dan. "Beyond Waterboarding: The Science of Interrogation." *New Scientist* 205 (2010).

Jorgensen, Nina. *The Responsibility Of States For International Crimes*. New York: Oxford University Press, 2000.

Kafka, Franz. "In the Penal Colony." In *Kafka's Selected Stories*, edited by Stanley Corngold. New York: W.W. Norton. 2007.

Kamen, Henry. *The Spanish Inquisition: A Historical Revision*. New Haven, CT: Yale University Press, 1998.

Kaplan, Robert D. *Balkan Ghosts: A Journey Through History*. New York: Vintage, 1993.

Katz, Steven T. *The Holocaust in Historical Perspective.* New York: Oxford University Press, 1944.

———. "The Uniqueness of the Holocaust: The Historical Dimension." In *Is the Holocaust Unique?*, edited by Alan S. Rosenbaum. Boulder. CO: Westview Press, 1996.

Kern, George M. and Leon H. Rappoport. "Discussion: Of Pierre Papazian's a Unique Uniqueness?" *Midstream* 30, no. 4 (April 1984).

Kittichaisaree, Kriangsak. *International Criminal Law.* Oxford: Oxford University Press, 2001.

Kramer, Matthew H. *Torture And Moral Integrity: A Philosophical Enquiry.* New York: Oxford University Press, 2014.

Kreimer, Seth F. "Too Close to the Rack and the Screw: Constitutional Constraints on Torture in the War on Terror." *University of Pennsylvania Journal of Constitutional Law* 6 (2003).

Kuhn, Thomas. *The Structure Of Scientific Revolutions.* 3rd edition. Chicago: University of Chicago Press, 1962.

Kuper, Leo. *Genocide: Its Political Use in the Twentieth Century.* New York: Penguin Books, 1981.

———. "Theoretical Issues Relating to Genocide: Uses and Abuses." In *Genocide: Conceptual and Historical Dimensions*, edited by George J. Andreopoulos. Philadelphia: University of Pennsylvania Press, 1994.

Lacquer, Walter. *A History of Terrorism.* New Brunswick. NJ: Transaction Publishing, 2001.

———. *Voices of Terror: Manifestos, Writings and Manuals of Al Qaeda, Hamas, and Other Terrorists from Around the World and throughout the Ages.* Naperville, IL: Sourcebooks, 2004.

———. *No End to war: Terrorism in the Twenty-first Century.* New York: Continuum Publishing Group, 2004.

Lagnado, Lucette. M. *Children of the Flames: Dr. Josef Mengele and the Untold Story of the Twins of Auschwitz.* New York: Penguin Books, 1992.

Langbein, John H. *Torture and the Law of Proof: Europe and England in the Ancien Régime.* Chicago: University of Chicago Press, 2012.

Lea, Henry Charles. *A History of the Inquisition of the Middle Ages.* Vol. 1–2. New York: Macmillan, 1887, 1901.

Lee, Win-chiat. "International Crimes and Universal Jurisdiction." In *International Criminal Law and Philosophy*, edited by Larry May and Zachary Hoskins. New York: Cambridge University Press. 2010.

Leeuwen, Theo van and Carey Jewitt, eds. *Handbook of Visual Analysis.* London: Sage Publications, 2001.

Lemarchand, Rene. *The Dynamics of Violence in Central Africa.* Philadelphia, PA: University of Pennsylvania Press, 2009.

———. *Rwanda and Burundi.* London: Pall Mall, 1970.

———. *Rwanda: The State of Research.* Online Encyclopedia of Mass Violence, 2013.

———. "Disconnecting the Threads: Rwanda and the Holocaust Reconsidered," *Journal of Genocide Research* 4, no. 4 (2002).

Lemkin, Raphael. *Axis Rule in Occupied Europe: Laws of Occupation, Analysis of Government, Proposals for Redress.* Washington. DC: Carnegie Endowment for International Peace, 1944.

Letgers, Lyman H. "The Soviet Gulag: Is it Genocide?" In *Toward the Understanding and Prevention of Genocide,* edited by Israel W. Chaney. Boulder, CO: Westview Press, 1984.

Levi, Primo. *The Drowned and the Saved.* New York: Summit Books, 1988.

Lewis, Bernard. *The Assassins.* New York: Basic Books, 2003.

Liddick, Donald R. *Eco-Terrorism and Radical Environmental and Animal Liberation Movements.* New York: Praeger, 2006.

Lima, Maria Antónia. "The Dark Side of the Mediterranean—Expressions of Fear From the Inquisition to the Present." *Babilónia* no. 8/9 (2010).

Lippman, Mathew. "The Development and Drafting of the United Nations Convention Against Torture and Other Cruel, Inhuman, or Degrading Treatment or Punishment." *Boston College International and Comparative Law Review* 17 (1994).

Lockwood, Alan H., Richard J. Salvi, and Robert F. Burkard. "Tinnitus." *New England Journal of Medicine* 347 (2002).

Longman, Timothy. *Christianity and Genocide in Rwanda.* New York: Cambridge University Press, 2010.

Luban, David. "A Theory of Crimes against Humanity." *Yale Journal of International Law* 29 (2004).

Luban, David and Henry Shue. "Mental Torture: A Critique of Erasures in U.S. Law." *Georgetown Law Journal* 100. no. 3 (2012).

MacDonald, R. St. J. "Fundamental Norms in Contemporary International Law." *Canadian Yearbook of International Law* 25 (1987).

Mamdami, Mahmood. *Saviors and Survivors: Darfur. Politics. and The War on Terror.* New York: Three Rivers Press, 2010.

———. *When Victims Become Killers: Colonialism, Nativism and the Genocide in Rwanda.* Princeton: Princeton University Press, 2002.

———. *A People Betrayed: The Role of the West in Rwanda's Genocide.* New York: Zed Books, 2000·

Margalit, Avishai and Gabriel Motzkin. "The Uniqueness of the Holocaust." *Philosophy And Public Affairs* (Winter 1996).

Markusen, Eric. "Genocide and Modern War." In *Genocide in Our Time,* edited by Michael N. Dobkowski and Isidor Walliman. Ann Arbor, MI: Michigan: Pierian Press, 1992.

May, Larry. "Habeas Corpus as Jus Cogens in International Law." *Criminal Law and Philosophy* 4 (2010).

———. *Crimes Against Humanity: A Normative Account.* Cambridge, UK: Cambridge University Press, 2005.

Mayer, Jane. *The Dark Side: The Inside Story of How the War on Terror Turned into a War on American Ideals.* New York: Knopf Doubleday Publishing Group, 2008.

McCoy, Alfred W. "Beyond Susan Sontag: The Seduction of Psychological Torture." In *Screening Torture: Media Representations of State Terror and Political Domination*, edited by Michael Flynn and Fabiola F. Salek. New York: Columbia University Press, 2012.

Mosler, Hermann. *The International Society as a Legal Community.* New York: Springer, 1980.

Mueller, John. "Has the Threat from Terrorism Been Exaggerated?" *Commentator* (January 8. 2014).

Mumford, Andrew. "Minimum Force Meets Brutality: Detention. Interrogation and Torture in British Counter-Insurgency Campaigns." *Journal of Military Ethics* 11. no. 1 (2012).

Murphy, Cullen. *God's Jury: The Inquisition and the Making of the Modern World.* New York: Houghton Mifflin Harcourt, 2012.

Myers, John E.B. "A Short History of Child Protection in America." *Family Law Quarterly* 42 (2008–2009).

———. *Child Protection in America: Past. Present, and Future.* New York: Oxford University Press, 2006.

Møller, Aage R. "Similarities between Chronic Pain and Tinnitus." *American Journal of Otolaryngology* 18 (1997).

Nielsen, Christian Axboe. "Surmounting the Myopic Focus on Genocide: The Case of War in Bosnia and Herzegovina." *Journal of Genocide Research* 15, no. 1 (2013).

Nolte, Ernst. "A Past Will Not Pass away—A Speech it was Possible to Write, but not to Present." *Yad Vashem Studies* 19 (1988).

Norman, Sir Henry. *The People and Politics of the Far East.* London: T. F. Unwin, 1895.

Nowak, Manfred. "What Practices Constitute Torture?: US and UN Standards." *Human Rights Quarterly* 28 (2006).

O'Boyle, Garrett. "Theories of Justification and Political Violence: Examples of Four Groups [Provisional IRA. Red Army. al-Qaeda. anti-abortion]." *Terrorism and Political Violence* 14, no. 2 (2002).

O'Connell, Mary Ellen. "*Jus Cogens*: International Law's Higher Ethical Norms." In *The Role of Ethics in International Law*, edited by Donald Earl Childress III. Cambridge: Cambridge University Press, 2012.

Palmer, Alison. "Ethnocide." In *Genocide in Our Time*, edited by Michael N. Dobkowski and Isidor Walliman. Ann Arbor, MI: Pierian Press, 1992.

Papazian, Pierre. "A 'Unique Uniqueness'?" *Midstream* 30 no. 4 (April 1984).

Paris, Roland. "Kosovo and the Metaphor War." *Political Science Quarterly* 117, no. 3 (2002).

Parry, John T. "What Is Torture, Are We Doing It, and What If We Are?" *University of Pittsburgh Law Review* 64 (2003).

———. "Escalation and Necessity: Defining Torture at Home and Abroad." In *Torture: A Collection*, edited by Sanford Levinson. New York: Oxford University Press, 2006.

Perini, Laura. "The Truth in Pictures." *Philosophy of Science* 72 (2005).

Pimentel, David. "Criminal Child Neglect and the 'Free Range Kid': Is Overprotective Parenting the New Standard of Care?" *Utah Law Review* no. 2 (2012).

Posner, Richard. *The Problems of Jurisprudence*. Cambridge, MA: Harvard University Press, 1990.

Potter, Will. *Green is the New Red: An Insider's Account of a Social Movement Under Siege*. San Francisco, CA: City Lights Publishers, 2011.

Pound, Cuthbert W. *"Inquisitorial Confessions."* *Cornell Law Quarterly* 1, no. 2 (1916).

Primoratz, Igor. "Philosopher Looks at Contemporary Terrorism." *Cardozo Law Review* 29 (2007–2008).

———. *Terrorism: A Philosophical Investigation*. Cambridge, UK: Polity, 2013.

Prunier, Gerard. *From Genocide to Continental Wars: The Congolese Conflict and the Crisis of Contemporary Africa*. London: C. Hurst, 2009.

———. *The Rwanda Crisis: History of Genocide*. New York: Columbia University Press, 1995.

Pustilnik, Amanda C. "Pain as Fact and Heuristic: How Pain Neuroimaging Illuminates Moral Dimensions of Law." *Cornell Law Review* 97 (2012).

Read, Piers Paul. *Alive: Sixteen Men. Seventy-Two Days. and Insurmountable Odds— The Classical Adventure of Survival in the Andes*. New York: Harper, 2005.

Reeves, Shane. "To Russia with Love: How Moral Arguments for a Humanitarian Intervention in Syria Opened the Door for an Invasion of the Ukraine." *Michigan State Law Review* 22. no. 1 (Fall 2014).

Reichel, Philip L. *Comparative Criminal Justice Systems*. Engelwood Cliffs, NJ: Prentice Hall, 2012.

Richards, Anthony. "Conceptualizing Terrorism." *Studies in Conflict & Terrorism* 37, no. 3 (2014).

Richardson, Louise. *What Terrorists Want: Understanding the Enemy. Containing the Threat*. New York: Random House, 2006.

Robin, Corey. *Fear: a History of a Political Idea*. Oxford, Oxford University Press, 2008.

Robinson, Paul H. and Jane A. Grall. "Element Analysis in Defining Criminal Liability: The Model Penal Code and Beyond." *Stanford Law Review* 35 (1983).

Roch, Michael P. "Forced Displacement in Former Yugoslavia: A Crime under International Law?" *Dickinson Journal of International Law* 14 (1995).

Rorty, Richard. *Philosophy and Social Hope*. New York: Penguin Books, 1999.

Rosenbaum, Alan S., ed. *Is the Holocaust Unique?* Boulder, CO: Westview Press, 1996.

Rosenberg, Alan and Evelyn Silverman. "The Issue of The Holocaust as a Unique Event." In *Genocide In Our Time*, edited by Michael N. Dobkowski and Isidor Wallimann. 47. Ann Arbor. MI: Pierian Press, 1992.

Rosenberg, Alan. "The Crisis in Knowing and Understanding the Holocaust." In *Echoes from the Holocaust: Philosophical Reflections on a Dark Time*, edited by Alan Rosenberg and Gerald E. Myers. 379–95. Philadelphia: Temple University Press, 1988.

Rosenfeld, Alvin H. *The End of the Holocaust*. Bloomington, IN: University of Indiana Press, 2011.

Rosman, Adam L. "Visualizing the Law: Using Chats, Diagrams, and Other Images to Improve Legal Briefs." *Journal of Legal Education* 63 (2013).

Rummel, R. J. *Statistics on Democide: Genocide and Mass Murder Since 1900*. New Brunswick, NJ: Transaction Publishers, 1997.

Sadat, Leila Nadyra, ed. *Forging a Convention for Crimes Against Humanity*. New York: Cambridge University Press, 2011.

Saul, Ben. "The Legal Response of the League of Nations to Terrorism." *Journal of International Criminal Justice* 4, no. 1 (2011).

———. *Defining Terrorism in International Law*. Oxford: Oxford University Press, 2006.

Schabas, William A. "State Policy as an Element of International Crimes." *Journal of Criminal Law and Criminology* 98 (2008).

———. *Genocide in International Law: The Crimes of Crimes*. Cambridge: Cambridge University Press, 2000.

———. *Unimaginable Atrocities: Justice, Politics and Rights at the War Crimes Tribunals*. New York: Oxford University Press, 2012.

Schachter, Oscar. "International Law In Theory and Practice: General Course in Public International Law." *Recueil des cours* 178, no. 21 (1982): 336.

Schlink, Bernhard. "The Problem with Torture Lite." *Cardozo Law Review* 29 (2007): 85, 86.

Seeskin, Kenneth. "What Philosophy Can and Cannot Say about Evil." In *Echoes From the Holocaust: Philosophical Reflections on a Dark Time*, edited by Alan Rosenberg and Gerald E. Myers. 91–104. Philadelphia: Temple University Press, 1988.

Shanahan, Timothy. *The Provisional Irish Republican Army and the Morality of Terrorism*. Edinburgh: Edinburgh University Press, 2007.

Shue, Henry. "Torture." *Philosophy & Public Affairs* 7, no. 2 (1978).

———. "Torture in Dreamland: Disposing of the Ticking Bomb." *Case Western Reserve Journal of International Law* 37 (2006).

Simma, Bruno and Philip Alston. "The Sources of Human Rights Law: Custom. Jus Cogens. and General Principles." *Australian Yearbook of International Law* 12 (1988–1989).

Simon, Thomas W. *The Laws of Genocide: Prescription for a Just World*. Westport, CT: Praeger Security International, 2007.

———. "A Theory of Disadvantaged Groups." In *Democracy and Social Injustice*. 71–107. Lanham, MD: Rowman & Littlefield, 1995.

———. "Defining Genocide." *Wisconsin International Law Review* (Fall 1996).

———. *Democracy and Social Injustice: Law, Politics and Philosophy*. Lanham, MD: Rowman and Littlefield, 1995.

———. "Genocide, Evil, and Injustice: Competing Hells." In *Genocide And Human Rights, A Philosophical Guide*, edited by John K. Roth. New York: Palgrave Macmillan, 2005.

Skolnick, Jerome H. and James J. Fyfe. *Above the Law: Police and the Excessive Use of Force*. New York: Free Press, 1993.

Sluka, Jeffrey A. *Death Squad: The Anthropology of State Terror*. Philadelphia: University of Pennsylvania Press, 1999.

Song, Jiewuh. "Pirates and Torture: Universal Jurisdiction as Enforcement Gap." *Journal of Political Philosophy* (2014).

Sontag, Susan. *On Photography*. New York: St Martin's Press, 1977.

———. *Regarding the Pain of Others*. New York: Penguin, 2004.

Speke, John H. *Journal of the Discovery of the Source of the Nile*. London: Blackwoods, 1863.

Stannard, David E. "Uniqueness as Denial: The Politics of Genocide Scholarship." In *Is the Holocaust Unique?*, edited by Alan S. Rosenbaum. Boulder, CO: Westview Press, 1996, 163–208.

Sternberg, Robert J. "A Duplex Theory of Hate: Development and Application to Terrorism. Massacres, and Genocide." *Review of General Psychology* 7 (2003).

Suhke, Astri and Bruce Jones. "Preventative Diplomacy in Rwanda: Failure to Act or Failure of Actions?" In *Opportunities My Opportunities Seized: Preventive Diplomacy in Post-Cold War World*, edited by Bruce W. Jentleson. Lanham, MD: Rowman & Littlefield, 2000.

Sussman, David. "What's Wrong with Torture?" *Philosophy & Public Affairs* 33. no. 1 (2005).

Sztucki, Jerzy. *Jus Cogens and the Vienna Convention on the Law of Treaties: A Critical Appraisal*. New York: Springer-Verlag, 1974.

Takashima, Yoshio, Richard L. Daniels, Wendy Knowlton, James Teng, Emily R. Liman, and David D. McKemy. "Diversity in the Neural Circuitry of Cold Sensing Revealed by Genetic Axonal Labeling of Transient Receptor Potential Melastatin 8 Neurons." *Journal of Neuroscience* 27 (2007).

Takemura, Hitomi. "Big Fish and Small Fish Debate: An Examination of Prosecutorial Discretion." *International Criminal Law Review* 7 (2007).

Thomas, Laurence. "Characterizing the Evil of American Slavery and the Holocaust." In *Jewish Identity*, edited by David Theo Goldberg and Michael Krausz. Philadelphia, PA: Temple University Press, 1993.

Thornberry, Patrick. *International Law and the Rights of Minorities*. Oxford: Clarendon Press, 1991.

Tushnet, Mark. "Critical Legal Theory (without Modifiers) in the United States." *Journal of Political Philosophy* 13, no. 1 (2005).

Verdross, Alfred von. "Forbidden Treaties in International Law." *American Journal of International Law* 31 (1937).

———. "*Jus Dispositivum* and *Jus Cogens* in International Law." *American Journal of International Law* 60 (1966).

Verwimp, Philip. "Testing the Double-Genocide Thesis for Central and Southern Rwanda." *The Journal of Conflict Resolution* 47. no. 4 (2003).

Volcansek, Mary L. and John F. Sack. Jr., ed. *Courts and Terrorism: Nine Nations Balance Rights and Security.* New York: Cambridge University Press, 2011.

Waldron, Jeremy. "The Coxford Lecture. Inhuman and Degrading Treatment: The Words Themselves." *Canadian Journal of Law & Jurisprudence* 23 (2010).

———. "Torture and Positive Law: Jurisprudence for the White House." *Columbia Law Review* 105 (2005).

———. "What Is Natural Law Like?" In *Reason. Morality, and Law: The Philosophy of John Finnis,* edited by John Keown and Robert P. George. New York: Oxford University Press, 2013.

———. *Torture, Terror, and Trade-Offs: Philosophy for the White House.* New York: Oxford University Press, 2010.

Walzer, Michael. *Just and Unjust Wars.* 3rd edition. New York: Basic Books, 2000.

Weil, Prosper. "Towards Relative Normativity in International Law." *American Journal of International Law* 77 (1983).

Weinreb, Lloyd L. "Natural Law and Rights." In *Natural Law Theory: Contemporary Essays,* edited by Robert P. George. Oxford: Clarendon Press, 1992.

———. *Law and Justice.* Cambridge, MA: Harvard University Press, 1987.

Weinstein, Harvey M. "Victims. Transitional Justice and Social Reconstruction: Who Is Setting the Agenda?" In *Justice For Victims: Perspectives on Rights, Transition and Reconciliation,* edited by Inge Vanfraechem, Antony Pemberton and Felix Mukwiza Ndahinda. New York: Routledge, 2014.

Weisberg, Michael. *Simulation and Similarity: Using Models to Understand the World.* New York: Oxford University Press, 2013.

Weisburd, A. Mark. "The Emptiness of the Concept of *Jus Cogens,* as Illustrated by the War in Bosnia-Herzegovina." *Michigan Journal of International Law* 17. no. 1 (Fall 1995).

Weller, Marc. "The Crisis in Kosovo. 1989–1999: From the Dissolution of Yugoslavia to Rambouillet and the Outbreak of Hostilities." *International Documents & Analysis* 1 (1999).

Wharton, Francis. *Wharton's Criminal Evidence.* 11th edition. Vol. 2. Clark, NJ: Lawyer's Cooperative Publishing Co., 1935.

Wicker, Benjamin D. *Status: Inquisition in the Catholic Church.* Catholic Education Resource Center. http://www.catholiceducation.org/articles/history/world/wh0029.html.

Wiesel, Elie and Merle Hoffman. "I am against Fanatics." In *On Prejudice: A Global Perspective,* edited by Daniela Gioseffi. New York, Anchor Books, 1993.

Wisnewski, J. Jeremy. *Understanding Torture*. Edinburgh: Edinburgh University Press, 2010.

Wolfendale, Jessica. "The Myth of 'Torture Lite'." *Ethics & International Affairs* 23 (2009).

Yarwood, Lisa. "Defining Torture: The Potential for Abuse." *Journal of the Institute of Justice & International Studies* (2008).

Case Law

International

Barcelona Traction, Light and Power Company, Limited. (Belgium v. Spain). Judgment. ICJ Reports 1970.

Case Concerning East Timor (Portugal v. Australia) ICJ (1995).

Husayn (Abu Zubaydah) v. Poland. Application No. 7511/13. Judgment. (Eur. Ct. H.R. July 24. 2014). http://hudoc.echr.coe.int/sites/eng/pages/search.aspx?i=001-146047.

Prosecutor v. Akayesu. Case No. ICTR-96–4-T. Judgment (Int'l Crim. Trib. for Rwanda Sept. 2. 1998). http://www.unictr.org/Portals/0/Case/English/Akayesu/judgement/akay001.pdf.

Prosecutor v. Akayesu. ICTR-96–4-T (Int'l Crim. Trib. for Rwanda Sept. 2. 1998). http://www.unictr.org/Portals/0/Case/English/Akayesu/judgement/akay001.pdf.

Prosecutor v. Elizaphan Ntakirutimana and Gerard Ntakirutimana. ICTR-96–10-T (February 21. 2003) and ICTR-96–17-T (December 14. 2004).

Prosecutor v. Jean-Paul Akayesu. Case No. ICTR-96–4-T. Judgment. (Int'l Crim. Trib. for Rwanda Sept. 2. 1998).

http://www.unictr.org/Portals/0/Case/English/Akayesu/judgement/akay001.pdf. *adopted in* Prosecutor v. Delalić. Case No. IT-96–21-T. Judgment. 478–79 (Int'l Crim. Trib. for the Former Yugoslavia Nov. 16. 1998). http://www.icty.org/x/cases/mucic/tjug/en/981116_judg_en.pdf.

Prosecutor v. Radislav Kristic, Case No. IT-98–33-T, Trial Judgment (August 2, 2001).

Prosecutor v. Zeljko Raznjatovic (Arkan), IT-97–27, Indictment (September 23, 1997).

South-West Africa (Liberia v. South Africa. Ethiopia v. South Africa). ICJ (1966).

United States

Ashcraft v. Tennessee. 332 U.S. 143 (1944).

Blackburn v. Alabama. 361 U.S. 199 (1960).

Bram v. United States. 168 U. S. 532 (1897).

Brown v. Mississippi. 297 U.S. 278 (1936).

Brown v. Walker. 161 U. S. 591 (1896).
Chambers v. Florida. 309 U. S. 227 (1940).
Chambers v. Florida. 309 U.S. 227 (1940).
Cooper v. State. 86 Ala. 610 (1889).
Counselman v. Hitchcock. 142 U. S. 547 (1892).
Cross v. State. 221 S.W. 489 (Tenn. 1920).
Elizaphan Ntakirutimana v. Janet Reno et al. 184 F. 3d 419 (5th Cir. August 5, 1999); and 528 U.S. 1135 (2000) (certiorari denied).
Enoch v. Commonwealth. 126 S.E. 222 (Va. 1925).
Gross v. State. 817 N.E.2d 306 (Ind. Ct. App. 2004).
In re Kemmler 136 U.S. 436 (1890).
Jacobellis v. Ohio. 378 U.S. 184.
Matter of J-E-. 23 I & N Dec. 291. 300–01 (B.I.A. 2002).
Matter of Surrender of Ntakirutimana. 988 F. Supp. 1038 (S.D. Tex. 1997).
McKune v. Lile. 536 U.S. 24, 41 (2002).
Pennsylvania v. Muniz. 496 U.S. 582 (1990).
Ullmann v. United States. 350 U.S. 422 (1956).
United States v. Fullmer. 584 F.3d 139 (3d Circuit 2009).
United States v. Viehl. 2:09-CR-19 (US District Ct. D Utah. Central Div. 2010).
Wilson v. Seiter. 501 U.S. 294 (1991).
Zubeda v. Ashcroft. 333 F.3d 463 (3rd Cir. 2003).

European Union

Husayn v. Poland. App. No. 7511/13. Eur. Ct. H.R. (July 24, 2014). *Available at* http://hudoc.echr.coe.int/sites/eng/pages/search.aspx?i=001-146047.
Ireland v. United Kingdom. App. No. 5310/71. 25 Eur. Ct. H.R. (ser. A) (1978).

United Kingdom

R v. Gen. Medited by Council. [2004] EWHC (Admin) 1879. [2005] Q.B. 424.

Israel

Demjanjuk v. Israel, Crm. App. No. 347/88 (Supreme Court, July 29, 1993).
The Public Committee Against Torture in Israel v. The Government of Israel, HCJ 5100/94 53(4) P.D. 817 (1999).
The State of Israel v. Ivan (John) Demjanjuk, Crm. Case No. 373/86 (Jerusalem, July 29, 1999).

Legislation

Illinois Comprehensive Statatues.
Annotated Code Of Maryland, Family Law.

Arkansas Code Annotated.
French Criminal Code.
New Zealand Bill of Rights Act.
Prevention of Terrorism Bill.
South African Constitution.
U.S. Code.
United Kingdom Terrorism Act.

Reports

InternationalAmnesty International. "Amnesty International Report 1984." AI
Index POL 10/004/1984 (May 1, 1984).
————. "Report on Torture." AI Index ACT 40/001/1973 (Jan. 1, 1973).
Association pour la prévention de la torture (Genève). *Defusing the Ticking Bomb
Scenario: Why we must say No to torture, Always.* (Association for the Prevention of
Torture, 2007). http://www.apt.ch/content/files_res/tickingbombscenario.pdf.
Evans, Gareth. "The responsibility to protect." Fifth Committee of the General
Assembly. GA/AB/3837 (March 4, 2008).
Millenium Report, Annan, Kofi. "We the Peoples—The Role of the United Nations
in the 21st Century." March 2000.
National Academy of Sciences. "Rates of Physical and Sexual Abuse Have
Declinedited by But Not Child Neglect." *Science Daily.* Sept. 12. 2013. http://
www.sciencedaily.com/releases/2013/09/130912143940.htm.
Office of the High Commissioner on Human Rights. "Interpretation of
Torture in the Light of the Practice and Jurisprudence of International
Bodies." 2011. http://www.ohchr.org/Documents/Issues/Torture/UNVFVT/
Interpretation_torture_2011_EN.pdf.
Report of the Independent Inquiry into the Actions of the United Nations During
the 1994 Genocide on Rwanda, UN Doc. S/1999/1257 (1999).
Truth and Reconciliation Commission, Amnesty Committee. "Application in
Terms of Section 18 of the Promotion of National Unit and Reconciliation Act.
No.34 of 1995." AC/2001/003. http://www.justice.gov.za/trc/decisions/2001/
ac21003.htm.
United StatesBates, Elizabeth Stubbins. *Terrorism and International Law:
Accountability. Remedies, and Reform, A Report of the IBA Task Force on Terrorism.*
New York: Oxford University Press, 2011.
Bybee, Jay S. "Memorandum for Alberto R. Gonzales, Counsel to the President.
Re: Standards of Conduct for Interrogation under 18 U.S.C. § § 2340–2340A."
(United States, Department of Justice, Office of Legal Counsel. Aug. 1, 2002).
Reprinted in Mark Danner. *Torture and Truth: America, Abu Ghraib, and the War
on Terror.* 115 (2004).
Center for Constitutional Rights. "Shadow Report." Apr. 2014. (Prepared for the
52nd Session of the UN Committee Against Torture in Connection with its
Review of the Holy See.)

Children's Bureau of U.S. Department of Health and Human Services. "Child Maltreatment 2012." (2013). xi. http://www.acf.hhs.gov/sites/default/files/cb/cm2012.pdf; Childhelp. "Child Abuse Statistics & Facts." http://www.childhelp.org/pages/statistics (last visited July 29, 2014).

Child Welfare Training Institute. "Evolution of Federal Child Welfare Legislation." (2007). http://php.ipsiconnect.org/CWTI/Law/textOnlyLaw.html.

Committee on the Formation of Customary International Law. American Branch of the International Law Association: "The Role of State Practice in the Formation of Customary and Jus Cogens Norms of International Law" (January 19, 1989).

"Pain Receptor." Psychologycs. http://www.psychologycs.com/pain-receptor.htm (last visited Sept. 19, 2014).

"Report of the Comm. on Foreign Relations." S. Exec. Rep. 101–30 (1990) (Reports on the Convention Against Torture and Other Cruel, Inhuman, or Degrading Treatment or Punishment).

Smith, Melinda and Jeanne Segal, *Child Abuse & Neglect*. Helpguide.org. http://www.helpguide.org/mental/child_abuse_physical_emotional_sexual_neglect.htm (last updated July 2014).

Sofaer, Abraham D. Legal Adviser. Department of State. "Convention Against Torture: Hearing Before the S. Comm. on Foreign Relations" *101st Congress* 9 (1990) (Prepared Statement).

U.S. Department of Justice, FBI. *Terrorism in the United States*, 1988 (Terrorist Research and Analytic Center, Counter-Terrorism Section, Criminal Investigative Division. Dec. 31, 1988).

News Reports

Assault, Kosovo. "Was Not Genocide." *BBC News* (Sept. 7. 2001). http://news.bbc.co.uk/2/hi/europe/1530781.htm.

Estrin, Robin. "Don't Let Sleeping Tots Lie. Parent Learns." *Los Angeles Times*. Apr. 6. 1997. http://articles.latimes.com/1997-04-06/news/mn-45952_1_parent-learns.

Hastings, Deborah. "22 Month-Old Georgia Boy Left to Die in Hot Car had Scratches on Face and Head." *New York Daily News*. Jul. 5. 2014. 12:00pm. http://www.nydailynews.com/news/national/22-month-old-ga-boy-died-hot-car-scratches-head-article-1.1855937.

Lelyveld, Joseph. "Interrogating Ourselves." *New York Times*. Jun. 12. 2005. http://www.nytimes.com/2005/06/12/magazine/12TORTURE.html?pagewanted=all&_r=0.

Mayer, Jane. "A Deadly Interrogation. Can the CIA Legally Kill a Prisoner?" *New Yorker*. Nov. 14. 2005. 44. http://www.newyorker.com/magazine/2005/11/14/a-deadly-interrogation.

Mikkelson, Randall. "CIA Says Used Waterboarding on Three Suspects." *Reuters*. Feb. 5. 2008. 6:13pm EST. http://www.reuters.com/article/2008/02/05/us-security-usa-waterboarding-idUSN0517815120080205.

Warner, Judith. "Dangerous Resentment." *New York Times*. July 9, 2009. http://opinionator.blogs.nytimes.com/2009/07/09/dont-hate-her-because-shes-educated/?_php=true&_type=blogs&_r=0.

Treaties/International Documents

African Charter on Human and People's Rights. 1520 U.N.T.S. 217. June, 27, 1981.

Arab Convention on Suppression of Terrorism. Cairo 1998.

Committee on Civil and Political Rights. General Comment. U.N. Doc HRI/GEN/1/Rev. 1 at 30 (1992).

Comprehensive Convention on International Terrorism.

Convention Against Torture and Other Cruel, Inhuman or Degrading Treatment or Punishment. 1465 U.N.T.S. 113 (10 December 1984).

Convention for the Protection of Human Rights and Fundamental Freedoms. 513 U.N.T.S. 222. November 4, 1050.

Convention for the Suppression of Unlawful Acts against the Safety of Civil Aviation. Montreal. September 23. 1971.

Convention for the Suppression of Unlawful Acts against the Safety of Maritime Navigation. Rome. March 10, 1988.

Convention for the Suppression of Unlawful Seizure of Aircraft. Hague. December 16, 1970.

Convention on Offences and Certain Other Acts Committed on Board Aircraft. Tokyo. September 14, 1963.

Convention on the Marking of Plastic Explosives for the Purpose of Detection. Montreal. March 1, 1991.

Convention on the Prevention and Punishment of Crimes against Internationally Protected Persons, including Diplomatic Agents. General Assembly. December 14, 1973.

Convention on the Prevention and Punishment of the Crime of Genocide. 78 U.N.T.S. 277. Res. 2670. GAOR 3rd Sess., Pt. 1. U.N. Doc. A/810. General Assembly. December 9, 1948.

Convention on the Suppression of Unlawful Acts Relating to International Civil Aviation Beijing. 2010.

European Convention on Human Rights. 213 U.N.T.S. 222. November 4, 1950.

First U.N. Congress on the Prevention of Crime and the Treatment of Offenders. Standard Minimum Rules for the Treatment of Prisoners. 1955.

Geneva Convention Relative to the Treatment of Prisoners of War. 75 U.N.T.S. 135. August 12, 1949.

Hague Convention for the Suppression of Unlawful Seizure of Aircraft. 1970.

Hersch Lauterpacht. Report on the Law of Treaties. U.N. Doc. A.CN.4/63. 1953.

ILC Commentary. ILC Report. UN Doc A/6309/Rev. 1 (1966).

ILC Report. UN GAOR. 49th Sess. Supp. No. 10. 29–40. UN Doc. A/49/10 (1994).

Inter-American Convention on Human Rights. Nov. 22. 1969. 1144 U.N.T.S. 123.

International Convention against the Taking of Hostages. Adopted by the General Assembly of the United Nations/ 17 December 1979.

International Convention for the Suppression of Acts of Nuclear Terrorism New York. Adopted by the General Assembly of the United Nations on 13 April 2005.

International Convention for the Suppression of Terrorist Bombings. Adopted by the General Assembly of the United Nations on 15 December 1997.

International Convention for the Suppression of the Financing of Terrorism. Adopted by the General Assembly of the United Nations on 9 December 1999.

International Covenant on Civil and Political Rights. Art. 7. Dec. 16. 1966. 999 U.N.T.S. 171.

Montreal Convention for Suppression of Unlawful Acts Against the Safety of Civil Aviation (1971).

Official Records. First Session (Vienna. 26 March–24 May 1968). New York 1969. 327–28 (as quoted in Haimbaugh. *"Jus Cogens*: Root & Branch." 203).

Protocol for the Suppression of Unlawful Acts against the Safety of Fixed Platforms Located on the Continental Shelf. Done at Rome on 10 March 1988.

Protocol on the Suppression of Unlawful Acts of Violence at Airports Serving Convention on the Physical Protection of Nuclear Material. Signed at Vienna on 3 March 1980.

Protocol on the Suppression of Unlawful Acts of Violence at Airports Serving International Civil Aviation. (Supplementary to the Convention for the Suppression of Unlawful Acts against the Safety of Civil Aviation.) Signed at Montreal on 24 February 1988.

Protocol Supplementary to the Convention on the Suppression of Unlawful Seizure of Aircraft (Beijing 2010).

Report of the International Commission of Inquiry on Vilations of International Humanitarian Law and Human Rights Law in Darfur. UN Doc. S/2005/60. Paras. 491. 4.

Report of the International Law Commission on the work of its forty-sixth session. UN GAOR. 49th Sess. Supp. No. 10. UN Doc. A/49/10 (1994).

Reservations to the Convention on Prevention and Punishment of the Crime of Genocide. Advisory opinion. 1951 I.C.J. 23.

Rome Statute of the International Criminal Court. 17 July 1998. 2187 U.N.T.S 90. UN Doc. A/CONF 183/9. 37 ILM 1002 (1998).

Special Rapporteur on Torture and Other Cruel, Inhuman or Degrading Treatment or Punishment. *Report on Torture and Other Cruel, Inhuman or Degrading Treatment or Punishment.* Human Rights Council. U.N. Doc. A/HRC/13/39/ Add.5 (Feb. 5. 2010) (by Manfred Nowak).

Terrorism Convention of the Organization of the Islamic Conference (Ouagadougou,. 1999).

Texts of the Agreement for the Establishment of an International Military Tribunal and Annexed Charter. 5 U. N. T. S. 251.

Tokyo Convention on Offenses and Certain Other Acts Committed on Board Aircraft (1963).

UN Committee Against Torture. "General Comment 2, Implementation of article 2 by States parties." UN Doc. CAT/C/GC/2 (Jan. 24, 2008).

UN Committee Against Torture. Consideration of Reports Submitted by States Parties under Article 19 of the Convention: Convention against Torture and Other Cruel. Inhuman or Degrading Treatment or Punishment: Initial Reports of States Parties Due in 2003: The Holy. 8 March 2013. CAT/C/VAT/1.

Unanimously Adopting Resolution 2150 (2014), Security Council Calls for Recommitment to Fight against Genocide. SC/11356.

United Nations General Assembly. A/RES/377 (V).

Universal Declaration of Human Rights. G.A. Res. 217 (III) A. U.N. Doc. A/RES/217(III) (Dec. 10. 1948).

UNSC 56th Sess. 4370th mtg. Verbatim Report. September 12. 2001. UN Doc S/PV.4370.

Index

CPSIA information can be obtained at www.ICGtesting.com
Printed in the USA
BVOW06*0217020316

438728BV00005B/17/P